Walking the Old Road

WALKING THE OLD ROAD

*A People's History of Chippewa City
and the Grand Marais Anishinaabe*

STACI LOLA DROUILLARD

University of Minnesota Press
Minneapolis • London

The University of Minnesota Press gratefully acknowledges the generous assistance provided for the publication of this book by the Margaret S. Harding Memorial Endowment, honoring the first director of the University of Minnesota Press.

Published by the University of Minnesota Press
111 Third Avenue South, Suite 290
Minneapolis, MN 55401-2520
http://www.upress.umn.edu

ISBN 978-1-5179-0340-4 (pb)
A Cataloging-in-Publication record for this book is available from the Library of Congress.

Printed in the United States of America on acid-free paper

The University of Minnesota is an equal-opportunity educator and employer.

25 24 23 22 21 20 19   10 9 8 7 6 5 4 3 2 1

To the grandmothers, mothers, aunties, and sisters
who carried us until we were ready to walk

Contents

Chippewa City and Minnesota's North Shore ix

Prologue. The Old Road 1

Chapter 1. We Used to Sneak in There and Play:
The Chippewa City Church 9

Chapter 2. A Gateway for the Ages:
The Anishinaabeg Arrive at the Pigeon River 25

Chapter 3. At the Pleasure of the United States:
The Land Changes Hands 53

Chapter 4. Here Were Many Wigwams:
The Grand Marais Chippewa 71

Chapter 5. Nishkwakwansing:
At the Edge of the Forest 99

Chapter 6. Nokomisag miinawaa Mishoomisag:
Grandmothers and Grandfathers 115

Chapter 7. Indian Maidens and Plastic Tomahawks:
How to Make a Living 143

Chapter 8. A Call from Longbody:
North Woods Neighbors 171

Chapter 9. We Are Buried Here:
The Old Cemetery 193

Chapter 10. I Guess Sometimes I'm Torn:
Life between Two Worlds 209

Chapter 11. Divide the Land, Divide the People:
Land and Identity 225

Chapter 12. Signed with an X:
Katie's Point 243

Chapter 13. Jiigewayaazhagamay:
She Walks along the Water's Edge 255

Epilogue. A Return Home 269

Miigwech 277

Notes 281

Index 299

Chippewa City and Minnesota's North Shore. Map by Brad Herried.

St. Francis Xavier Church, as seen from the Old Road, circa 1975.
Courtesy of Cook County Historical Society.

→ Prologue ←

THE OLD ROAD

So MUCH OF IT has to do with being from somewhere—of being able to trace the history and footsteps of those who came before us. The "Old Shore Road" is what they called it, though it was really a well-worn walking path to and from Grand Marais, Minnesota, a small town located a mile's walking distance from Chippewa City on the North Shore of Lake Superior. The path wove along Thunder Hook Point, past basalt outcroppings and pebbled beaches, along jagged cliffs and steep overlooks. There is not much left of that old trail now. Most of it has been taken back by the woods or turned into lawns and driveways. There are even a few warning signs posted along the old road, threatening prosecution for "criminal trespass" to discourage anyone from traveling through. But it didn't used to be that way.

Jim Wipson, a member of the Grand Portage Band of Chippewa and veteran of World War II, was born in Chippewa City in 1918 and lived there with his grandmother Catherine (Kate) Frost until he was ten years old. Jim had fond memories of that old road, which he traveled often, walking alongside her on the way to town:

When I was a little boy, her and I used to walk that little old road. It was a mile from Chippewa City to Grand Marais. To us, we thought it was a long ways. Just to show you my grandma thought it was a long ways, she'd even take a little lunch along, and halfway between Chippewa City and Grand Marais we'd sit on the little cliff and have our little lunch. Then we'd journey the rest of the way to Grand Marais.[1]

When I first began interviewing my elders about the history of Chippewa City, I felt compelled to try to find the old road itself. Like trying to find hidden treasure without the help of a map, uncovering old pathways and searching for buried truths often becomes a pockmarked road of best guesses and tangled roadblocks, both real and imagined. True, the old path is now overgrown with dogwood brambles and impasses. But in addition to the physical barriers, I have my own internal potholes and fences to navigate. As a kid, I often felt disconnected from the place where my great-great-grandparents came from, and I knew very little about our Anakwad ancestors. My family is from Grand Marais. It's where my dad Francis Drouillard was born and where he and my mother, Joyce, raised my younger sister Dawn and me. The Drouillards were one of several mixed-blood Chippewa families who had never lived at Grand Portage until years later, when the Indian Reorganization Act of 1934 provided for self-government and job opportunities on the reservation. Until then, my dad and his six siblings lived in the woods between Grand Marais and Chippewa City.

My Grandma Lola, originally of the Linnell family who lived in Mineral Center, comes from Dutch and English parents, and Grandpa Fred was half Ojibwe and half French. Although my grandfather was a fluent Ojibwe speaker, he spoke only English to his kids, reserving his conversations in Ojibwemowin for other adults. Growing up, my sister and our close cousins were taught a few words and silly phrases, as that was all our parents remembered. Our Aunt Doreen Drouillard Voce, who used to run the Happy Fisherman restaurant in Colvill, around nine miles up the shore from Grand Marais, loved to tell us stories about "the old days" and some of her memories of Chippewa City. She encouraged us to be proud of our family heritage and of who we are.

So, I suppose that's where our family's place in this story began— with Aunt Doreen. She knew what it felt like to grow up poor, to work very hard, and to sometimes walk down paths that seemed to go somewhere only to be met with a dead end. But Aunt Doreen was never afraid to bushwhack her way through the woods, and her brave

No Trespassing. Photograph by the author.

spirit continues to inspire me to keep exploring our family history and the places that we come from.

TRYING IN VAIN TO LOCATE the old road and the cliff where Jim and his grandmother might have sat side by side, eating their carefully packed sandwiches, I am struck by the relationship between the physical place that used to be and my own identity as an Ojibwe descendant of Chippewa City. What so many of the people I interviewed longed for—what I long for—is the ability to return to the place where our ancestors lived and be welcomed there, as part of the living, breathing story of the people who call it home.

Chippewa City as a village was as culturally rich as it was economically poor. If you live in Minnesota you will recognize many notables with Chippewa City roots. The modern artist George Morrison was born and raised there, and so was Ruth Myers, a woman known as Minnesota's "Grandmother of Indian Education." John Beargrease, the legendary mail carrier and namesake of the annual sled-dog race between Duluth and Grand Portage, also lived there for periods of time with his family. After John died in 1910 in Beaver Bay, his wife

Louise Wishkop moved back to Chippewa City, where her family was from. She was taken by influenza in 1918 and is buried in the cemetery at Chippewa City. Her remains share a common grave along with the remains of her son Peter and brother-in-law George.

My great-grandmother Elizabeth Anakwad Drouillard is also buried there, as is my great-grandfather John Drouillard. I have returned to the place where they are buried many times, never knowing the exact location of their graves. Our family's remains, like so many other ancestral graves that were once marked with wooden crosses, spirit houses, or stone markers, have been lost to memory.

So, where does history begin, when so much of what came before remains a mystery? On each of my trips back to Chippewa City, I've tried to find the answer to that question. Does it begin with a gravesite or with the first written evidence that your ancestor existed? Does it begin with a specific memory or a point on a map? Does it require written or scientific evidence to be true? My cousin, the poet and writer Bob Swanson, helped answer some of my questions about

John and Louise Beargrease and family, circa 1895. Courtesy of Cook County Historical Society.

reconnecting with our family history in Chippewa City by illuminating the cultural significance of stories within Anishinaabe culture. He shared this with me, in one of our many e-mail exchanges, while connecting the dots between the Drouillard and Anakwad family ancestors that we share in common:

> In the Anishinaabe tradition, a story or legend is considered both animate and inanimate. It is a single item but it is also something that lives and in living not only remains, but changes . . . the story changes as people bring forth old remnants and put them in place to create a new story. That story, Bimaadizi Aadizookaan, lives and continues to grow, but only the people can determine if the story is remembered.[2]

I find great comfort in knowing that everything changes. Because this means that we all have the opportunity to change the trajectory of our story. Like a river gradually breaking apart an ice dam in the spring, perhaps we can begin to shift the often static and heavily weighted stories of our past by welcoming in the dynamic voices of the people who were often conveniently left out of our region's written history.

While the stories of Chippewa City are not unlike the stories of other Native communities who are fighting to protect and preserve their history, culture, and homelands, the words, memories, perceptions, and historical truths that the people I interviewed shared are a unique and important addition to our collective history—because the story of this place, Nishkwakwansing, has never been comprehensively told through the voices of the people who lived there and called it home.

In my college Ojibwe-language class, my professor Collins Oakgrove taught us that in Ojibwemowin you tell your name and then you tell where you are from.

Staci indizhinikaaz. Kitchi-bitobig indonjjibaa.

We do this because telling where you are from is just as important as your name. It helps tie us together and gives us a strong and solid place to speak from. It is my hope that the stories of Chippewa City will be heard, shared, and remembered, and that the story of Chippewa City and the Grand Marais Chippewa will continue to grow. By being a part of the living narrative, Bimaadizi Aadizookaan, together we can create a new story about what was, what is, and ultimately, what will be.

Chippewa City Church with congregation, late 1800s.
Courtesy of Cook County Historical Society.

→ *Chapter 1* ←

WE USED TO SNEAK IN THERE AND PLAY

The Chippewa City Church

HIGHWAY 61 MEANDERS between Duluth and the Canadian border, winding its way through the rocky cliffs and along the pebbled shore of Lake Superior. Cars, like river water, flood its lanes in spring, summer, and fall, while winter traffic becomes a slow but steady trickle of skiers, snowmobile enthusiasts, and Canadian pulpwood trucks. Just northeast of Grand Marais, 110 miles northeast of Duluth, the road guides traffic closely past an old church whose white siding has gleamed brightly in the sun of summer and settled into the stark drifts of winter for 120 years. Unlike other buildings that border Highway 61, the church turns its back to the road and its front door faces south, and out across the commanding expanse of Lake Superior.

As a child growing up in Grand Marais, I remember the old church as a frequent target for rock throwing by local children. The windows on all sides were shattered and grass grew so tall it obscured the stairs. The church was a great curiosity to most of us, and somewhat of a local fright. Schoolkids would sometimes boast about seeing phantom faces peering out from behind its boarded-up windows or claim that candlelights could be seen glowing from inside the sacristy late at night. It was even said that sometimes you could hear the bell ringing in the tower as if guided by a ghostly hand, trying to send a message from the long-forgotten past.

Someone driving by would have very little indication—other than a neatly designed historical marker—that the understated old church was once the center of life in Chippewa City. From the outside looking in, there is no clue that the parish was built to withstand the harshest of winter winds, or that the interior stays remarkably cool, even on a hot day.

Formally named St. Francis Xavier but known more commonly as the "Chippewa Church," it is the only complete, structural remnant of Chippewa City, a village that was once home to at least one hundred families of full- and mixed-blood Ojibwe people and was the only Catholic parish to serve Grand Marais during its years in service, from 1895 until 1916. The building itself is still in good condition, thanks to the care and investment of the Cook County Historical Society, which worked to have it placed on the list of National Historic Places in 1985. As kids, we never went inside the church. The windows were boarded shut and the doors locked from the outside with old-fashioned iron padlocks.

I would not go inside the building for the first time until George Morrison's funeral in 2000. Because the Catholic diocese gifted the building to the Cook County Historical Society, certain rules are attached to the use of the space. You cannot use it for religious ceremonies, for example. But because of the Morrison family's deep connection to the church, an exception was allowed that day. Perhaps for the first time in eighty years, all of the pews were filled to capacity. There was a birch-bark basket set out on the old woodstove, and it was filled to overflowing with cards and sprigs of cedar. We could hear the drum from outside the main entrance, where my dad and I stood, along with many others, to pay our respects to one of Chippewa City's own.

Today the church has been given new life, with a fresh coat of white paint, restored siding, and new shingles. The interior walls are painted robin's-egg blue, with wooden pews painted reddish clay and gray. Its windows are no longer broken, and if the bell rings today, it is most likely at the hand of a sightseer or Jerry and Kay Sivets, stalwart Cook County Historical Society volunteers who open the church to visitors on the weekends in spring, summer, and fall.

Each time I visit St. Francis Xavier, I am struck by the smallness of the interior, the perfection of the tightly woven, dovetail corners, and the ornately decorated altar where the priest once stood. But more profoundly, an immensity of spirit still resides within the church's four walls, because it is not simply a building to the people who lived there—it is a place filled to the rafters with stories. When I go back there, I carry with me the memories of the people who generously shared their stories about the church with me. There are so many voices—first recorded on an old-fashioned tape recorder, then transcribed into a computer, and later printed on paper and filed by name. But when I'm inside the church, it's not the words that I read on paper that make the space seem alive—instead, it's the voices that I hear. The memories of Jim Wipson, Mike Morrison, and George Morrison, all of whom had deep connections to the church. And Vivian Waltz and Gladys Beckwith, who attended church here as little girls. I can hear all of them clearly in my mind, just as clearly as I heard the drum on the day of George's memorial.

DOROTHY DROUILLARD JOHANSEN was one of the first of my elders who agreed to talk with me about Chippewa City. She lived there when she was nine years old, where her father, Bill Drouillard, made a living as a commercial fisherman in the late 1930s.

Their house was right on the shore of Lake Superior, with the church located straight up the hill. Years later as an adult, she longed to return to St. Francis Xavier, preferably on foot, via the "Old Road," just the way she did when she was little. Even though Dorothy was in her eighties when I interviewed her in her apartment in Duluth, her voice chimed like a child's toy bell when she spoke of wanting to visit the church again after so many years:

> We walked [the Old Road] all the time. I remember one time when they started having Mass on the Fourth of July at the old Indian church, I wanted to go so bad, and I never got there. So, I told my son one day, "You know, I think I'm going to go in

[to Grand Marais] on the bus and then I'll walk to church." He said, "Mother, do you know how far that is?" I said, "I walked it all the time when I was a kid!"

Dorothy and her cousins Vivian Waltz and Gladys Beckwith would often reconnect each year during Rendezvous Days and Pow Wow at Grand Portage, and Dorothy told me that one year they vowed that they would all go back to Chippewa City together. They eventually did:.

So, I finally got to go. And I'm a very weepy person. I walked into that church and I was just overcome. I wanted to cry. It's just, it's so tiny. And I remembered all the time going to church there and where my family sat, and where the Morrisons sat, and it was very . . . emotional.[1]

Then Dorothy let out a tiny giggle and confessed in a soft whisper, "we used to play in there. We used to sneak in there and play."

Much of Chippewa City community life was centered around the activities of the church. George Morrison shared how his grandfather served as an usher and a keeper of the bell:

Dorothy Johansen on the porch of her home in Chippewa City around 1932. Courtesy of Dorothy Johansen.

My grandfather, James Morrison Sr., was one of the elders and founders of St. Francis Xavier Church . . . He usually sat in a gray pulpit chair he had built. The chair was always located to the left of the church door where he greeted people and officiated as the bell ringer. When I stand on Chippewa Beach and look up to see the church, it is the only remnant of my grandfather. The church remains a symbol of the community and our life here.[2]

When you enter the church today, it is easy to imagine the lanky figure of James Morrison Sr. standing just inside the double doors, ushering in his fellow congregates for Sunday Mass. The Morrisons, like most other Chippewa City residents, were devout Catholics. Before St. Francis Xavier was built, Mass was often held in the Morrison home, with John or James Morrison leading the service.

Congregation in front of St. Francis Xavier, with Antoine Fillison (*far right*), Charlotte Wishkop, Mr. and Mrs. Jim Morrison, Jane Zimmerman, Elizabeth LeSage, and others, late 1800s. Courtesy of Michael Morrison.

Michael Morrison, a younger brother to George, was very proud of his family's relationship to the church. Throughout his life, he carefully documented the history of St. Francis Xavier and in 1975 wrote a succinct and well-researched history of the church and Chippewa City called "19th Century Town." I interviewed Michael three times about Chippewa City. He was nearly eighty years old by then, had survived a stroke, and though his voice often wavered, the passion he had for the church always came through loud and clear. He spoke with pride about his family's many contributions to the parish, and how the people, long before there was a church to pray in, managed to conduct religious services as regularly as possible:

Although the missionaries had been coming to care for the Indians in Grand Portage as early as 1731 ... Father Charles Mesaiger, S.J., is the first of whom there is definite record ... the people along the North Shore were not so blessed. As there was only a priest visiting from Canada who came once a month, John Morrison Sr., offered his home for the celebration of Mass. Children as well as adults who had received instructions make their First Holy Communion in his home. On one occasion about twenty received communion.[3]

The Community Builds a Church

There had been no regular visits from a priest to the Grand Marais area until the arrival of Father Joseph Specht in 1880, who served as priest on the North Shore from 1880 until 1898. During the spring and summer of 1895, Father Specht directed the construction of the St. Francis Xavier Catholic Church on land donated by Antoine and Antoinette Fillison.[4] The 0.7-acre parcel was part of a larger tract of land (150 plus 80/100th acres) claimed by Fillison as a homesteaded property, as allowed by the Homestead Act of 1862.

According to Catholic birth records kept by the Thunder Bay, Ontario, diocese, Antoine Fillison is a half brother to the Anakwad family,

The interior of St. Francis Xavier. Photograph by Dick Gilyard.
Courtesy of Cook County Historical Society.

my great-grandmother's people. Anakwad in the Ojibwe language
means "cloud." Born in 1834, he is an uncle to my great-grandmother
Elizabeth Anakwad. Antoine was married to Antoinette (Shingibbiss),
and Fillison's name appears on many of the early land transactions in
Chippewa City. The Fillisons, like many of the Ojibwe families who
owned land outside of tribally held reservation lands in the mid-1800s,
had either secured a land patent through provisions of the Homestead
Act or were living on lands allotted to them, as defined by the terms
of the 1854 Treaty of LaPointe. Land transactions recorded as part
of the Chippewa City Plat do not include the sales price. As was the
convention at the time, the record shows that the Fillisons transacted
the land to the Catholic diocese for one dollar. If money above that
amount changed hands, it was not customary to include that information on the land deed. In 1884, for example, the Fillisons deeded land
to Martell and Therese Anakwad, my great-great-grandparents, for
one dollar. They in turn deeded smaller lots within that parcel to their
family members Elizabeth Anakwad Drouillard, Charles Anakwad,

and George Anakwad, all showing a one-dollar transaction fee. From the Fillison land abstract you can ascertain the chain of ownership for each lot, including the deed recorded in 1895, when they handed Lot Twelve over to the Catholic church.

Once the land was donated and deeded to the Catholic diocese, construction of the church began. In order to raise money for the building project, the congregation held "basket socials" where they offered up hand-made birch-bark baskets that were filled with home-baked sweets and other specialties. Lumberjacks who were camped in the area, having been hired to harvest the plentiful timber stands from the surrounding forest, snapped up the baskets of goodies, helping to raise the money needed to build the church.

The building was designed in the American half-dovetail style and built by Ojibwe carpenter Frank Wishkop from hand-hewn tamarack timbers that met in dovetailed corners, like precisely fitted puzzle pieces. The heft of the logs Wishkop used to frame the walls of the church is impressive when you see them in person because old-growth trees in good health, and of that size and straightness, are rare. The strength and thickness of these solid wood walls can be credited, in large part, for the longevity of the building. The original church building measures just twenty-five by thirty feet and has sitting room for around eighty people. The 225-pound bell and pews were added in 1896, under the supervision of Father Specht. At that same time, a lean-to was added to the north side of the parish, measuring eight by fourteen feet. This is where the visiting priest would sleep until a much roomier sacristy was added by Father LaMarche in 1903.

Father LaMarche oversaw the congregation from 1901 to 1906 and was followed in 1907 by Father Simon Lampe, whose missionary work required that he travel 140 miles from Cloquet to Grand Marais, and then up the shore to the Holy Rosary Catholic Church in Grand Portage, another thirty-five miles. Father Simon would visit Chippewa City most often during the summer months; winter visits were more sporadic. In the winter he would occasionally travel by snowshoe or dog team, housing himself inside the shelter of the sacristy and boarding his dogs inside the lean-to shed not far from the back door. It is somewhat astonishing to imagine Father Simon's arrival, mushing his team of dogs into the snowy churchyard, a dark figure against the gray sky of a winter afternoon. The sheer will it would take to journey such a distance, and in such a way, clearly shows his dedication to the parish and the hard-fought delivery of his work as a Catholic missionary.

The parishioners were an equally dedicated lot. Because there was one priest to cover the many miles between worshipers, the people often had to volunteer their services to the parish, especially given the forbidding winter weather on the North Shore. Many people remember the services and hymns being conducted in the Ojibwe language when a priest was not available to conduct the worship services. Dorothy Johansen recalled:

> *This was before my time, but at Christmas, the Indian people would gather at the church in Chippewa City and if the priest wasn't there, they would have their own service. They would probably sing hymns in Chippewa and I think that Jim Morrison would probably read the Bible.*[5]

There is a black leather-bound prayer book housed in the collection of the Cook County Historical Society; it is the same size and shape of most other prayer books, except that when you open it to the first page, all of the songs, scriptures, and verses are written in the Ojibwe language and not in English or Latin. This little hymnal perfectly symbolizes the state of flux that the people of Chippewa City experienced at the turn of the twentieth century, when many of them had fully accepted and adopted the words of Catholicism, but the way the words were communicated and shared were exclusively on their own terms.

St. Francis Xavier served as the community gathering place for the people of the village as well as many of the people living in Grand Marais with ties to Chippewa City. In most cases, those who lived in

Grand Marais and attended services at Chippewa City were relatives and friends of the people there, or had lived in Chippewa City at one time. Jim Wipson describes this community connection:

> *Everybody that was able would go to church on weekends. They'd all meet up at the Catholic church and then after church everybody would stand outside and jabber for an hour or so. It was just an old tradition. And then there was a few Indians that lived in Grand Marais. They'd come to that church on Sundays and that's how people got to meet each other.*[6]

When the church was blessed in 1895, many baptisms, first communions, and confirmations were given and received. That year, my great-aunt Mathilde (Tilly) Drouillard was baptized at St. Francis Xavier by Father Specht. Listed as her sponsors are "the Chief" Addikonse and

Ojibwe prayer book, 1925. Courtesy of Cook County Historical Society.

Catherine Nabagadwi. Tilly's older sister, Josephine Drouillard Zimmerman, was the first person to receive the sacrament of confirmation in the church on May 8, 1896.

In a letter written in 1971 to Olga Soderberg, then director of the Cook County Historical Society, Mrs. Zimmerman fondly recounted her lifelong connection to St. Francis Xavier:

Dear Miss Soderberg,

Here are a few captions on the Chippewa City as I recall them.

Josephine Zimmerman and Alice LaPlante. Courtesy of Vivian Waltz.

In about the years 1884 to 1900 I would say, there were between 75 and 100 families that lived in Chippewa City. There were the Morrisons, Kadunces, Caribous, Wishcops, Paros, Drouillards, Fillisons, MacLorens, Frosts, LaPlantes, Newtons, Anakwads and many more.

Many of the homes were burned in the fire of 1907. The Catholic Church was newly built at that time.

I distinctly remember the fire. It was in the month of September and after I had made all my berry preserves for the winter. I had 3 children at the time, Carrie who was 4, Robert who was 2 and Eva was the baby. The fire was so bad that we buried most of our furniture along with my preserves in the sand down on the lake shore. We, along with hundreds of other families were put up in Army tents. There were two big vessels out in the harbor ready to take people aboard in case the fire reached the shore lines. It was the sailors off these boats that saved the church from burning.

I was married in this church on November 10, 1902. Most of my eleven children were baptized there also. The first cemetery I recall was between what is now Backlunds and Beckwiths, below the road and close to the lake. There was a huge cross erected there. When they acquired the land where the cemetery is now, they moved all these bodies.

There was a huge statue of Jesus that was in the church for many years and then it was moved to the Catholic Church in Grand Portage. I don't know whether it is still there or not. I received my first communion in a private home. It was the home of John Morrison, Sr. as we only had a visiting priest who came once a month from Canada. There were about 20 of us who received at this time. Mrs. Anna Corcoran was one of them. Then we took our confirmation in the church at Chippewa City when it was blessed. There were many converts at this time. Many received their first communion, confirmations, baptisms and many couples had their marriages blessed.

Much of the money raised to finance our new church was by basket socials. The baskets were made by hand out of birch bark and of course all the food was home baked. The Lumber jacks in the vicinity (and there were many of them) were our best customers.

I hope that this will be of some assistance to you.

Sincerely,
Mrs. Josephine Zimmerman[7]

In an Independence Day dedication for the church written by Olga Soderberg in 1975, she identifies the person responsible for the two boats sent to rescue St. Francis Xavier from the fire as Mrs. Albertina Hedlund, who she describes as "an invalid from rheumatism" who lived on Maple Hill, about four miles inland from Chippewa City, and her nearest neighbor, August J. Johnson, a local businessman described by Soderberg as "very civic-minded."[8] Mr. Johnson

A grave at St. Francis Xavier on the lake side of the church, late 1800s.
Courtesy of Cook County Historical Society.

and his family were closely involved in the establishment of Cook County as a municipality—they were a relatively well-to-do family of Swedish settlers and were instrumental in business and economic development mostly through the acquisition of land, timber, and mineral leases. Mrs. Hedlund convinced August Johnson to use his political ties and "send word to the Governor to send relief ships to be stationed in the harbor. With this assistance at hand, everyone felt considerably, more safe."[9]

The sailors operating from the safety of the bay were able to contain the blaze, and the little Chippewa church was saved. Tragically, the Zimmerman home and many of their possessions were lost in the fire. But because they had been safely dug into the cool and wet beach gravel along the edge of the water, we can presume that Mrs. Zimmerman's jars of berry preserves were enjoyed by all that following winter.

Father Simon would continue his work on the North Shore until early 1923. His tenure saw the construction of a new Catholic church,

St. John's, in 1916, located within the city limits of Grand Marais. There were now two Catholic parishes a mile away from each other. Because there was only one priest, Mass was alternated between the two churches for several years, with people from Grand Marais occasionally attending services in Chippewa City and vice versa. Many Grand Marais Chippewa families chose to continue to attend services at St. Francis Xavier, even after the Catholic church was built in Grand Marais.

One attendee who stayed at St. Francis Xavier was Vivian Waltz, the daughter of Carrie Drouillard Paro, whom I interviewed at her apartment in Duluth in 1991. Vivian was a beautiful and soft-spoken woman. Every time I saw her, her silver hair was perfectly styled and she always had bright lipstick on. The Paros had lived between downtown Grand Marais and Chippewa City until Highway 61 was built in in the late 1920s, when they were forced to move. When I asked her why her family chose to attend church in Chippewa City even though the new church was closer to their home in Grand Marais, Vivian explained:

> I think my mother liked going there, and we had to go to church, you know. Of course, it's a ways to walk from Grand Marais to Chippewa City. We used to walk along the highway, along the lakeshore on the old trail.[10]

FATHER SIMON WAS REPLACED by Father Thomas Borgerding in 1923—and by this time the population of Chippewa City was in decline. Between 1923 and 1936, the parish would have two more priests assigned to it. When Father Boniface Axtman delivered the last Mass for the Feast of Christmas in 1936, the number of families living in Chippewa City had diminished to just five or six original families, including Jim and Joe Morrison, the LaPlantes, and a few others.

Since 1895, St. Francis Xavier has survived the great forest fire, raging winter storms, and a changing roster of priests and parishioners. But in the years following 1936, the church would face its most difficult test: surviving the decay brought on by poverty, prejudice, and community division, three factors that ultimately led to the final decline of the village and a long period of neglect for the Chippewa church.

During those years of division, the church wore its abandonment like an old ragged coat. Hidden behind a tangle of mangy, overgrown grass, the fractured windows allowed the cold wind and snow to blow through the building and out through the cracks. For many years, there was no sign of the people who used to care for it, who had built it with their hands and blessed it with their faith. There was no longer any indication of where the people came from, what they looked like, who their relations were, or the roads they had traveled to get here. The weathered wooden sign stuck into the ground on the south side of the highway gave the only clue: all it said was *St. Francis Xavier Chippewa Church.*

Red Rock Bay in Grand Portage. Courtesy of Grand Portage National Monument.

Chapter 2

A Gateway for the Ages

The Anishinaabeg Arrive at the Pigeon River

EVEN THOUGH I HAD PASSED BY that old St. Francis Xavier church sign hundreds of times, I had never really given it much thought. Leaving home for college, it may have been the last thing on my mind when there was so much to explore in the big world outside of my little hometown. At home, there was just one road in and out of town—and because of Lake Superior, you always knew what direction you were headed. Trying to find my own version of true north in the heart of the city I struggled to find my way, dropping out of college and tripping and falling my way through life away from home. I would begin to regain my footing while walking through the dingy, industrial-tiled hallways that led to and from a stuffy basement classroom at the Minneapolis College of Art and Design. It was 1988, and I was going to night school while working full-time during the day. The course was "Native American World Views," an anthropology class taught by Ruth Voights. The books that Professor Voights guided us through that semester were by authors who changed the way that I thought about literature and history; *Ceremony* by Leslie Marmon Silko, *Black Elk Speaks* by John G. Neihardt, and *Night Flying Woman* by Ignatia Broker. I saw myself in these books, and for the first time in my life felt a sense of belonging and a desire to learn more about why these stories felt so at home to me.

She had given us an assignment to interview someone about their own Native American experience and write an essay about them, incorporating some of the philosophy and cultural teachings we were reading about. I thought immediately of the artist George Morrison, because I knew both of our families had a connection to Chippewa City, which, at that time, I knew very little about.

With my parents' help, I called George on the phone and gave him a quick outline of what I wanted to talk to him about. He was cordial, yet quite formal, and we arranged for a visit to his studio in Grand Portage. My sister Dawn was still living at home in Grand Marais where she was in her senior year at Cook County High, and I asked if she wanted to come along for the interview. It was a clear, warm day, and we had baked chocolate chip cookies to share with George. I was nervous. It wasn't every day that you met a world-famous artist, and I didn't know what to expect. I had been warned that George was a very private person and that he was busy with an upcoming three-museum exhibit that would take place the following year. We arrived on time and there was a note on the door that said, "Come in and holler up." The door opened into a large workshop with bright white walls, high ceilings, and warm, natural light. George stood behind a huge work-table overflowing with the pieces and parcels of his life and work. He wore a plaid flannel shirt and jeans that fit him loosely, as if he had recently lost a fair amount of weight. He said "hello" and welcomed us inside.

The benches in the workshop were covered with tools, stacks of books, and pieces of wood by the hundreds. A lot of George's works at that time were abstract wood collages, inspired by the landscape and the horizon of Lake Superior. His home studio was on the shore of Red Rock Bay on the Grand Portage reservation, and the whole south side of the house was floor-to-ceiling windows facing the lake. There was a front deck with stairs trailing down to the beach, a jumble of rocks in rare colors of red ocher, granite, black, and clay. He ushered us back outside to the beach, pointing out the various features at the water's edge. It was clear that he spent a lot of time out here, and that this was the place where a lot of his art came from, both literally and figuratively. On one side of the deck was a drying rack for the wood George used to create his collages. Some of the wood drifted ashore and was left in its natural state, and some of it was gathered from other places, arriving in larger chunks and then cut and sized to fit. The rack allowed the wood to weather naturally in the sun and storms.

We moved back inside, my eyes wandering from object to object, trying to take it all in. Everything had a place of its own and seemed to be put there for a reason—the lack of randomness in his studio was remarkable. He pointed out some of his works in progress, including a series of relatively small paintings he called his "Small Horizon Series." He had recently been ill and had chosen to work on a much smaller scale that allowed him to sit and paint. Rich in color and texture, each painting was a testament to the ever-changing palette of colors, weathers, lighting, and moods of Lake Superior. When he felt that we had sufficiently toured his home, he started the interview process himself by pulling up a comfortable chair and saying, "You said on the phone that you wanted to talk about Chippewa City."

"Okay," I said, "what was Chippewa City like when you were growing up?"

He began to speak in what I can only describe as "George's way," using long, thoughtful pauses between answers, taking plenty of time to formulate his responses, and all throughout, emphasizing his phrases with stern and authoritative inflection. He began:

> At the turn of the century, Chippewa City was a very active vil-
> lage with upwards of one hundred to two hundred people at one
> time. The families that lived there are related to the families in
> Grand Portage now. It was an extension of Grand Portage. Like
> a reservation, in a sense. It was on the decline when I was growing
> up there. There were only four or five families left. It disintegrated
> mainly because people were moving to work in the Twin Cities
> and to Duluth. My mother separated and eventually divorced my
> father and moved to Duluth. My father [Jim Morrison] and his
> brother Joe were part of what I call the remnants, the old Indians,
> of Chippewa Village. They died in the late 40s and early 50s. I was
> living in New York at that time.[1]

We visited with George for almost four hours that day. He talked about Chippewa City and how the people who lived there interacted with the people who lived in Grand Marais, an aspect of the cultural history of Chippewa City that is key to understanding the greater context of my research, and of my own family history. He related stories from his own life, helped us to understand his vision, and shared many keen observations about art, art history, the cultural context of his work, and the creations of others. George was so generous

George Morrison. Courtesy of Cook County Historical Society.

with his time that any apprehension I had about meeting with him, or any initial shyness I felt about intruding on his private life, quickly melted away. He made us feel at home, and many of his Chippewa City recollections from that day formed the basis of inquiry into my early research about Chippewa City. In some ways, there would never be a *Walking the Old Road* without George's help, and many of the stories he told us are shared throughout the pages of this book.

He made us coffee to go along with the cookies we had brought, boasting that he could make "a good imitation of café au lait." He tantalized us with a few breathtaking and personal stories about our Drouillard relatives from Chippewa City, including great-grandmother Elizabeth Anakwad, who, according to George, was called "Chi'zubet" or "Big Elizabeth." I asked him if his own grandmother was proud of "the old ways":

> *Sure, she was. There is a certain pride in every nationality. Each has special qualities and uniqueness in their own way. But I felt I wanted to deliberately go away from that and go to art school in*

Minneapolis to a completely different world. There were—are—a lot of Indians in the Twin Cities. There has been a tremendous influx from surrounding reservations. Becoming white men in a sense by adapting everything. Thinking, education, white art, but underneath one can never leave that. There is something inside that always comes through. Gradually, the landscape themes crept through into my art. The indirect influences of land, water, and wood. I have never tried to prove that I was Indian by doing baskets, or painting feathers.[2]

Before we headed back to Grand Marais, George opened up two of his notebooks for us to look at. They were full of beautiful and original sketches, ideas for paintings and sculptures, his thoughts, and some quotes that he enjoyed. We had also made tentative plans to watch the movie *Powwow Highway* together sometime. He told us, "I hope you have gotten something out of this little exchange."

"Quite a bit," I replied.

In retrospect, George's so generously opening up his studio and answering our questions that day did teach me quite a bit. Not just about our shared past, but also how to listen and not talk over someone during an interview, how to wait and let an elder finish his or her thoughts before you speak, and how to treat whatever information is exchanged with respect. George's sharing his family history with us, and in turn some of our own, made me feel like I was part of a cultural tradition that until then had seemed inaccessible to me. To hear him acknowledge that "there is something inside that always comes through" made me realize that George was not only talking about his own life, he was talking about my life, and about anyone who has traveled far away from home in search of identity, only to discover that our true selves—the part that always comes through—are shaped by the people and places we come from. For the first time in my life, I was made to feel included and welcome to explore the places where my own worldview meshed with that of other Native American people.

Meeting George, and having him verify our shared historical connection, helped to clear away some of the first roadblocks I encountered on the long way back to Chippewa City. This was the first time that I turned my head and *really* looked back—something that was hard to do, because I was trying so desperately to keep my momentum moving forward. And now that I had learned a little bit more about "the old days" in Chippewa City and was given new, intriguing insights about my great-grandmother Chi'zu-bet's life, I was forced to reconcile my desire to blaze ahead with the realization that sometimes it's necessary to backtrack—to revisit some of the places of our past in order to have a full picture of who we are as individuals, as family, as a community. In order to find my way home, I would have to go way, *waaay* back, to the time when Anishinaabe people set out on the inland water route that would take them from the East Coast all the way to present-day Ojibwe country on the North Shore of Lake Superior.

A Gatekeeper for the Ages

Today, there are no signs or plaques to mark the place where our ancestors first arrived in Grand Portage. It is very remote, requires a boat, and the road to the landing is hard to find. There is nothing there to indicate its historical value or flaunt its importance as the place where our Ojibwe ancestors found the home promised to them in the prophecies.

Each year the Grand Portage Band of Lake Superior Anishinaabe hosts a Fourth of July Fishing Contest on the Pigeon River, attracting families in boats and seasoned fishermen who hope to break last year's record walleye or northern pike. This is by far the most activity one will find on the river—for the rest of the year, the Pigeon is a reverentially peaceful place where you can see eagles, otters, and the occasional moose traipsing across the sandy bottom of the river. Here, the water is churned into a perpetually muddy flow that has traveled

Pigeon River, looking east. Courtesy of Grand Portage National Monument.

through the elevated border country, over the steep cliffs of High Falls, and on through the valley where it eventually meets Lake Superior. These are international waters, serving as the boundary between the United States and Canada. Since the terrorist attacks in 2001, the security of the border has usurped recreational or casual adventures, and it's now common to see Border Patrol boats cruising the mouth of the river or hear reports about tribal fishermen being stopped and questioned by the authorities. Once, when my nephew Francis was a toddler, our family was fishing on the river in my dad's old fishing boat. We stopped to let Francis run around on the Canadian side, an innocent enough excursion—we just wanted the kid to stretch his legs. Minutes later a Coast Guard patrol boat came charging across the bay toward us. We quickly piled back into the boat and made a run for the landing. The Coast Guard cruiser didn't follow us into the shallow part of the river. Either it didn't want to run aground or the officers decided that we weren't an actual threat to national security.

It's important to remember that long before 9/11 and the strict enforcement of a hard border, the land that straddles the Pigeon River was once the territory of Chief Peau de Chat, who participated in treaties with both Canada and the United States in the mid-1800s.[3] It's also important to know that many centuries before 1899, when the chain of lakes and rivers from Lake of the Woods all the way to the mouth of the Pigeon were identified and marked by the International Border Commission, this river valley was just one of many remote and wild tributaries located in the heart of Anishinaabe country. Unless you are fishing close to the bridge that now connects the United States to Canada, it's easy to strip away the rigid and unnatural associations of the river as a boundary to be crossed, and instead experience it the way that our ancestors did: as a quiet, protected, and welcoming place that is teeming with life. Because the river has remained relatively unchanged for so many years, and because Anishinaabe people still rely on the river for so many things, it's a place of historic significance that conjoins us to our past, present, and future. On the Pigeon, time and space become untamed and fluid, just like the water that flows steadily between the banks of the river.

One day in 2016 my dad and I were fishing the river in that same old boat. It was a hot, sunny day, the kind of afternoon when the fishing is easy and time slows to a trickle. We rounded a bend in the river and carefully plotted our way through the shallows, taking care to keep the motor from running aground on a newly formed underwater island—islands appeared and disappeared regularly at the whim of shifting sediment. We fished our way toward Lake Superior to the place where our ancestors first arrived. The bay was now in sight, but there was movement in the air and we realized that we weren't alone. There was Migizi, a bald eagle, who was also fishing the mouth. As we approached, the bird continued flying low and slow across the opening of the bay, its wings heralding our arrival.

"There he is," I thought as I watched the bird gracefully police the entrance to the river, "a gatekeeper for the ages."

But unlike the humans who now guard the border, this one seemed easily distracted from his duties by the lure of a fat trout. The eagle quickly disappeared over the tall trees on Pigeon Point, no badge or license needed to assert its authority over the land. It's strange to think that this peaceful domain of eagles also serves as a two-way street to our past. Like the flight of Migizi and the drifting, sandy bottom of the Pigeon, the story of how our Anishinaabe ancestors got here involves all the elements of a successful

Dad with Pigeon River walleye, 1990s. (The fish was released.) Photograph by the author.

passage—resistance and tenacity, a sense of exploration, a strong current, good fishing, and sometimes the help of a guide.

THE MIGRATION STORY of the Ojibwe has been passed along through Anishinaabe oral tradition for centuries and is corroborated on paper by the Ojibwe-French historian William Warren and others. According to Warren, the ancestors of the modern Anishinaabe people once lived far away, on the East Coast of the Atlantic near the mouth of the St. Lawrence River.[4] Part of a larger group of northern Algonquin-speaking people, the Anishinaabe people were recognized by the name of their clan (totem or *doo-daim*) and had not yet coalesced into one tribe. In the late 1880s, an Ojibwe elder and storyteller explained to William Warren that our ancestors received a message from the sacred megis, a spiritual guide:

> *"My grandson," said he, "the megis I spoke of, means the Me-da-we [Midewiwin] religion. Our forefathers, many string of lives ago, lived on the shores of the Great Salt Water in the east. Here it was, that while congregated in a great town, and while they were*

suffering the ravages of sickness and death, the Great Spirit, at the intercession of Man-ab-o-sho [regionally known as Naniboujou, Nenabozho, Maniboujou, or Wenabozho][5] the great common uncle of the An-ish-in-aub-ag, granted them this rite wherewith life is restored and prolonged. Our forefathers moved from the shores of the great water and proceeded westward."[6]

And so the people traveled from the shores of the Atlantic to Mackinaw Island, where Lake Michigan converges with Lake Huron. Known by the French as "Saulteurs," or "people of the Sault," this group would divide into three tribes—the Anishinaabe, Ottawa, and Pottawatomi. The Ottawa stayed at Mackinaw, the Pottawatomi moved northwest into what would later be present-day Michigan, and the Ojibwe began their migration north toward Lake Superior with a large group settling at La Pointe on Madeline Island on the south shore of Lake Superior. According to Warren, all of the bands of the southern Ojibwe originally came from Madeline Island, which at one time encompassed a three-mile-long expanse on the western end of the island.[7] A smaller group of Anishinaabeg did not stay at La Pointe, but instead moved further north. This group of northern people are the ancestors of the modern Ojibwe bands who live in Thunder Bay, on Lake Superior, Lac La Croix, Lake of the Woods, and Rainy Lake. Wrote Warren:

The Northern division formed the least numerous body, and consisted chiefly of the families claiming as Totems the reindeer [caribou], lynx, and pike. They proceeded gradually to occupy the north coast of Lake Superior, till they arrived at the mouth of Pigeon River (Kah-mau-a-tig-wa-aug). From this point they have spread over the country they occupy at the present day along the British and United States line, and north, far into the British possessions.[8]

The actual arrival date of the Ojibwe to the Lake Superior region can be different depending on whom you ask. Bineshiikwe's account as shared in the book *Talking Rocks* by Ron Morton and Carl Gawboy places the Ojibwe people in the wild rice territory surrounding Lake Superior at least a thousand years ago.[9] This differs by about four hundred years from the timeline offered by Carolyn Gilman, the author of *The Grand Portage Story*, which has the ancestors of the Ojibwe arriving at La Pointe in the early 1600s and by 1730 completing their migration north, having established villages at the present site of Thunder Bay, Ontario, where they traded furs with the French as middlemen to the western Cree.[10]

Many Ojibwe scholars and teachers have explained that timelines and historical roadmaps are often the work of others, who may or may not have an agenda to impress upon the historical record, or an end goal that requires chronological proof in order to confirm validity. "It's a two-way street," my Ojibwe professor Collins Oakgrove once said, regarding the widely theorized Bering Strait route of migration to North America. In *A History of Kitchi Onigaming—Grand Portage and Its People*, the narrator writes that "oral tradition tells us that the Chippewa always have lived in North America. Indeed, they always have called themselves Anishinabe—the original people."[11]

My experience has taught me this: when you are interviewing an elder whose family has lived here for multiple generations, who was taught how to maple sugar in the spring, fish the waters of Lake Superior in the summer, harvest wild rice in the fall, and wait until winter to talk about the wild creatures that surround us, you come to understand that as Ojibwe people, we have always been here. So, when Bineshiikwe tells of the Ojibwe people knowing how to find and process rice for one thousand years, dating the people to roughly the year 1000, we know it to be true. It's just a different way of keeping track of time, and a different way of recording history. What I find to be the case, most often, is that the oral traditions passed along by our elders will eventually be corroborated by another voice, and that more often than not a historical fact will appear in the written record that supports the memory of an elder. Sometimes the evidence simply washes up on shore, to the delight and amazement of anyone who has ever found an ancient arrowhead, a bit of copper, or a well-worn trade bead, drenched in the colors of Lake Superior. As students of Native American history, we learn to trust that stories are indeed alive and well, that they speak to us in many different forms, and are most often spoken in more than one language.

Learning How to Speak Ojibwemowin
༶

My college Ojibwe-language teacher Collins Oakgrove used to refer to his class time as "chatting with Collins in the morning." If the class got changed to the afternoon in the next quarter, he changed the name to "chatting with Collins in the afternoon." Language lessons often came during the second half of the hour, because his teaching style was based on a holistic approach that taught us how to speak the words and phrases of Ojibwemowin from the inside out. Using joviality and humor, Collins had the ability to emulsify words and language into much greater messages about life. On the first day of class, before we learned the basics like *indizinikaaz* (my name is . . .), he taught us the difference between the words used by others to describe Ojibwe people and the words used by the people to describe themselves.

Traditionally, Native American people are Anishinaabe, which in the Ojibwe language means "spontaneous man"[12]—or, to put it another way, a human appearing out of the elements spontaneously. This idea of being "first" or "instant" human beings can be applied to Native people everywhere. For each tribe, all across North America, there is a unique origin story that places the people on earth as the first people.

The native people of Lake Superior are most commonly known as Ojibwe (pronounced phonetically as O-jib-way) and also as Chippewa. The origin and meaning of the most accepted name, Ojibwe, is somewhat contested. Like much of Anishinaabe history, the answer can change depending on whom you ask or where you look. Scholars often cite the Ojibwe historian William Warren, who noted that

"Ojibway" was a name given to the people by enemy tribes such as the Cree and was not part of their own lexicon of words.

Ojibwe's literal translation is "to roast till puckered up" and is based on the terrible practice of torturing prisoners of war by fire.[13] This version of the name is considered by some to be just plain "gruesome," as aptly described by the writer Louise Erdrich.[14] Many people believe instead that the origin of the word describes the puckered stitch found on the toes of traditional Ojibwe moccasins.[15] This interpretation is more widely used in modern histories. The Ojibwe language is based on detailed descriptions and animated interactions with the world around us, such as a specific style of moccasin. It includes clear divisions between living things and nonliving things, such as the word for "bread," which is considered to be animate, or living, because it rises up when baked: *bakwezhigan.* Perhaps the most culturally appropriate interpretation of the word *Ojibwe* is its relation to the root word *ozhibii'ige,* which means "write" and most likely comes from the Ojibwe custom of writing on birch-bark scrolls.[16] This theory is favored by many modern Ojibwe historians and writers including Anton Treuer, Louise Erdrich, and others.

To further confuse history, the word *Chippewa* is actually a nonsense word. It is, in fact, a mispronunciation of the word *Ojibwe,* which in historical records and early maps created by French explorers is written as "Oh-chip-e-way" or "Chip-eh-wa." Despite its somewhat dubious origins, the word *Chippewa* is found in most of the U.S. government treaties and official tribal documents. This is the name used for the group of regional bands known as the Lake Superior Chippewa Tribe, and also appears in many regional placenames, including Chippewa City. In 2016, the Grand Portage Reservation changed the wording on the sign that visitors see as they cross over the reservation boundary from the west. Where it used to say "Grand Portage Chippewa" it now says "Grand Portage Anishinaabe Nation." This is a good example of how words, like land, and like history, are constantly in the process of reclamation and change in Ojibwe country.

Professor Oakgrove taught us that in the Anishinaabe worldview, language is culture, and, like culture, language can, and should, change over time. This is a valuable lesson because learning to speak Ojibwemowin meant learning to live the language in real time; Ojibwe life and Ojibwe language are never viewed as separate from one another. Early on, the words that we said over and over in class would begin to insert themselves into my daily routine. I would begin the day with *makade-mashkikiwaaboo* (black medicine water) and would often bring the language with me into my dreams at night. To speak it is to live it—and once I began to learn the language, my grasp of the history of my Chippewa City ancestors would grow and change the way that I thought about almost everything.

The Men of the Waving Stick
~&

Kah-mau-a-tig-wa-aug, the Pigeon River, the gateway of our ancestors, was recorded on paper for the first time by the Jesuit missionary Claude-Jean Allouez, who traveled by canoe along the North Shore in 1667 and clearly marked the mouth of the river on a map.[17] It's believed that the French explorers Pierre-Esprit Radisson and Médard Chouart des Groseilliers had also passed by just prior to Allouez, during their illegal 1655 trading expedition. Regardless of whether their business was religious conversion or scouting for trade routes, the French were known to the Ojibwe as *wemitigoozhiwag* or "men of the waving stick," in reference to cross-bearing Jesuits such as Allouez and Father Jean-Pierre Aulneau, a Jesuit missionary who paddled the rivers from Lake Superior to Lake of the Woods in 1735.

By 1678, twenty years after Radisson and Groseilliers, the French traders would have a semipermanent presence on the North Shore. Although they did not carry big crosses like their Jesuit countrymen, the French explorers and traders who came a bit later did carry big expectations about making their fortune as traders and exporters of goods to Europe. They were reliant on the furs supplied by Ojibwe,

Dakota, and Cree trappers, as well as on help from indigenous people to survive in what was a very remote, rugged, and dangerous landscape. There was also the sticky relationship between the Ojibwe and the Dakota, who, at that time, controlled areas south of the Great Lakes.

On the first of September, 1678, Daniel Greysolon (commonly known as Sieur du Lhut), left Montreal for Lake Superior. In 1679, du Lhut was present at a council meeting between the Anishinaabe and the Dakota at the current site of his namesake city, Duluth. Early on, he established himself as an "agent of empire" in the fur trade.[18] He encouraged the Anishinaabe to develop commercial trading partnerships with the Dakota. In exchange for a reliable source of trade goods, the Anishinaabe would be permitted to migrate along the south shore, eventually to Chequamegon and Keeweenaw, where game was more plentiful.[19] Chequamegon would become the central location of Anishinaabe life, where a year-round settlement was established. Du Lhut is also known for encouraging intermarriage between the Dakota and the Anishinaabe,[20] because having the Ojibwe and Dakota at war with each other stood in the way of French profits. This marriage of people and cultures created a new genealogical reality for many families from the Chequamegon area, including the scholar William Warren, who claimed both Ojibwe and Dakota heritage. These people of mixed heritage were considered part of the Ma'aingan (Wolf) clan, one of twenty-two Anishinaabe *doo-daims.*[21]

After that fateful council meeting, du Lhut followed the North Shore past the Pigeon River to the mouth of the Kaministiquia, a river that crosses through what is now the city of Thunder Bay. This is also where the Pike, Catfish, and Caribou clans of the Anishinaabeg would base their summer village. Here, du Lhut established the first trading post in the region, relying on the help of the Northern Ojibwe to obtain furs, subsist on the resources of the forest, and build his forts and settlements on what is now the city of Thunder Bay, Ontario.

By 1680, the Lake Superior fur trade centered around several military posts, including Kaministiquia, Nipigon in Canada, and

The Pigeon River just below the Grand Portage Trail. Courtesy of Grand Portage National Monument.

Chequamegon Bay across Lake Superior on the south shore. Trade was under the jurisdiction of French military officers and regulated by the French government. In competition with English posts at Hudson Bay, the French government proposed to increase fur trade by increasing the number of trading posts in the region in an effort to sway Native American trappers with the convenience of a "home delivery" system.[22] This would bring the fur trade very close to home, making Grand Portage and the Pigeon River the port of entry for the delivery of North American beaver pelts and other trade goods to the rest of the world.

Words Are the Bones of Stories

Because of the active role Grand Portage played in the fur trade, cultural exchange between the Anishinaabe and European traders began quite early within the context of Indigenous history. In 1731, Pierre

Gaultier de Varennes, Sieur de La Vérendrye, and his company explored the lakes and rivers along the Pigeon River route. By that time, Britain's Hudson's Bay Company had already established several posts in the interior. However, the British posts followed a strict system of racial segregation, with direct trade and interrelations strictly prohibited between the fur traders and Indigenous people. The French smartly learned to adapt to Ojibwe and Cree trading customs, and they did not discourage or outlaw intermarriage, which would ultimately lead to long-standing French and Ojibwe alliances, as well as a good number of French and Ojibwe children all throughout Ojibwe country—my own family included.

When the French and Indian War began in 1754, the Ojibwe took up the French cause against the British and eventually helped the French and Ottawa alliance defeat the British at Mackinaw under the leadership of Chief Pontiac. The French would ultimately surrender Canadian territories to the British, and the Ojibwe would be forced to do business with the British fur traders.

Interestingly, an Englishman named Alexander Henry (the elder) was nearly killed during Pontiac's uprising at Mackinaw in 1763. His life was spared; "only the mercy of an Indian woman, who hid him in an attic, kept him alive while all the other white men were massacred in the yard below."[23] After surviving Pontiac's rebellion, Henry traveled to the North Shore, scouting the area for business opportunities. Described as a "Yankee" from New Jersey, he left Grand Portage in 1775 and paddled inland along the border route.[24] According to his journal, his men did not encounter any people living along the waterway until they reached Saganaga Lake, a five- or six-day journey from Grand Portage, and found what was left of a trading post located at the mouth of the Granite River. In his diary entry for July 20, he reported that

> there was formerly a large village of the Chipewa here, now destroyed by the Nadowessies [Dakota]. I found only three lodges filled with poor, dirty and almost naked inhabitants, of whom I bought fish and wild rice, which latter they had in great abundance.

When populous, this village used to be troublesome to the traders,
obstructing their voyages and extorting liquor and other articles.[25]

As a very early description of the Lake Superior Anishinaabe, it's
vitally important to put Henry's perceptions about the people who
were living at the mouth of the Granite River into the proper historical context, because his words set the stage for all of the other local
historical accounts that would follow, including that of Peter Pond, a
countryman of Henry's, the Treaty of Ghent commissioners Dr. John
Bigsby and Major Joseph Delafield, who wrote about the Gunflint
Trail Anishinaabe in 1823, and Alexander Henry the younger, who also
did a fair amount of travel writing about the Gunflint Trail area and
the Indigenous people who lived there.

"Poor," in this case, is juxtaposed with Alexander Henry's experience as a relatively wealthy Englishman from New Jersey. "Dirty"
could very definitely be construed as a prejudicial judgment, based
on his own preconceived ideas about "cleanliness," which at the time
were equated with religious devoutness and puritanical ideology. His
observation about the people being "almost naked," while shocking to
Henry, might simply have been an indication of the weather that day.
Anyone who has been fortunate enough to spend time on Saganaga
Lake in late July can appreciate being in a state of "almost naked," and
feeling well fed on deepwater trout and wild rice. It's all a matter of
perspective.

Henry's view of the Saganaga Ojibwe exemplifies how many early
non-Native historians used their words to dismiss Indigenous people
because they did not fit neatly into their own worldview. The Ojibwe
word *Saganaga* means "twisting lake with many islands."[26] Saganaga,
like all of the lakes and rivers along the border, is an important part of
the human history of Minnesota, including the history of the Anishinaabe people who have hunted, fished, riced, and paddled the borderlands for centuries. Henry and other early travelers of the border route
used their own words to shape others' perceptions about the Lake Superior Ojibwe without ever making room for the other side of history.

Ojibwe woman paddling near the Border Route. Her identity is not known. Courtesy of Cook County Historical Society.

Words are the bones of our stories, and they are alive and carry weight. That is why the historical works of William Warren, Anton Treuer, and other Ojibwe historians are so important. We, as Anishinaabe people, are challenged to counter the mainstream historical record, which is so often composed of ugly words, spoken with ill intent. Feeling the sting of "poor," "dirty," and "almost naked," I can't help but wonder what the Ojibwe people's description of Alexander Henry might have been on the day they sold him fresh fish and wild rice. I wish that they had been asked to record that moment, when they served as guides and helped an Englishman prepare for the next leg of his trip. My questions for them would be pointed and specific. I would like to know, for example, what kind of fish they caught that day, and how they caught them. Did they use nets? Had they made their own lures out of wood? I'd ask why the Ojibwe decided to let him and his crew pass that day, instead of turning them back. I wish that Henry had shown them as much mercy as his Indigenous savior at Mackinaw had shown to him when his own life was in danger. I wish that their Anishinaabe words to describe that summer day had survived and been able to fill in the historical gaps missing from the pages of his journal. Without their story, the historical record is crushed under the weight of one man's voice, and history becomes tilted and out of balance, like a canoe with all of the packs loaded to one side.

The Great Carrying Place

In 1729, half a century before Alexander Henry paddled the Pigeon River with his men, the Nipigon commandant Pierre Gaultier de Varennes, Sieur de La Vérendrye, was given a map of the route connecting Lake Superior to the northwest via an inland trail known by the French as the "Grand Portage." At eight and a half miles, the Grand Portage bypasses a series of waterfalls along the Pigeon River border route that connects the western water routes to Lake Superior and all points east and west. The Grand Portage trail itself precedes written history. It is believed to have been a common route for prehistoric people and migratory animals long before the first mention of the passage in written accounts. According to the Ojibwe migration story, the route was used by the people who first arrived at the Pigeon River and then continued west to eventually settle at Lac La Croix, Rainy Lake, and Lake of the Woods. This is a route that continues to be used today by the Grand Portage Anishinaabe, or anyone with a sense of adventure and a love of the deep woods.

The hydrological force of the Pigeon River at High Falls, the primary impasse circumvented by the fur traders headed inland on the border route, is so impressive that it makes its own weather at certain times of the year. It creates rain and snow, and it's common to see multiple rainbows when the sun penetrates the trees and bounces off the misty spray that hangs in the air where the river cascades over the cliff. When you visit High Falls in the spring, sometimes the spray of water ricocheting up and out of the gorge will drench spectators standing on the observation deck a hundred yards away. Further upriver is Partridge Falls, another impasse, albeit with a much smaller vertical drop. Our family has enjoyed many fine grouse dinners from these woods. And while the grouse are plentiful, this is legendary moose country, where the giant beasts still roam and browse the high branches of the quaking aspen and poplar trees.

Thinking back on the ancient history of the Pigeon River route as a conduit to move hunted and trapped animals out of the forest, I feel grateful to know the river as a wild and untamed place with no rules other than if things go wrong, you had better have your wits about you.

My dad has had many successful moose hunts on the river, even into his seventies, when the population was still healthy. He doesn't believe in hunting them anymore, and he has been outspoken about postponing the tribal moose hunt, or at least just agreeing to take a few bulls every fall to feed the Grand Portage elders and honor the traditional ways, without further threatening the strength of the herd. Back in the day, he would often put his boat in just above Partridge Falls and motor upriver before the sun was up, so that he could get into position before the pitch-black *moozoog* started moving into the shallow rushes where the lily pads grow. One time he was out there all alone. He put his boat in, as usual, and turned away to grab his gun and other gear out of the back of his truck. When he turned back, he saw his boat beginning to float away, headed right for the falls. Fortunately, he had not yet transferred the set of moose horns he had in his truck into the boat. During a hunt, he used these antlers to call in moose during the rut season, clacking them together to mimic the sound of two bulls locking horns over a female. Thinking quickly, he tied a rope around one of the horns and, standing on the bank of the river, held on to one end and aimed the heavy antler at his boat. He tossed the horn up into the air and in his first attempt landed it in the bow of the metal boat. Slowly reeling the rope in, he managed to catch the gunnel with one pointed tip of the antler. Hand over hand, he pulled his boat back to shore, managing to save what would otherwise have been a disastrous day on the Pigeon.

Partridge Falls on the Pigeon River. Courtesy of Grand Portage National Monument.

This river is of great importance to life at Kitchi Onigaming, the Grand Portage, which in Anishinaabemowin means the "great carrying place." It is one of the most well-documented historical sites in Minnesota—not only because of the extensive written records from early traders, and the many books written about the fur trade, but also because of what has been found buried in the ground surrounding the former depot. Since 1922, the earth around the original location of the trading post on the shore of Lake Superior has been meticulously excavated, dredging up the bits of history that the European traders left behind. The collection of artifacts is housed at the Grand Portage Monument at the foot of Mount Rose, a reproduction of the fort and stockade built at the location of the original trading post.

Based on the number of objects in the collection, the French and British trappers and traders who used Grand Portage as a rendezvous in the late 1700s lived well and left their footprints deep into the landscape. They also left behind their place-names and surnames, a heritage that remains buried in the blood and guts of history. And although the early French traders left their marks on the Lake Superior region, there is a great distinction to be made between those early European traders and trappers, who took what they could, and then moved away, and the Anishinaabe, who continue to honor traditional ways and proudly care for the land and waters where our ancestors first came to live after the great migration from the east.

In Their Tracks

After it cascades past Partridge Falls and crashes over High Falls, the water slows down and meanders through a swampy valley where the river bottom rises and falls with every drought and every rainfall. At the mouth, where the Pigeon River meets Lake Superior, there is a narrow beach where the Canadian shore lazily collects driftwood from the surf. My family has come here often to pick through the piles of sun-bleached branches and beaver cuttings, hoping to find the perfect walking stick or some other treasure washed up by the waves. We've left our tracks here in the dark sand many times, my nephew's tiny feet growing bigger and leaving deeper impressions with each passing summer. When you stand on the beach facing Pigeon Point, it is remarkably easy to picture the ancient ones hugging the shoreline in their birch-bark canoes, propelled by hand-carved paddles and weighted down with the necessities of their long journey from east to west. Although we can't possibly know if their boats faced rough water out of the east on the day they arrived, or if they were welcomed to the inlet by the calm waters accompanying a west wind, we do know for certain that they were the first to mark this sandy beach as home, and that their descendants are the people who have stayed here, long after our ancestors' tracks were erased by the waves.

So often, history treats Indigenous people as part of our world's past but not as part of its future. As we move through the Anishinaabe history of the North Shore, it is critical to remember that the people are still here—and in many cases don't live very far from the place where our ancestors first arrived. In fact, all of the people who live on the Grand Portage Reservation today have a shared connection to the land. Each family keeps its own stories, and most everyone comes together for annual events like the Elders' Pow Wow in May and Rendezvous Days the second weekend in August. And even the people who don't live on the reservation have family connections to the people there.

But my own family connection is fleeting. Because we did not live on the reservation until much later, Grand Portage has never felt like my home. For a long time, I did find beauty and peace there. As a band member, my dad put his name on a piece of tribal land right on the shore of Lake Superior, just a few miles past Reservation River, not far from great-grandmother Elizabeth's 1887 allotment. Because the parcel was held in a tribal trust, our family did not own title to the land but had the right to live there, as long as we were able to care for it. Over the years, my dad built a small house, and then added a guesthouse and a garage. Their view looked out on Blueberry and

Pancake Islands and included a closer, smaller chunk of rock that we nicknamed Seagull Island. A fisherman since he was eight years old, my dad put in his own boat launch, and we spent many summer days catching trout off of the reefs that run along the shore. He set up his deer stand up on the hill, just across the highway, which was adjacent to a prolific blueberry patch, and built a fire pit near the water where

Moon over Seagull Island. Courtesy of Stephan Hoglund.

our family spent many hours sitting and talking and experiencing the spectacularly unpredictable moods of the Lake. True to nature, Dad made sure we had everything we needed, and he kept his promise to care for it impeccably.

It was a happy time for us. My sister's wedding was held there and it's where my nephew took his first steps, inside the little kitchen of that house. My mother ran an antiques and collectibles shop for a number of years that led her to many friendships and acquaintances. Many people would just stop in and ask if they could walk the path down to the lake, or take photographs of the water, the islands, or the wild irises that bloom every summer out on the rocks. The land got inside of me and I still carry it around with me, although visits to Grand Portage are now infrequent and can be sorrowful. This severed connection to the reservation was all wrapped up with my own questions about identity and cultural belonging. But the truth is, I never trusted that that place would ever belong to us. Because my sister and I do not meet the blood quantum requirement put in place by the U.S. government and enforced by the Minnesota Chippewa Tribe, we would never inherit the right to live there. Not unlike our ancestors before us, we had land only to have it taken away. This is an important and complicated part of the story for many Anishinaabe descendants who find themselves somewhere in between. Perhaps this is why the story of Chippewa City feels so close to my heart. To walk in the footsteps of our ancestors is not always easy. The paths they took and the bridges they crossed were often treacherous and washed out by loss and sadness. And while the history of our ancestors is one of migration and often-forced displacement—through it all, the people have always kept walking, and talking. It's an essential part of being Anishinaabe.

Mrs. Blue Sky (*left*) and Mrs. Shingibbiss in Chippewa City, late 1800s.
Courtesy of Cook County Historical Society.

→ *Chapter 3* ←

AT THE PLEASURE
OF THE UNITED STATES

The Land Changes Hands

THE ELEMENT OF CHANGE—whether purposeful or by surprise—is present all throughout the living story of the Anishinaabeg and serves as the catalyst for major shifts in the landscape of Anishinaabe history. This is also true about life in the wilderness, which requires a degree of acceptance and adaptation in order to survive. If there is one certainty about North Shore life, it's that the water and the sky are in a constant state of flux. It was a source of great inspiration for artists like George Morrison, who found a new painting in every Lake Superior horizon. To live here year-round requires both flexibility and good planning, a fact not lost on anyone who has intended to spend a day on the water only to be sidetracked by a wicked wind out of the east, or a lightning storm that comes up so fast you barely have time to reel in your fishing line. Like my dad pulling in his stray boat hand over hand, understanding that the complex history of Indigenous people and the Anishinaabe relationship to land requires thought, good source material, and a very long rope that can reach all the way back to when the people traveled all over the land, unimpeded by Europeans, treaty arrangements, or imaginary borders.

Our family was raised on the water—in fishing boats, on snowmobiles over frozen water, and swimming in the lakes inland from Grand Marais. I've continued this tradition as an adult, spending a lot of time on the lakes and rivers that straddle the Canadian borderlands. Today, when you paddle or motor the old water routes from the interior lakes and along the Canadian border route toward Grand Portage, it is difficult to imagine how the French and British new-comers to the area could possibly have traversed their way through the deep and often treacherous wilderness without help from the Ojibwe. Every ancient route used by the fur traders had already been carefully navigated by those who came before. Stone tools and primitive arrowheads found on the upper Gunflint Trail have been carbon-dated at seven thousand years old. Both the ancient woodland people and the modern Anishinaabe people have used these same historic routes to travel to and from the wild rice lakes on the Canadian side of Saganaga Lake in *Dagwaagin* (fall), and to the *Biboon* (winter) hunting grounds further south, where the moose were abundant and the caribou moved in dense antlered herds. Winter camps were built in the shelter of the boreal forest and with the help of hand-meshed snowshoes made of cedarwood and sinew, and a cache of preserved meats and berries called pemmican, the people would, for the most part, survive the harsh and unforgiving winters that last almost half the calendar year.

Each season brought with it harbingers of the next. When the top of the snow hardened into a crust, the people knew it was time to move to the sugar bushes in the maple woods that run along the high country above Lake Superior, which would be full of running sap when the warm days and cold nights of *Ziigwan* (spring) began the thaw. When the spring rains came and the waterways and trails opened up again for travel, the people would move to village sites along the shore of Lake Superior, where fish were plentiful just off the rocky points and reefs that protected the shoreline from storm surges and treacherous waves. This is where the people would build the round frames for their wigwams and set up their *Niibin* (summer) villages.

Before the first Europeans arrived, Anishinaabe people moved freely throughout most of northern Minnesota and Ontario, Canada. It's very common for people with Grand Portage ancestry to have relatives all over Anishinaabe country. My great-grandmother's family, the Anakwads, share Bad River and Grand Portage relatives. Because it was customary for Ojibwe women to move to where their husband's family lived, Ojibwe clans and totemic groups have roots all over the Ojibwe Nation. Because it was common for people to have relatives at different reservations and Canadian reserves, traditional Ojibwe life included a lot of travel and adaptability. There are accounts of people traveling as far north as Hudson Bay and as far west as Rainy Lake or Lake of the Woods, to visit relatives, trap, hunt game, or conduct trade. Espagnol, the principal leader at Grand Portage in the 1820s, was known to have fished, hunted, and riced across a huge territory, ranging from the Kaministiquia River in Ontario, Basswood Lake, near Ely, and over to the trout waters near the Palisades at Beaver Bay.[1] And the Maymashkawaush family and other families from Grand Portage spent a lot of their time fishing, foraging, and hunting on Isle Royale, paddling thirteen or more miles each way from Pie Island to the closet western point at Isle Royale.[2] In her book *Chi-mewinzha,* Leech Lake elder Dorothy Dora Whipple put it this way:

> *Our Indians were all over. A long time ago, they were all over. That's how they used to talk to me about it, that I should put down tobacco. Wherever I go, I think about the Indians long time ago. My relatives were all over.*[3]

A seasonal lifestyle and the ability to survive on the resources that surround us on the North Shore have often been the cause of great misunderstanding between Anishinaabe people and non-Native people. When the first treaties were struck between tribal nations and the newly formed U.S. government, the freedom inherent in a seasonal lifestyle and the uninterrupted access to traditional food sources such as wild rice, moose, deer, and fish, as well as an unrestricted proximity to the unsullied waters of our homelands, would be the only bargaining chip that mattered to the tribes. Even when the earliest treaties were being drafted, Ojibwe Nations were already experiencing the early effects of European encroachment. Soon they would also be subjected to the will of U.S. politicians and frontiersmen. It was a tide of expansion that came in from the east and, like an extreme wind shift on a calm day, forced the people to change course, or be swamped by the unrelenting waves.

The Inherent Rights of the Ojibwe and the Early Treaties

One of the first agreements struck between Indigenous people and the U.S. government was the Treaty of 1783, which stated that "no citizen of the U.S. could settle on Indian lands," making it illegal for any non-Indian person to settle in the Great Lakes area.[4] This would be the first consequential treaty for the Grand Portage Anishinaabe because it effectively divided the traditional homelands with an arbitrary boundary. As part of this treaty, the Pigeon River was designated as the fixed border between the United States and Canada.

In 1794, an agreement known as "Jay's Treaty" called for all areas south of the Great Lakes to be "off limits" to non-Indian people. The status as an Indian territory would quickly be altered by the Treaty of Greenville in August 1795. In return for goods and annuities ranging from five hundred dollars to one thousand dollars per tribe, this treaty ceded all of Ohio and made special provisions for the U.S. government to build military posts inside the Northwest Territory. The agreement specifically recognized the rights of the "Chippewa" and other tribes to "hunt, fish, gather roots and berries, make maple sugar, and harvest wild rice."[5] This would be a significant moment in Anishinaabe history because it was the first time that the inherent rights of the people, as original inhabitants of the land, were recognized in a government treaty, which also acknowledged the importance of the traditional, seasonal way of life. If the government agreed to protect these rights, then the Chippewa would agree to cede their lands to the U.S. government and not to the British. This treaty forced the British to abandon their post at Grand Portage and move operations north to British territory across the border at Fort William, Ontario, the modern location of the city of Thunder Bay. By 1804, the once lucrative North West Company had moved northwest, abandoning the Pigeon River trade route for the sea route through Hudson Bay.

At the close of the war of 1812, a new U.S. Congress passed an act excluding "foreigners" from the fur trade in American territory. At that time, the American Fur Company purchased the Northwest Company's posts south of the Pigeon River, including those at Grand Portage. In 1823, it established a trading post thirty-five miles south of Grand Portage at Grand Marais, nicknamed "Fort Misery" by the tradesmen who frequented the area.[6] The establishment of this post brought the first European traders to the place now known as "Grand Marais."

Because of its natural harbor, the area around the trading post was deemed suitable for use as a port for the export of furs and other goods. It was also an ideal staging place for the American Fur Company's expansion into the commercial fishing business. When the fort was in operation, a number of North Shore Ojibwe families used the harbor for fishing grounds and seasonal living. At this time, Ojibwe bands lived in scattered settlements at Grand Marais, Beaver Bay, Red Sucker Bay on Saganaga Lake, Rove Lake, Moose Lake, and Gunflint Lake near the narrows, with a small core remaining at Grand Portage.[7] Most of the North Shore Ojibwe belonged to the moose, bear, marten, pike, lynx, crane, or reindeer (caribou) clans, with kinship to a particular clan closely connected to a geographic area.[8] For example, the Kadonce family belonged to the bear clan, and they lived west of Grand Portage at the mouth of the river that is now named for them.[9] And even though a friend once pointed out that "Kadonce" is the sound your car tires make at that particular dip in the road, it's really the place where that family lived. Modern maps and road signs spell the name "Kadunce," an indication of how changing just one letter can confuse things many years later. These totems, or, in Anishinaabe-mowin, *doo-daims,* form the social structure of Ojibwe life, help to maintain sustainable family groups, and serve as an effective way to prevent intermarriage between common family members. Children are born into the clans of their fathers and are taught the ways of their *doo-daim,* which to the Anishinaabe is just as important as what your name is and where you come from.

Fort Misery (the fur-trading post at Grand Marais) would be collateral damage in the governmental efforts to take control of Anishinaabe lands. In 1840, despite their attempts to tame the wilderness from their lonely outpost on the North Shore, John Jacob Aster and the American Fur Company were forced to abandon the business and give up on attempting to create a commercial fishing enterprise. The early treaties contained clear provisions that guaranteed Ojibwe people the continued right to live within and subsist on the resources of the land and barred non-Native people from settling in "Indian Territory." The treaties also required any trade activity on unceded lands to secure a permit issued by the U.S. government, which also required approval by the local Chippewa tribe. This restriction, along with the challenging weather, rugged landscape, and the remote location, contributed to the post's reputation as being a difficult, if not impossible, place to do business.

In the 1842 Treaty of La Pointe (not to be confused with the 1854 treaty, also signed at La Pointe), the "Chippewa Nation" was divided into the "Chippewa of the Mississippi" and the "Lake Superior Chippewa." This separation was owing to the discovery of copper and iron deposits on the North Shore and was an overt attempt to isolate the North Shore Anishinaabe for the purposes of negotiating mineral rights in the Lake Superior region.[10] This document included articles that outlined additional land cessation along the south shore of Lake Superior, adding the provision that "the Indians residing on the Mineral district, shall be subject to removal therefrom at the pleasure of the President of the United States."[11]

This meant that the early treaties that cleared the way for the copper boom on the south shore now included the active removal of Anishinaabe people from the landscape. Even now, almost two hundred years later, reading the words *removal* and *pleasure* buried together in the same government decree highlights the need to recognize and name the layers of historical trauma that shroud any telling of Native American history. For historians like me, who strive to tell a more balanced story, the language in these documents exposes how the government has historically treated the Anishinaabe people. Our ancestors were treated similarly to the way lumbermen treated the tall timbers of the north woods—simply as objects to be removed at the pleasure of the industry, an approach that was sanctioned by the U.S. government.

In 1847, fifty-nine "chiefs" from Lac du Flambeau to Grand Portage marked their names with an "X" signifying their agreement to cede vast amounts of territory along the upper Mississippi in exchange for a payment of seventeen thousand dollars. Article I of this document optimistically promises "that the peace and friendship which exists between the people of the United States and the Chippewa Indians shall be perpetual."[12]

In addition to the payment, which would be meted out over the course of six months, the tribes and the U.S. government agreed on some additional provisions, including the commitment to establish schools at designated locations throughout Chippewa territory and the promise that each Chippewa band would be assigned a blacksmith, teachers, and laborers who would be paid by the government but serve as employees of the various tribal communities. This provision would forever change the course of my own family history, because it would provide passage for my great-great-grandfather, Narcisse (Nelson) Drouillard, to Grand Portage. Nelson, a thirty-one-year-old, skilled builder and metalsmith, was hired to serve as the first blacksmith at Grand Portage, thereby fulfilling at least one of the benefits that were promised to the Grand Portage Anishinaabeg in the Treaty of 1847.

The Mountain with Two Names

Anishinaabe culture has built-in activities that have been practiced and perfected for thousands of years. In the time leading up to the signing of this series of land-cessation treaties, the balance between cultures tilted heavily toward traditional ways. Before there were fish markets and trading posts, the people would often travel inland for long periods of time in the spring to harvest maple sugar, hunt moose, caribou, and other big game, or gather wild rice in the fall. Winters were often spent trapping beaver, mink, fox or marten, and setting up camps along inland waterways and lakes. The families would then return to the shore of Lake Superior to their summer fishing grounds. This is not that different from what our modern families still do— flocking back to the lakes and rivers when the trout are biting and the sun warms the southern facing slopes along Lake Superior.

The people continued to live a migrant lifestyle well after cultural contact was under way with the early European settlers and well after the early treaties were signed. Even though a certain degree of acculturation was already taking place, the people stayed true to their seasonal traditions. Timothy Hegney was installed as the first schoolteacher at Grand Portage in 1856, a government position provided for by the Treaty of 1847, like the one that brought my great-great-grandfather to Grand Portage to serve as blacksmith. In his "Schools Annual Report" for October 1, 1856, to September 17, 1857, the teacher provided some historical perspective on the seasonal lifestyle of his students:

> *The roving habits of the parents are a great drawback to the children. During the five weeks at the Sugar Bush last spring, I had but four white children and two half-breeds attending school. The vacations were a fortnight at Christmas and a week at Easter. The Indians are preparing to go to their fishing stations, so, if I have hard times, I get easy starts; I take some pleasure in doing as much as I can for them while they are here.*[13]

It is difficult to determine the actual Ojibwe population of the North Shore in the mid-1850s because no one was keeping close track. But that would soon change. From 1854 to 1890, there would be a gradual but steady increase in non-Native business interests and the vast resources that could be found in the waters and forests of the North Shore. As more and more people arrived in boats from all directions, the increasingly valuable commodities of land, minerals, and timber would begin to tip the scales toward a white majority population. When Hegney wrote his report, he and his family were part of a small minority of non-Native people who were sent deep into the heart of ceded territory to bring English words and European skills such as farming and carpentry to the moose, marten, pike, lynx, and caribou clans.

My great-great-grandfather Narcisse (Nelson) Drouillard was installed as the first government blacksmith on the Grand Portage Reservation in 1851. A transplant from Detroit, he arrived ahead of his young family and was put to work immediately building the school where Hegney would hold classes, a barn, a warehouse to store treaty goods, and a blacksmith shop. In the absence of a government farmer, he was also charged with clearing land for a garden and encouraging "the Indians to build 'more comfortable' homes."[14]

BLACKSMITH SHOP.

NELSON DROUBILLARD, Pro.

Bayfield,   •   •   Wi..

THE undersigned has re-opened his shop on Third street, and is now ready to do all kinds of blacksmith work on short notice. Terms strictly cash. No money, no work. Call and see me at the old shop.
        n22-v2-tf   N. DROUBILLARD.

Nelson Drouillard, blacksmith. Drouillard Family Collection.

Nelson's wife Archange Chauvin Drouillard and their three-year-old son John joined him in Grand Portage six months after his arrival. I found John Drouillard, my great-grandfather, listed on the Grand Portage school register in 1856, when he was eight years old.[15] According to the roster, he was reported to be making "good" progress reading and writing on the slate. It's quite likely that he was one of the four white children who reported for school during maple sugar season in Hegney's 1856–57 report to the government about his work at Grand Portage.

Even well after the Treaty of 1847 was signed, the North Shore Ojibwe did not stay in one place but would make the trip to Grand Portage when their treaty payments arrived by boat. Reporting on the first annuities payment in 1851, the year that great-great-grandfather Nelson arrived at Grand Portage, the Annual Report to the Commissioner of Indian Affairs stated:

> *There would be over two thousand Indians in Grand Portage on days when payment was made. Runners would go out and call them in. They would come as far as Vermilion Lake and Lake of the Woods, or from wherever they were located in Northern Minnesota.*[16]

Henry C. Gilbert, the government agent in charge of annuities distribution for the Treaty of 1847, was on the same boat that brought my great-great-grandmother Mrs. Archange Drouillard and her son John to be reunited with Nelson. They arrived at Grand Portage Bay in the company of John Godfrey and his daughter Josephine. The other non-Indian people living in Grand Portage at that time included Hugh H. McCullough, the general manager for the American Fur Company; John McClaren, company clerk; Sam Howenstine; brothers William and Henry Elliot; the teacher Tim Hegney, his wife Mary, and their young daughter; and a few other families who lived on the Pigeon River.[17]

In the written family history that describes the Drouillard family's arrival, it is said that Agent Gilbert, upon

> *seeing the highest point of the mountain on the east side of Grand Portage ... thought he would like to go to the top of it. He asked some of the party to go with him, and invited Mrs. Drouillard and Miss Josephine Godfrey, to go along. They went, and were the two first white women to ascend this peak, which has ever since that day been known as Josephine Mountain.*[18]

I had hiked this trail before I knew that great-great-grandmother Archange had also climbed the mountain on the fateful day that she arrived in Grand Portage from Detroit. Treading along the path that leads to the summit of Mount Josephine is a bit like going back in time. The climb is steep and long and the rocks and trees that line the trail are heavy with history. When you reach the peak, the wind swirls around you from all four directions, because up there you are elevated far beyond any of the surrounding bluffs. In the old stories, this high vantage point is believed to be where the thunder beings—the mighty spirits of the sky and protectors of the Anishinaabe—would gather, ready to throw lightning bolts down at any force or malevolent spirit that threatened the people. When you are at the top, it's very easy to imagine the sound of massive wings fluttering overhead—so easy, in fact, that your intuition tells you that you should not linger there for very long.

After discovering this family history about Mount Josephine and its English name, I've come to think about the mountain in a different way. There is a clear sense of pride in knowing that your great-great-grandmother was one of the first white women to climb Mount Josephine, but also a bit of shame that is rooted in the deep-seated recognition that any claims to the naming of this sacred place by white settlers, even if you are related to them, is colonialism, pure and simple.

At the summit of Mount Josephine. Courtesy of Grand Portage National Monument.

The Ojibwe name for the mountain is not known by any of the elders I interviewed. But there are clues, such as the mountain's being identified as "The Thunder" by the fur trader John Johnston.[19] Perhaps the Ojibwe name is remembered by a relative I have not yet met, or perhaps it will come back to our people in a dream, the way other names are given and found. Until then, we will continue to honor those who leave their prayers along the pathway to the summit and offer tobacco to all of our relatives who have walked there before us, whether they walked in moccasins or in pointed leather shoes. At the top, we will look out on the vast horizon, with an eagle's view of Wauswaugoning Bay (bay where they spearfish by torchlight), Minong (Isle Royale), and the Susie Islands. This is the place where we will sit and wait for the lost answers to rejoin our lingering questions.

The Treaty of La Pointe
⟶❦

In spite of the annuities, debt forgiveness, and other payouts promised as part of the great land cession of 1842, the Lake Superior Ojibwe were not amenable to the government's efforts to remove the Chippewa people from ceded lands. President Millard Fillmore received a Chippewa delegation in Washington, D.C., in 1852 and was convinced by the delegates to rescind the order for removal. The president, in council with the commissioner of Indian affairs, "noted that in order to get these bands to cede their rich mineral lands on Lake Superior's North Shore, they might have to be allowed to remain on small reservations." Government agent Henry Gilbert, the man who accompanied my great-great-grandmother to the top of Mount Josephine, advocated for the tribe's position, warning that the Ojibwe "will sooner submit to extermination than comply" with the order to remove them from their homelands.[20]

Weighing the options, the commissioners acquiesced. In Article II of the treaty, reservation lands were designated for the L'Anse, Vieux de Sert, Ontonagon, La Pointe, Lac du Flambeau, Lac Court Oreilles, Fond du Lac, and Grand Portage bands. In 1854, these Ojibwe bands signed a treaty with the U.S. government in which they agreed to the largest land cessation in the history of the Lake Superior Ojibwe. Known as the "Treaty of La Pointe," it relinquished 51,840 acres of land at Grand Portage alone.[21] As part of this treaty the Lake Superior Chippewa were to receive payments worth nineteen thousand dollars per year for twenty years, plus a onetime bonus of goods in exchange for their land.

At that time, the people living at Grand Marais were led by Addikonse (Little Caribou), who shared political leadership with the "first man" at Grand Portage, Zhaganasheence (also known as Grand Coquin or Little Englishman), as well as with two other clan leaders, Waywaygewam and Maymushkowaush (Most Powerful One).[22] Addikonse, born in 1789, was a stately and diplomatic individual who was well known as a great orator and negotiator for the people.[23] As a tribal leader, Addikonse helped to guide the people across the bridge that joined traditional ways and the ways of the European traders and businesspeople. He would serve as a staunch defender of his people's rights throughout the next phase of Ojibwe and government relations, and in fact, he was the last of the Ojibwe leaders to sign the treaty on September 25, 1854.

Addikonse, or Little Caribou, is one of the oldest names to appear in the early, written accounts about the Grand Marais Anishinaabe. His grandson Joe Caribou lived at Chippewa City and the Caribou family have relations all across Anishinaabe country. Observers in attendance at the treaty signing in La Pointe, Wisconsin, reported that Addikonse "long stood, solitary and alone, pitting himself, nobly, against the Government orators, and insisting that the proffers of annuities, &c., were inadequate."[24]

Annuity payment day, Bad River, Wisconsin, 1870. Photograph by Charles Zimmerman. Courtesy of Grand Portage National Monument.

The *Annuities List of the 1854 Treaty* divides the people into regional bands or family groups. It includes separate annuities lists for the Grand Portage band at Grand Portage, the Addikonse band at Grand Marais, the Maymoshkawash band, and others. The annuities payment records show that Zhaganasheence received $10.59 in treaty annuities, with Addikonse, the leader at Grand Marais, receiving $7.06.[25]

A primary objective of the Treaty of La Pointe was to clearly define where Ojibwe people could and could not live. Immediately after the signing, many of the North Shore Anishinaabe lived within the modern borders of the Grand Portage reservation, though this was not enforced owing to the lack of an organized government presence on the North Shore at that time. At this point in history, the Anishinaabe people remained the majority ethnic group on the North Shore, a fact that is often underplayed by early European accounts. The following recollection on the very day that the Treaty of La Pointe was signed provides a deceptive description of the Chippewa presence at Grand Marais:

> on or near the 25th of September, 1854, [a group of mineral prospectors] pulled into the harbor, finding five Frenchmen from Detroit already there, having arrived just two days ahead of the McLean party. Apparently, before the arrival of that group, "there was not a soul, Indian or white men, living at Grand Marais."[26]

What is important to note is that the date of the signing is in the early fall of the year, and would likely find the Ojibwe people in the height of the hunting and ricing season, requiring them to move far inland to Gunflint Lake, Northern Light Lake, the Royal River, or across the Pigeon River to Whitefish Lake in Ontario. This would leave the convenient impression that Grand Marais was uninhabited territory. In the book on Grand Portage people, *Kitchi-Onigaming*, the seasonal lifestyle of the people is recorded in detail. The book, published by the Minnesota Chippewa Tribe in 1983 and written as a collaboration between Grand Portage historians and scholars, documents that in springtime the people moved from their winter camps to maple sugar groves at Grand Portage, Grand Marais, Beaver Bay, and on the Canadian side of the Pigeon River. In the summer, it is reported that the people kept gardens at Maple Hill above Grand Marais and harvested fish on the reefs east of Grand Marais.[27] This included the Scott family, who lived at the mouth of Kimball Creek, as confirmed by Bill Amyotte, whose mother Maggie Scott was born there:

> *[my mother] said that [Grandpa Scott] would follow the net or fish from along the shore . . . Salt trout. I think she said we got ten cents a pound for it.*[28]

The Treaty of La Pointe essentially opened up all of the North Shore to European settlers, mineral hunters, and business opportunists. According to the historical accounts reported by Cook County historian Will Raff and others, many men were impatiently awaiting news of the treaty's signing, with some particularly overzealous prospectors waiting in boats inside the Grand Marais harbor, just a short distance offshore, ready to stake their claims to the land once news of the signing was made official.[29]

After a very short time, the North Shore became inundated with fortune seekers. Less than two months after the treaty was signed there were so many copper prospectors that surveyor Thomas Clark II observed on his late fall 1854 trip to the remote village of Grand Marais that while "landing at a half breed fisherman's dock," the owner "has gone up to Superior leaving his wigwam and traps to care of themselves. Such is the confidence all have in each other that we have no fear of thefts. But not so with the copper hunters and claim makers; they are jumping, crowding and crushing each other's tracks in all directions."[30]

With the signing of the 1854 Treaty of La Pointe, the once easily traced footprints of our ancestors would soon be obscured by the leather-soled tread of prospectors, copper hunters, gold miners, and entrepreneurs looking for a new place to do business on the North Shore.

The old birch tree in front of the Birch Terrace Supper Club in Grand Marais.
Courtesy of the Minnesota Historical Society.

→ *Chapter 4* ←

HERE WERE MANY WIGWAMS

The Grand Marais Chippewa

WHEN YOU STAND ON HIGHWAY 61 and look up the hill at the Birch Terrace Supper Club, you'll see a gnarled and age-old birch tree on the west side of the yard. Unlike the younger tree growing just to the east, this older birch tree has a massive trunk and, over the course of many years, has expanded the reach of its branches out in all directions. In my parents' photo album there is a picture of me as a little girl taken inside the Birch Terrace Supper Club, which was for many years the most popular restaurant in town. I'm wearing a flowered jumper and sitting at a table covered with a red and white checkered cloth. Our family favorites were dinners of fried walleye or surf and turf, served with homemade brown rolls and an old-fashioned relish tray. Like other Grand Marais families, we were following in the tradition of

the Johnson family's hospitality. The man who built it as his second home, Charles Johnson was known for hosting lavish parties for his friends and visiting dignitaries. He was one of the first European homesteaders to make a claim in Grand Marais, which was once known by an entirely different name.

The author at the Birch Terrace Supper Club, circa 1969. Drouillard Family Collection.

In Ojibwemowin, *Kitchi-bitobig* means "the great duplicate water; a parallel or double body of water like a bayou."[1] It's role as a central location for fishing, hunting, and exploring the surrounding wilderness appears in this romantic account from Dr. F. B. Hicks, who wrote an article titled "Historian Tells of Early Beginnings of Grand Marais as an Indian Trading Post" for the *Duluth Tribune* in 1929:

> *Indian legend tells a mythical story of a wonderful medicine man named Ogi-mah-quish-on, who lived at a place on the shore of the great lake where the huge cliffs nursed two wonderful bays that were separated by a point of rock and an isthmus of gravel. One bay made a deep indentation into the land. Its water was shallow. In places grasses and flowering plants sprang up from the water, which was calm and peaceful even when the big sea waves were most fierce. The other had sloping, gravelly banks. Here were many wigwams, for fish and game were plentiful and to these bays trails and canoe routes led from all directions.*[2]

Of course, now the town and the waterfront look quite different than in 1929, when Dr. Hicks shared his perceptions about Grand Marais, but it continues to be the hub of activity for this small town of 1,500, which grows to fifty thousand or more people every summer. The sign marking the entrance to the city limits uses the French voyageur description—Grand Marais—which refers to a great harbor, or refuge.[3]

In a report written in 1939 about the Grand Marais harbor, the U.S. Army Corps of Engineers in a section titled "Indian Inhabitants" makes the claim that "The Sioux Indians, the earliest inhabitants recorded by history, were occupying the region about the time Columbus discovered America. Later they were driven out by Chippewa tribes who migrated to that part of Minnesota about 1550." The report goes on to say that "A Chippewa village was located at the present site of Grand Marais and Indians occupied the entire region, except for occasional white explorers, trappers and fur traders."[4]

In Dr. Hicks's history of Grand Marais, he suggests that Radisson may have stumbled upon Kitchi-bitobig in 1657, when the explorer "recorded that Grand Marais was a popular Indian village." Hicks also states that when a trader named Malhoit was on the North Shore, he recorded in his diary on Tuesday, June 20, 1830, that "At 3 o'clock in the afternoon I camped at the Grand Marais because the savages told me I should have good fishing there."[5] Given that the Grand Marais harbor continues to be a place where prized lake trout, coaster brook trout, and coho salmon are regularly caught, it can be determined with confidence that the "savages'" recommendation to Malhoit was genuine.

There is plausible evidence that Chippewa people lived all along the western hillside well before more modern houses were built by the early European settlers. On a map created by the historian and photographer M. J. Humphrey and revised by Grand Marais resident John Blackwell Jr., there is an "Indian Burial" on the east side of Sixth Avenue West, just across the street from where early Scandinavian settler Charles (Charlie, Chas) Johnson built his second home.[6] The house, made of native stones and local timbers, is situated on the crest of the hill. During construction, Johnson's crew found it necessary to

Longbody and others at Chippewa City. Courtesy of Cook County Historical Society.

avoid several graves on the hillside that were covered by ceremonial grave houses. It was also reported that the crew had to "take care not to dig down too deeply and disturb the grave contents" while putting in the drive.[7] In an interview with Pat Zankman, former director of the Cook County Historical Society, Charles Johnson's son, Lloyd K. Johnson, was asked about the presence of graves on what are now the Birch Terrace Restaurant grounds. He explained:

> There was an old Indian burial ground on the Birch Terrace. When we leveled out the ground we hit into some of the graves and my father made little mounds over so he wouldn't touch the graves.[8]

Catherine Jones was the wife of the physician Dr. Henry Jones, who served as the town doctor from 1898 to 1902. She was one of few white women living in Grand Marais at the time, and her diaries reveal, in both banal and colorful ways, what life was like in the remote village at the turn of the century. She and Dr. Jones had been befriended by Charles Johnson, and in this entry from Sunday, March 12, 1898, she recalled a dinner at Johnson's place that was called to honor six men visiting from Hovland:

> The townspeople entertained the Chicago Bay boys at Charlie Johnson's for supper. I sent over pans of escalloped potatoes, a cake and loaf of bread. About 25 were present and seemed to have a good time.[9]

Historian Will Raff also wrote about the festive parties hosted by Charles Johnson, including the unusually extravagant trappings that could be found inside his home. According to Raff, Johnson owned a pump organ as well as some other rare objects, including

> an expensive cocoa set of delicate porcelain china, with large pitcher and cups, a treasure still preserved in his son's Duluth home. Surely these were not the usual possessions of a stereotyped

*"frontiersman"; but then, there was much about Charlie Johnson
that defied any stereotypes. It was surely a departure from North
shore norms, too, that Charlie had a Japanese "house-boy" and
cook to supervise the household and the overworked kitchen.*[10]

The Johnson house was just one of several homes and businesses
owned by Charles Johnson at the turn of the twentieth century. He
also built the first post office and one of the first general stores in
downtown Grand Marais. His house on the hill would serve as the
gold standard of fine living on the North Shore and would become
a focal point for others living in the vicinity of Grand Marais. As it
happens, the house also provided respite from high water, an improvement over the Johnsons' first house that was built closer to the water.
In the spring of 1899, Catherine Jones alludes to a rainy spell that
lasted from April 23 through the 28th, when the storm subsided and
sunny weather finally returned to the settlement:

*Very pleasant and warm. Water nearly covers Chas Johnson's
yard. Doctor and I went along the lake shore picking up stones.*[11]

Second home of Charles Johnson. Courtesy of Cook County Historical Society.

After some particularly tumultuous spring storms, water has been known to flood the lowlands and settle in deep pools along the marshy areas close to shore. This is perhaps why Grand Marais's rumored French nickname is "Great Marsh." The floodplain makes itself known every spring, when the ground is still frozen and the first of the spring rains combine with meltwater to create shallow ponds that are known to overtake basements, buildings, and parking lots that are close to the water.

Irene Paro Sullivan was a Grand Portage band member who grew up between Grand Marais and Chippewa City, and she remembered these floods. As a young girl, her playground was the area around the east bay, the current location of a number of hotels and stores. Before Highway 61 was built, and before there were parking lots at the edge of the water, the spring floods were a natural part of the ecosystem:

Irene Sullivan. Courtesy of Mary Stack.

> *There was a big sand pit where we used to play and a big red barn down near the cranberry bog. I don't know if anyone picked cranberries there, but I remember the bog because my mother used to talk about it.*[12]

The Anishinaabe who lived here long before the harbor was deepened, and before the break walls were built, lived on the high ground above the lake. This is also where they buried their family members, resting them up on the hill to keep the graves safe from the spring rains or the big seas encroaching from the harbor in the fall. And this, smartly, is also where Charles Johnson built his second house, just north of the old birch tree. That old tree has seen it all, from the time when people chose the hillside as an eternal lookout for their families, and through the days when we sat and dined on corn fritters and T-bone steaks. It's one of the few holdouts, and it gives witnesses to history an opportunity to imagine what the hillside might have looked like before it was cleared to make way for the foundation and driveway.

The presence of graves on Birch Terrace hill is not disputed by the Johnson family and has become a point of interest to people familiar with local history. The current owners of the establishment even tout the existence of "Indian graves" on their menu, right alongside the list of entrees. But nowhere do they acknowledge the names, birthdays, causes of death, or even the tribal affiliation of those who are buried there. Standing on the sidewalk below, it is easy to imagine the house vanished—and in its place a collection of mounds dotted with wooden and stone grave markers. The old birch tree serves as the only remaining monument to the bones of our ancestors. They are still there, buried underneath the pavement, cement, and masonry.

Francis Roussain Lays Claim to Artists' Point

The Treaty of La Pointe that opened up the North Shore to European settlement was also the first treaty to divide land individually between tribal members. Each head of household or single person over twenty-one years of age could select his or her own parcel of land within the boundaries of ceded territory, an area encompassing all of northeastern Minnesota. It is important to note that the treaty did not require the selection of land, nor were parcels of land "assigned" to tribal members, as was the case of the Dawes Severalty Act thirty-three years later. The Dawes Act, also known as the Allotment Act, divided reservation lands into forty- to 160-acre tracts, with the overall goal being "the dissolution of tribal boundaries by giving the land to the Indians in severalty."[13] These tracts were to be held in trust by the government for twenty-five years, with the "full rights of citizenship" made a guarantee to all who stayed on the land for the duration of the trust period.[14] The Dawes Act also opened up all unpatented or unclaimed reservation lands to white settlers, making available for sale any acreage that remained unassigned. The Dawes Act resulted in historic losses of land and resources all over the United States, including tribal lands at Grand Portage and all throughout Ojibwe country.

In contrast, the allotment provisions of the 1854 Treaty of La Pointe did not include land inside the newly formed Grand Portage Reservation borders. Nor did the 1854 allotment provision have the overt goal of tribal and cultural destruction by stripping away their connection to lands held in trust by the tribes. It did, however, hope to "induce individual Indians to 'progress' one more increment along the idealized pathway to 'civilization'";[15] the government viewed the "civilization" of the Ojibwe as compensation for their loss of land. And so, the seventh clause of Article 2 of the 1854 treaty states:

> *Each head of a family, or single person over twenty-one years of age . . . shall be entitled to eighty acres of land, to be selected by them under the direction of the President, and which shall be secured to them by patent in the usual form.*[16]

Between 1859 and 1870, lots in the newly formed township of Grand Marais, which lies inside ceded territory, were divided into these voluntary allotments, all with the potential to be selected by Chippewa individuals or families as part of the 1854 treaty. The chunks of land were registered as "homestead" patents and tagged with references to the treaty.

Buried deep in the official *Record of Patents Delivered, 1861–1868* are all of the first homestead patents ever made within the newly ceded 1854 treaty lands. The name "Francis Roussain" is written here in delicate cursive, along with the details of his land selection: a parcel totaling 93 and 50/100 acres that encompassed most of the west bay of Grand Marais and included the peninsula now known as "Artists' Point." This spit of land continues to be one of the most recogniz-

Artists' Point. Courtesy of Cook County Historical Society.

able geographic features along the North Shore. Almost anyone who
has vacationed or grown up here probably knows the rocks, paths,
impasses, and crevices intimately. Growing up in Grand Marais, we
always knew it simply as "The Point."

It is where my sister and I first learned to run across the sharp
rocks without fear and how to tell when the stones were slippery
and when they were just fooling us into thinking they were. It is the
place where I stayed awake all night for the first time, my friends and
I huddled together on the high rocks at the far end. We watched the
sun come up out of the eastern sky, signifying our first official morning of adulthood. My aunt Gloria Martineau told me that she was
forced to sink or swim out there, in the sun-warmed, shallow pools
left behind by the colder, deeper storm surges. It is where you can cast
a shiny metal trout spoon out into the surf and, if you're lucky, you'll
come back with a coaster, a salmon, or a steelhead. It is the subject
of countless works of art and has inspired poetry and narratives by
writers both famous and anonymous. In the process of uncovering the
history of Chippewa City, discovering that The Point was originally
a treaty allotment was particularly eye-opening because I had never
before considered that "Indian" land might have existed outside of the

Grand Portage Reservation. If this iconic landmark was once deeded
to a Chippewa resident, then what other lands also have a recorded
history of tribal ownership?

Grand Portage band member Richard Anderson described how
his grandmother, Katherine Boyer Scott, acquired land along the
shoreline seven miles northeast of Grand Marais as part of the Treaty
of La Pointe, where the Scott family raised their family and made a
living, fishing for trout just offshore:

> *In 1870 the President granted my grandmother, Katherine Boyer*
> *Scott, and I can remember what it said on the deed . . . "to Kath-*
> *erine Boyer Scott, an Indian, a mile of shoreline about seven miles*
> *east of Grand Marais." Our family had that for a long, long time.*
> *My sister still has the only remaining piece of property there. She*
> *has her home on it yet. That was east of Chippewa City.*[17]

It turns out that a good part of the acreage that is now the city of
Grand Marais, Chippewa City, and Croftville was at one time eligible
to be parceled out to individuals who qualified for land selection as
part of the Treaty of La Pointe. Because the treaty did not make this a
requirement, and the people still migrated seasonally, European land
claims in the area weren't difficult to obtain. In 1872 "the choicest land
remaining unpatented" was the whole western shore from a point
at the water's edge encompassing what is now the entire Recreation
Park, the current location of North House Folk School, extending east
to the middle of the west bay. This property did include "an active little
community of Indians," which Will Raff, in *Pioneers in the Wilderness,*
estimates to have been established "from the settlement of Grand
Marais in the 1850s."[18] While I don't want to discredit the good work
of Will Raff, who I had the pleasure of meeting and whose work has
done a lot to further the reach of local history, the Anishinaabe perspective is that the settlement dates for the Grand Marais Chippewa
go back much further than 1850, and that the Ojibwe people from this
area still carry the weight of this arbitrary and skewed timeline on our

Katherine Boyer Scott mends fishing nets, mid- to late 1800s. Courtesy of Cook County Historical Society.

shoulders. It should also be noted that many Anishiinaabe people who lived in seasonal groups all along the North Shore never chose an allotment or picked out a parcel of land to "own" as a permanent place of residence. At that time, only the ability to speak English and understand with great certainty the language of the treaties would actually "entitle" someone to select an allotment as promised by the treaty.

And so, when that prime piece of land in what is now the western shore of Grand Marais harbor was claimed by the settler Sam Howenstine in 1872, the Ojibwe people who lived along the water presumably moved east along the shoreline. The eastern border of the claimed property lay just past Wakelin's land claim of 1872, which would later become the unmarked border between Grand Marais and Chippewa City. Cac Hussey, an early resident of Grand Marais, recalled that in his time, Chippewa City stretched "as far down there as you can see" from a line east of what is currently First Avenue East.[19]

Half-Breed Scrip

The original patent for Artists' Point allotted to Francis Roussain is dated November 20, 1866. The document details the transaction as an 1854 treaty allotment and identifies Roussain as a recipient of the land based on "each head of a family or single person over twenty-one years of age at the present time of the mixed bloods, belonging to the Chippewas of Lake Superior."[20] According to Will Raff's research into this particular land deal, Roussain was of one-half Ojibwe descent.[21] This is where the lines begin to blur, in terms of how land was acquired and who was certified to obtain land in territory newly ceded to the U.S. government.

Francis Roussain was a fur trader at Fond du Lac, originally from Nett Lake. His French ancestry is linked to General Roussain, a leader during the French Revolution. Francis was married to a woman named Zoe from Fond du Lac. Described as "mixed-blood French and Chippeway," she and her husband had five children including their first-born son, Eustache. She is described as follows:

> From those who had known Zoe we are told that she had been a very beautiful Indian girl and become a charming woman ... their son Eustache, born in 1839, was claimed to have been the first white child born within the limits of Duluth.[22]

So, although Zoe's Ojibwe heritage is clearly documented, there is a conflict of identity when it comes to her children, who were viewed as "white" even though both parents claimed at least half "Indian" blood. The definition of who was considered to be an Ojibwe person was first instituted as part of the 1842 treaty, which acknowledges the tribe's request to include all Ojibwe people that share family or kinship ties:

> *Whereas the Indians have expressed a strong desire to have some provision made for their half breed relatives, therefore it is agreed, that fifteen thousand (15,000) dollars shall be paid to said Indians, next year, as a present, to be disposed of, as they, together with their agent, shall determine in council.*[23]

The treaty of 1847 takes this one step further by including all family members who "reside" with the tribe as a measurement of who legally qualifies as an Ojibwe person: "the half or mixed bloods of the Chippewas residing with them shall be considered Chippewa Indians, and shall, as such, be allowed to participate in all annuities."[24]

In the case of Francis Roussain, claiming a 50/50 blood quantum granted him the ability to pick a prime piece of North Shore waterfront with the following guarantee:

> *NOW KNOW YE, That the UNITED STATES OF AMER-ICA, in consideration of the premises, HAVE GIVEN AND GRANTED, And, by these presents DO GIVE AND GRANT, unto the said Francis Roussain and to his heirs, the said tract above described: TO HAVE AND TO HOLD THE same, together with all the rights, privileges, immunities, and appurtenances, of whatever nature, thereunto belonging, unto the said Francis Roussain and to his heirs and assigns forever.*[25]

The earlier treaty terms first provided money to be distributed to "half-breeds" whereas, as Melissa Meyer observes, the later treaties "encouraged 'half-breeds' to take allotments on the ceded lands or the public domain, away from the tribe. Policymakers expected these individuals to sever their tribal ties and journey further down the idealized yellow brick road to assimilation."[26] Unlike the treaty of 1847, the treaty of 1854 stated that "residence among the Anishinaabeg . . . did not determine 'half-breeds'' eligibility to take scrip. This broadly construed ruling allowed land speculators an entrance into Anishinaabe ceded lands."[27] This made it easier for area traders of mixed blood to take advantage of the government's offer to choose a parcel of land inside ceded territory, even without having an ancestral tie to that particular place. Roussain has a long history of land transactions in Minnesota, having made a number of claims throughout the mid- to late 1800s. Records show that he owned at least three thousand dollars in assets by 1860, an impressive show of wealth for that time.[28] Recorded carefully in a ledger housed at the Minnesota History Center in St. Paul, inside a book with the title *Chippewa Half Breed Scrip Locations,* penned in ink on the front cover are listings for a number of government allotments claimed by Francis Roussain, his wife Zoe, and some in his son Eustace's name. One entry for land at Bois Forte included all three of their names, each of them owning separate allotments of land; with Francis receiving 160 acres, Zoe receiving 160 acres, and Eustace receiving 80 acres. The land was given as part of the treaty of 1866 between the U.S. government and Bois Forte and preceded the Dawes Act by twenty-one years. Owning multiple allotments was not typical at that time, especially when the land acquired was located all over ceded territory, as was the case with Francis Roussain.

By the time the Grand Marais harbor project was completed in 1884, the infamous piece of land once allotted to Roussain as part of the treaty of 1854 had already changed hands several times. Two months after receiving the allotment in 1866, Francis Roussain and his wife Zoe sold the property to D. George Morrison and his wife Mary for $450. According to St. Louis County records, D. George Morrison was Francis Roussain's nephew from Superior, Wisconsin. The son of the Canadian American Fur Company trader William

Morrison, D. George Morrison never lived in Grand Marais and, like his uncle Roussain, never intended to. He and his wife kept the land for four years until they sold it to Eber H. Bly in 1871. Henry Mayhew, cofounder of the Grand Marais Real Estate and Improvement Company, bought it on August 9, 1873. In 1879, the piece of land was still intact, but during Mayhew's tenure it went in and out of tax forfeiture status several times. He was able to hang on to the property until June 1883, when he turned it over to a trust held by himself and a number of Milwaukee- and Chicago-based developers.

Chippewa Indian Peace Commission, Washington, D.C., 1854 (with Francis Roussain, D. George Morrison, and others). Courtesy of Grand Portage National Monument.

Henry Mayhew, Sam Howenstine, and Ed Wakelin would eventually own all of what is now downtown Grand Marais, including "Mayhew's Point" and much of the southern facing hillside. The fate of The Point remained in Mayhew's hands until 1903. That year, the old and increasingly feeble Mayhew sold all of his downtown properties to another avid local developer. The holdings and buildings were all purchased with a twenty-five thousand-dollar promissory note written to him from Charles Johnson.[29]

Johnson and Mayhew ran competing grocery stores for a number of years, but owing to location and other business snafus, the Mayhew grocery struggled to keep up with the Johnson enterprise. Johnson's move to buy out all of Mayhew's property with the promise of twenty-five thousand dollars seems to have been an offer that Mayhew couldn't refuse. Henry Mayhew died the following year and his estate refused to renew the loan. However, according to Will Raff, Charles Johnson "managed to raise the money and recover the note, on the last possible day of payment."[30]

The Point's early history as an 1854 treaty allotment that was acquired by a trader who never lived there reveals a number of hard truths about the rocks that we all walk on and our futile attempts to claim those rocks as belonging to us. It is just one example of how traditional Ojibwe hunting and fishing grounds have been eroded away one treaty provision at a time and have become complicated by layers of names written on countless stacks of paper. On the crumbling pages of the first land records, you will discover in archaic script the people and dates and legal descriptions that, on their own, weigh almost nothing, but in force have the power to shake the earth right out from underneath us. The span of time between the signing of the early treaties, when Addikonse stood up and fought for the rights of his people at Grand Marais, and when the number of early European homesteaders eventually overtook the number of Anishinaabe people on the North Shore, was a time of great change. The forests changed to accommodate the need for new homes and businesses, the economy changed by placing monetary value on resources, goods, and land,

and our waterways changed—especially at Kitchi-bitobig, the place of two bays.

Waiting on the Dock
~&

There are four women in the photograph, huddled closely on the dock. A few of their faces are blurred with movement, as if their images were resistant to capture. We know the picture was taken at the Grand Marais harbor because of the familiar, graceful slope of the Sawtooth Mountains, a glimpse of lumber stacked in a neat pile behind the women, and the rocks jutting out at the end of the dock, graced with young pines and a scrubby birch tree. The women are Anishinaabe, and they most likely walked a mile from Chippewa City, on the path that followed the shoreline of Lake Superior, over Aabita-ziibiing, Half-Way River, and down into the lowlands of the town. They are friends or family, judging by the way they are sitting tightly together. And they are dressed alike, in long skirts and warm coats, with scarves made from gingham trade cloth covering their heads. It's a warm spring day, or a cool fall day—it's hard to know for sure. But all of their backs are to the water to keep their faces out of the cold wind blowing off the surface of the lake. They cannot let the chill get inside their coats, because there's no telling how long they will have to wait.

Before the North Shore Road (the early incarnation of Highway 61) was built in 1899, the way to move goods and people was by steamship, which was dangerous all year and impossible during the icy winters. On December 12, 1875, the *Stranger,* a cargo ship that worked between Grand Marais and Grand Portage and was owned by American Fur Company manager John Bradshaw, disappeared out of the harbor carrying a captain and crew. Despite attempts to rescue the boat, the weather and lack of a breakwater prevented others from reaching the ship, and the *Stranger* drifted off into the storm, never to be seen again. This event was the catalyst for the first alterations to the natural harbor. In 1876, when the first dock was built in the west bay, the land was owned by Henry (Hazael) Mayhew. The industrious Mayhew brothers employed a number of local people, including my great-grandfather John Drouillard, to complete work on the dock project. Great-grandfather John was thirty-one when he worked for the Mayhew brothers, one of his many vocations at that time.

Because of a need to bring larger boats inside the harbor, the town leaders made recommendations to hire contractors from Duluth to dredge the harbor to allow large ships to enter. In 1879, the U.S. government appropriated ten thousand dollars for the project, and in 1880 the task was under way. At that time, the recorded population of Cook County totaled sixty-five people.[31]

The 1880 census has two sections—one for whites and one for "Indians." According to the census there were just nine white people who lived in Grand Marais in 1880 and forty-seven Ojibwe people. The family names listed include Anakwad, Fillison, Frost, Peters, Wemaskawaush (Maymashkawaush), Zimmerman, Howenstine, Morrison, and Scott.[32] By then the fur trade economy had dwindled, and commercial fishing and logging had become the primary ways

Anishinaabe women on the dock at Grand Marais harbor. Courtesy of Cook County Historical Society.

that people made a living. Because the retreating fur trade created a lack of employment opportunities at Grand Portage, a large number of families moved to Grand Marais to work on the harbor and break-wall construction. It was at this time that the population of Chippewa City grew to reach its peak—when Ojibwe people from all along the North Shore joined the people who were already living there to work on the harbor renovation project. The addition of an expanded harbor and lighthouse would make it much easier for more and more settlers to make their way to the remote village, and would increase the amount of exports leaving the port exponentially. Its purpose as a refuge was invaluable, as it was the only safe harbor between Agate Bay and the Pigeon River, a distance of 126 miles of coastline. A sea-going harbor would also become a lifeline for everyone who lived in

Harbor dredging at Grand Marais harbor. Henry Mayhew is in the foreground. Courtesy of Cook County Historical Society.

this remote place, including the Ojibwe, who at that time were becoming increasingly dependent on treaty provisions as promised to them by the U.S. government.

The Anishinaabe women waiting on the Grand Marais dock in that photograph are anticipating the annual shipment of treaty annuities from the president in Washington. En route from Superior, Wisconsin, the cargo ship will be laden with iron kettles, heavy wooden boxes full of hand-forged nails, and stacks of wool blankets. There will also be *zhooniyaa,* a specific number of American dollars made of paper and metal, some for each tribal member. This seemingly simple act of trade between two nations was complicated by the reality of history: it involved not just the exchange of money for land, but also required travel from great distances to claim one's payment, as well as differing views on what it means to own a piece of the world, misunderstandings about the symbolic value of paper, and other dirty tricks involving debts owed to the president for taxes, or penalties if you did not know how to write your name in English.

Most important, one needed to know the time and place that the Indian agent would arrive, because what these women have learned is that kettles, blankets, or *zhooniyaa,* even if owed, only belonged to them if they were there in person to receive the payments. If they arrived late, or got impatient, or sick, then their unclaimed annuities would become the property of the Indian agent sent to distribute them. They were not allowed the luxury of biding their time until the next shipment, which would not arrive until next year, or might never arrive. And so, they patiently wait.

Allotments, Timber Sales, and Staying Put
~&

When the photograph on the dock was taken, life for the area Anishinaabe was in transition. Subjected to the provisions of every treaty leading up to the turn of the nineteenth century and suffering the loss of land by government decree, the people struggled to provide for their families in an economic system that was increasingly leaving them behind. Named for Massachusetts Senator Henry Dawes, the 1887 Dawes Act was passed by Congress and implemented gradually, affecting tribal reservation lands from Massachusetts to California. The Dawes Act is considered one of the most destructive and damaging actions taken against Native tribes in the history of government interactions with Native nations. It set the stage for violent confrontations such as the Wounded Knee Massacre and many other violent actions taken against Native people. The act fostered an uncompromising state of dependency, which subjected generations of Indigenous families to physical and emotional trauma, poverty, cultural decimation, and, in some cases, the termination and extermination of tribal people and homelands.

One provision of the Dawes Act was to assign all enrolled members of the Grand Portage band eighty acres of land within the borders of the Grand Portage Reservation. According to the original list of land assignments from 1889, many of the people who were known to have lived at Grand Marais also received a land allotment on the reservation.[33] Names of Chippewa City residents that appear on the 1889 *Schedule of Land Allotments* include the Addikonse (Little Caribou) family, Catherine Frost (LeSage), Shingibbiss (Hill Diver), the LaPlantes, the Morrisons, the Anakwads (Cloud), the Drouillards, and others. My great-grandmother Elizabeth Anakwad's allotment was located on the eastern bank of Reservation River. There was no road access to her land, and because it was so far inland, many miles away from where she lived in Chippewa City, she never built a structure or lived there. In fact, when the Dawes Act was passed in 1887, the majority of the North Shore Anishinaabe did not live within the reservation borders defined by the treaty of 1854.

Designed to privatize reservation land, with the overt intention to assimilate Indigenous people into mainstream culture, the Dawes Act also favored business interests and settlers, ensuring that "lands that remained after all individuals received allotments were to be sold on the open market to would-be settlers."[34] As a final insult, the money generated from the sale of reservation land would be used to finance the government's assimilation programs.

The Dawes Act was met with active resistance by most Native American tribes, who were growing increasingly wary of U.S. government intentions. In response to growing tribal discontent, the government swiftly passed the Nelson Act of 1889, which declared that all of the Minnesota Ojibwe reservations, with the exception of Red Lake, would be dissolved, and the people forced onto one large reservation at White Earth unless they agreed to live on their assigned allotments. It should be noted that this act was ensured passage by allowing tribal members who were under age eighteen to sign, as well as using other coercive actions against the people, who at that time were growing increasingly dependent on the government.[35] The effect of this act on the Grand Portage Ojibwe was the eventual loss of 16,041 acres of reservation land, which was what remained after each of 304 band members received their allotments in 1889.[36]

The Dawes and Nelson acts ultimately paved the way for homesteaders on the North Shore—with one key provision of the Nelson Act stipulating that "all agricultural lands remaining after allotments had been made would be sold for $1.25 per acre under the Homestead Act."[37] This included both on- and off-reservation lands within ceded territory. The Minnesota Anishinaabe lands were also subjected to special treatment by the government because much of tribal land was located in the heart of the rich, timber forests of northern Minnesota. These pine-covered lands were not allotted, and instead were "appraised and sold in forty-acre plots at public auction."[38] This was a historic trend that gained speed soon after the treaty of 1854 and continued to be a government priority, leading up the Nelson Act in 1889.

Even though the treaty of 1854 included restrictions on how the lands ceded by Ojibwe people could be used, the Interior Department removed the constraints on land patents in 1882, allowing all land patentees the right to sell the timber resources and allow logging by non-Natives. According to the 1884 Annual Report of the Commissioner of Indian Affairs, "During the 1883–1884 season the Chippewa, with the guidance of the Office of Indian Affairs, signed eighty-eight contracts with white lumber companies, which felled over 48,000,000 feet of timber valued at more than $250,000."[39]

The U.S. Chippewa Commission was charged with enforcing the Nelson Act. It tried to convince the Anishinaabe that "the pine would be a constant source of trouble" and that they were better off giving up their land and selling their timber rights.[40] My great-grandmother Elizabeth sold the timber rights to her allotment on the Grand Portage Reservation, as did many others.

Because of the leadership of Kichi-onigaming headman I-ah-be-dway-waish-kung—Joe Caribou—Grand Portage was not dissolved, in spite of the U.S. government's stated intentions.[41] Joe Caribou was just thirty-five years old when the Nelson Act was suspended in 1902 at Grand Portage. The leader of the Caribou clan since the early age of twenty-three, Joe is the grandson of Addikonse, the Anishinaabe headman at Grand Marais who protested the signing of the treaty of 1854. Strong leadership, as well as a consequential provision of the Nelson Act that allowed people to choose an allotment on their own reservation rather than as part of the consolidated land at White Earth, effectively saved the North Shore Anishinaabe from forced relocation. This may explain the reason why many of the people who had never lived on the reservation prior to 1854 chose to remain in their homes at Grand Marais and other places, as opposed to moving to their respective allotments at Grand Portage. Those who chose to stay put included the Morrison family. As George Morrison said, "My people were not forced to relocate. They stayed where they were in Chippewa City."[42]

The Timber and Stone Act

The Grand Marais Real Estate and Improvement Company was established in 1887, the same year as the Allotment Act. According to historian Will Raff, the three businessmen who founded it—Ed Wakelin,

Henry Mayhew, and Sam Howenstine—had all established themselves in Grand Marais by 1870 or 1871.[43] The men used investment
capital from Duluth and Iron Range mining interests to generate plans
to build a railroad from Lake Vermilion to Grand Marais, with the
intention of making Grand Marais a mining port. The Grand Marais
Real Estate and Improvement Company would quickly acquire large
amounts of shoreline and inland acreage for the railroad in an effort
to forestall other development in the area. The business encouraged
settlement, offering land for sale at "reasonable prices," and going so
far as to advertise that "to public enterprises or manufacturing plants
they may be induced to donate sites on certain conditions."[44] This
amounted to a giveaway of land to anyone willing to put out a shingle
and brave enough to take a chance on the unproven solvency of business and industry on the North Shore.

A government incentive called the "Timber and Stone Act" was
passed in 1890 making it easier for early developers and prospectors
to gain control of land and resources in the area. The purpose of the
Timber and Stone Act was to encourage free enterprise in mineral

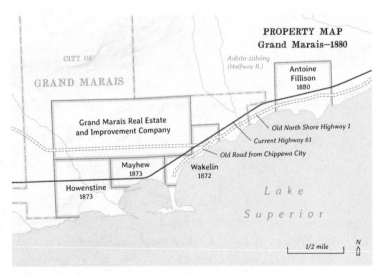

Wakelin, Mayhew, and Howenstine properties. Map by Brad Herried.

and timber harvesting on the North Shore. As a result of this act, the non-Native population of Grand Marais increased from 98 people in 1890 to 810 by 1900.[45] As more and more people arrived and got to work, the productivity and economic engine of the village also grew. According to shipping receipts from 1891, one year after the act was passed, the exports leaving Grand Marais Harbor were as follows:

Export	Tons
Cedar Posts	1,800
Building Stone	150
Fish	20
Miscellaneous	1

By 1905 there was an enormous jump in products being shipped out of the harbor, which included at least one surprising locally grown product—potatoes:

Export	Tons
Pulpwood	30,000
Telegraph Poles	24,500
Railroad Ties	14,389
Lumber	4,500
Shingles	1,500
Miscellaneous	963
Lath	225
Potatoes	45
Fish	35
Furs	1

Timber harvests were one of the fastest ways for people to make a relatively large amount of money fairly quickly. Unlike mineral and precious-metal mining that required up-front investment and infrastructure on a large scale before any profits could be pocketed, cutting down trees required relatively little investment. In addition to the large amount of timber products shipped out of Grand Marais, in 1901 there were 16,645 cedar ties, 4,600 cedar poles, and 1,427 feet of piling sold off of land at Grand Portage, for the total sum of $8,620.[46] Charles Johnson's father, August Van Johnson, was the registrar of deeds when he signed for a number of timber sales on the Grand Portage Reservation and elsewhere, including the trees from my great-grandmother Anakwad's allotment. A lot of the sales were purpose-fully written in his wife Stina L. Johnson's name, which put her in the same category as a number of large-scale timber barons of the time. His sons Charles and Van ran the busy lumber camps at Grand Portage, where they hired local hands and supervised the harvest, processing, and transfer of the logs from campsites at Reservation River and other places adjacent to a connected water route. These massive trees were floated by boom along the surface of Lake Superior to the Grand Marais harbor where they were counted and shipped out to markets in Duluth and across the lake to Ashland, Wisconsin. These were the years when the bay was stacked with floating logs so thick that kids would play the dangerous game of running across the moving surface of the logs from one side of the harbor to the other. My dad and my uncles all boasted about their best runs, and told teeth-chattering tales of the kids who slipped under the logs and came up hypothermic—not to mention the ones who weren't able to make it back to the surface from under the moving carpet of cedar and pine logs, never to be seen again.

Because many Grand Portage tribal members had sold off the timber on their individual allotments or, in some cases, the land or mineral rights to the land, many people were forced to seek homes and jobs off of the reservation. In 1909, only around a hundred of 328 enrolled Grand Portage band members lived on the reservation, with only five of the hundred residents living on their land allotments.[47] Predictably, the mass sell-off of what seemed to be an endless source of timber was not to last. Because of massive forest fires in 1907, much of the remaining timber at both Grand Portage and Grand Marais was lost. By the turn of the century, remaining lumber resources were not sufficient enough to sustain the economic needs of the local population. Soon the business leaders began to turn toward what would be the North Shore's economic mainstay: luring visitors from afar to bask in the scenic beauty, cool air, and freshwater of the North Shore.

The efforts of the Grand Marais Real Estate and Improvement Company to entice business development in Grand Marais would not find much resistance from the local Ojibwe population, who by then were being assaulted by government agencies as part of forced allotment as well as the corresponding attacks on their families, culture, and religious freedom—known as "assimilation." *Assimilate*—a nice word that refers to the attempted annihilation of Ojibwe culture and society. The combined effects of the early treaties—the Allotment Act, the Nelson Act, and the Timber and Stone Act—would contribute significantly to a diminishing population at Grand Portage and the growth of the Ojibwe population at Grand Marais. It was at this time that many Grand Portage people joined their relatives and friends in Chippewa City, where they were able to find jobs as loggers, road builders, trappers, and commercial fisherman. It was there that they were also able to find a shared sense of community off of the reservation.

Jim Wipson (*front right*), grandmother Kate Frost (*center*), Jim's mother Ida Frost (*far right*), Jim's uncle Martin Drouillard (*left*), and cousins in Chippewa City. Courtesy of the Patsy Drouillard Swanson Collection.

-» *Chapter 5* «-

NISHKWAKWANSING

At the Edge of the Forest

LIKE ANY QUEST OR JOURNEY, the trip back to Chippewa City was
not without wrong turns, quagmires, and false starts. As a graduate
student at the University of Minnesota, when I began to compile
research material for what would become an academic thesis about
the history of Chippewa City, many family members suggested that I
talk to a man in Grand Portage named Jim Wipson, who was born in
Chippewa City in 1918.

I called Jim on the phone and asked if we could arrange an interview. He was downright enthusiastic about the proposal; we set a
date. The first time we met was in March 2001. We had a spirited and
friendly talk where Jim put his trust in me, sharing two hours of his life
story on my old-fashioned cassette tape recorder. A few weeks later, excited about making progress on what was becoming a more extensive
oral-history project, I interviewed another subject and inadvertently
taped over half of Jim's original interview. This was one of the most difficult lessons I learned about collecting other people's history. Always
make a copy of the original tape and never, ever leave a tape unmarked,
without a title and a date. Most important, take great care to treat other
people's words with respect and caution. To a historian, other people's
words are more valuable than money. I was devastated.

In the embarrassing return phone call to Jim I explained what had
happened and how sorry I was. He was quiet for a little while, and then
said that he was OK with doing a follow-up interview. He and his wife
Lorraine kindly welcomed me back to their home in Grand Portage

the following May. Their trailer house was right next to the stone wall at the foot of Mount Josephine. They had hummingbird feeders dangling all along the porch railing and seed feeders full of fluttering songbirds perched just outside the kitchen window. I brought them a package of moose hamburger from a bull that my dad had hunted the previous fall, and everyone expressed thanks. Jim and Lorraine were both in very good spirits. Jim and I sat at the table, while Lorraine listened in from the kitchen, occasionally offering her own memories. In spite of my false start, Jim remained warmhearted and enthusiastic about repeating his stories of Chippewa City, especially the ones about his grandmother Kate Frost and the "Old Road" between Chippewa City and Grand Marais, which they had traveled often:

> *When I was a little boy, her and I used to walk that little old road. It was a mile from Chippewa City to Grand Marais. To us . . . we thought it was a long ways. Just to show you my grandma thought it was a long ways, she'd even take a little lunch along, and halfway between Chippewa City and Grand Marais we'd sit on the little cliff and have our little lunch. Then we'd journey the rest of the way to Grand Marais . . . every weekend I think we'd walk to town. And all these white people seen us walking around Grand Marais and they got to know us real good. In fact, lot of people got to say, "Hey, Katie, how are you?" And "Oh, you're here with your little grandson." And they all talked to us . . . and my grandmother used to love ice cream. And we'd stop at a little restaurant there, I think they called it LeSage's Restaurant . . . and we'd go in there and have our little ice cream, and she really enjoyed it. So, everybody in Grand Marais knew Kate Frost and her little grandson, who was me, Jimmy.[1]*

Jim spoke of that path to and from town as having a proper name, the Old Road. So much of our history is built around the construction of roads, both literally and figuratively. They not only join communities, but also serve as conduits between worlds. By entrusting me with his personal story, Jim not only gave me the gift of history, he also equipped me with some of the most important tools I would need to travel with care in both directions: forgiveness for my mistakes and the courage to tell the truth.

A narrow stream crosses the Old Road close to where Jim and his grandmother Kate would stop to eat lunch on their way to town. It has an Ojibwe name, Aabita-ziibiing, which means "Halfway River." To the best of my knowledge, that little stream does not have an English name. There could be two possible explanations for this— either no Englishman or Frenchman had a relationship to it or, once the Ojibwe people no longer used it as a landmark to determine the distance that remained to downtown, it wasn't deemed important enough to be given an English name. But when we name things, we bring them into the world. And once they are here, it's up to all of us to remember them.

Later that day, after I interviewed Jim for the second time, I pushed play on the tape recorder, hoping that I didn't mess up the recording again. The power was on, the volume was up, and I held my breath. I heard myself saying "Testing . . . 1 . . . 2 . . . 3" and then there was the sound of Jim's voice. He started talking with animated authority, as if he was speaking in front of a television news camera and not into a clunky tape recorder. His memory came through, shiny and bright. Accompanying him, and filling in the gaps between his words, were the sweet songs of the birds feeding outside the kitchen window. They spoke in languages no human could understand, but listening to their delicate chatter, I knew then, and with certainty, that Jim's voice and the voice of his grandmother Kate were coming through loud and clear. This time, they were safely preserved for all to hear.

Nishkwakwansing—at the Edge of the Forest

A large part of understanding the history of Chippewa City is coming to terms with the stories that have gotten lost along the way and accepting what is not yet known. For every local history, there are gaps in the archival records, or, as the case may be, lost tape recordings or voices that aren't yet ready to be heard. The detailed records kept by St. Francis Xavier Catholic Church helped to fill in many gaps in the historical record. But this applies only to the people who had converted to Catholicism at that time, and it requires a leap of faith that your relative was correctly identified and that their name is spelled correctly. Church records from that time are notorious for misspelling names. For instance, I've seen the name Anakwad spelled "Anaquot" or "Anakwadt" or "Anaquod" on various records, including tribal land rolls and the official U.S. census. Furthermore, it was common to record names in both Ojibwe (Anakwad) and English (Cloud), requiring a researcher to know both languages, and with a high degree of certainty, in order to follow the historical comings and goings of one's ancestors.

While I was very proud to discover that Addikonse, the Anishinaabe leader from my hometown of Grand Marais, was a brave man who stood up for the rights of his people, I am also saddened at the impasses I've discovered along the historical pathways of my research. For example, I've yet to confirm what clan the Anakwad family belongs to, or if my great-great-grandfather Anakwad lived in Grand Marais in 1854 when the treaty was signed, or if he was living at Grand Portage as part of Zhaganasheence's clan. I do know that his name was Mathias Anakwad and that he was baptized as a Catholic in Grand Portage in 1835 when he was twenty years old. His mother's name is Binesiwabe, but his father's name was not included on the baptismal record.

Because of the well-documented comings and goings of the Drouillard family, it has been easier for me to piece together that side of the family history. In 1856, when my great-grandfather John Drouillard was eight years old, he and his father, Nelson, the blacksmith at Grand Portage, would visit friends who worked the remnants of the American Fur Company post and fishing station in Grand Marais. They would brave the trip in a wooden rowboat, a distance of thirty-

five miles. This skill for traveling the waters and woods of the North
Shore would shape John's life and experiences, and the choices he
made as an adult. Although he was 100 percent French, he went to
school with Ojibwe children and lived his life among Ojibwe people.
He could speak French, English, and Ojibwemowin, a feat that would
enable him to be a cultural go-between all throughout his adult life.
Archange (Eliza I.) and Nelson had three more children while living
in Grand Portage: William, Caroline, and Eliza (II). Nelson continued
to serve as blacksmith at Grand Portage until 1857, three years after the
Treaty of La Pointe was signed. He was then transferred to the Red
Cliff Reservation in Wisconsin where he worked as the government
blacksmith for two years. Then, in 1864 he and his growing family
moved to the Bad River Reservation in Wisconsin, where he served
until 1867. That autumn, Nelson Drouillard and his wife Eliza moved
back to Bayfield, where he returned to his previous job as deputy
sheriff of Bayfield County. The family is listed in the 1870 Bayfield,
Wisconsin census:

> Nelson: age 50, male, white, blacksmith. Value of real estate $400.
> Value of personal property: $400. Born in Michigan.
> Eliza: age 40, female, white, wife of Nelson. Born in Michigan.
> John: age 21, male, white, blacksmith. Born in Michigan. Eligible
> to vote.
> Ellen, age 16. William, age 9. Caroline, age 8. Eliza, age 7. Clarisa,
> age 6. James, age 4. Henry, age 2.[2]

On July 14, 1872, twenty-three-year-old John Drouillard married
Mary L. Bachand at a Catholic church in Bayfield, Wisconsin. One
year later he was hired as interpreter to the government agent sent
to oversee payments at Grand Portage and Lake Vermilion. Part of
his job would be to accompany the payment agent to the two reservations, leaving his new wife behind on the south shore for long
stretches of time. He did return home to his wife Mary enough times
to grow a family of three. Sebastian was born in 1874 and Retta in 1876.

I also found a birth date for a third child named Adele, who was born in Bayfield in 1881. The year that his middle child was born in Bayfield, John was also known to have been working for the Mayhew brothers, who were building the first dock in Grand Marais harbor, the same dock where the group of Anishinaabe women are seen waiting for a ship bringing in government annuities, and the same dock where the first tourists to the area would disembark with their steamer trunks, ready to breathe in the cool northern air.

Following the trail of great-grandfather John Drouillard will eventually lead us to Elizabeth Anakwad, my great-grandmother, who at that time was living with her family in Nishkwakwansing, a descriptive phrase that means "at the edge of the forest." Like so many other places with two names, Nishkwakwansing is also known as the village of Chippewa City.

The Old Road

It has been a journey of many miles, arriving here at the edge of the forest. I've heard the story of the Anishinaabe and how they came from the east and how they navigated the rivers inland to find the homelands promised to them by the prophecies and lived their lives, following the rhythm of the seasons. I've found my relatives at the top of Mount Josephine and building a dock on the Grand Marais harbor, and have witnessed the survival of our Anishinaabe ancestors against all odds. Yet, there are still many questions that need answers, many paths left to explore. I believe that to truly understand a place you need to hear the story of everyday life in the voices of the people who lived there. And so, in some ways, I find myself back at the beginning, standing in the grass outside St. Francis Xavier Catholic Church and wondering what life at the edge of the forest was really like.

Dora Kasames is the granddaughter of Joe Caribou and Elizabeth Blackstone. She lived in Chippewa City as a girl and recognized that it was, at one time, an active village:

Mrs. Jim Morrison (*far left*), an unidentified friend, and Anna Caribou Smith holding Dora Kasames in the background, mid-1920s. Courtesy of Cook County Historical Society.

When the church was built, we had a white priest who talked Indian. He learned Indian from the Chippewas up there. He used to go to Grand Portage, Cloquet and Chippewa City . . . I don't know where the name came from, but there were a lot of Chippewas living there.[3]

The village reached its height between 1882 and 1901. By 1896, the people had built St. Francis Xavier church, moved one cemetery and secured land for a new one, built many hand-hewn log homes in the same style as the church, as well as many more portable-style homes in the traditional Ojibwe lodge design, which were made of birch bark, modern blankets, or hide that covered over a curved wooden framework of poles.

The village had no stores or trading posts, which meant that everything one needed to buy had to be found in Grand Marais. Although local fishermen did their part to provide the people with food, much of the commerce and trade was done with people outside of the village. With more and more people moving to Grand Marais and Chippewa City, there was a need for infrastructure and centralized places to do

Postcard, "A Typical Indian Tepee at Grand Marais," with Angus LeSage, Julia Caribou, and Paul Kadonce. Courtesy of Cook County Historical Society.

business. Essential to the community's growth was the added incentive of the government harbor development project in 1882, which created steady employment until its completion in 1901.

In addition to the harbor project, the need for adequate ground transportation made road building a priority. The work of cutting roads through the thick forests was made easier by following the existing trails. In *Pioneers in the Wilderness,* Will Raff has acknowledged that "Every time a land route was used along the North Shore . . . travelers naturally followed the primitive foot trail that had been used by generations of Indians."[4]

This is corroborated by a former Chippewa City resident, Irene Sullivan:

> *There were trails all over the place. The main trail that came from Chippewa City passed by our house and went to Grand Marais. It must have been an old Indian trail to the Canadian border because everyone called it the "Old Road."*[5]

In 1898, Cook County voters passed an eight-thousand-dollar bond that was designated for the lakeshore road from Grand Marais to Duluth, which until that time was suitable only for dog-team travel.[6] The *Duluth Tribune* reported in 1879 that "Forty miles of the new road has been opened on the Duluth Pigeon River wagon road, leaving but twenty miles to be cut in order to open the road for a one-horse team, for winter travel between Duluth and Grand Marais."[7]

This was just one of many new roads that were started and proposed in the late 1800s. Although there was a will to connect Grand Marais to all points west, north, and east, there was difficulty finding money and workers to keep the construction funded and on schedule. The newly formed local municipalities had already begun to tax area residents, with the hopes of paying for the priority infrastructure projects, of which roads and bridges were considered a high priority.

These were the years of seasonal isolation for some of the new settlers, who were not used to being cut off from the rest of the world for long stretches of time. Boats were still the primary way to transport goods and people to and from Grand Marais. The mail was most often brought in by canoe in the warm season, and by dogsled in the winter. Letters and packages had to be brought from Superior, Wisconsin, a treacherous undertaking at any time of year, especially when the tides of Lake Superior could turn a solid ice pack into shards at the whim of a change in wind direction. This responsibility was primarily in the hands of men like Louis Plante who took mail from Grand Marais northeast to the Pigeon River. This story is about a near miss involving Plante and bystander John Drouillard:

> *A Cold Bath—Mail Carrier Louis Plante had a very narrow escape from a watery grave last Friday. He was en route to Grand Portage from Hovland when off Howard's Point a heavy sea combined with a gale of wind capsized his boat. He managed to climb on top of it and hold on until John Drouillard, who witnessed the occurrence, could reach him ... Louis has a dangerous route at best*

Louis Plante with his team, led by lead dog Rover. Taken near Chicago Bay, Hovland, circa 1900. Courtesy of Cook County Historical Society.

and during the stormy weather which has prevailed this year the place has been especially hard and dangerous.[8]

John Beargrease was the man who brought the mail the first leg up the shore, from Superior all the way to Grand Marais. John is one of the better-known former residents of Chippewa City, and he is the namesake for the modern John Beargrease Sled Dog Race that is run every year between Duluth and Grand Portage.

John was often the sole source of news and correspondence during the winter months when the weather and harsh conditions isolated the North Shore from the rest of the world. Originally from Beaver Bay, he lived in Chippewa City at various times during his life as he had married Louise Wishkop, whose family lived in Chippewa City. The couple had five children.[9]

Beargrease reached the status of local legend during his fifty years as a contracted mail carrier. He carried not only correspondence but

John Beargrease (posed photograph), approximately 1898. Courtesy of Cook County
Historical Society.

also periodic weather reports, such as this one from March 1898:
"Beargrease reports good ice all the way to Two Island." A follow-up
report from early April that same year said, "John Beargrease reports
that the ice is solid from Beaver Point to Duluth."[10]

John Beargrease and Louis Plante made their final mail runs late
in 1899, when the Lake Shore Road was completed between Two
Harbors and Grand Marais, making the route accessible to horse and
buggy. After that, parcels, letters, and other shipments were delivered
by stagecoach.

We Were Born Here

The Ojibwe people's relationship to the Catholic church is complicated by the problems of unwanted occupation and assimilation, and
further tainted by the uncompromising role that Jesuit priests played

in early contact with the Ojibwe. But if it were not for the detailed and immaculate historical records kept by the church, the road back to Chippewa City might have ended here.

Because of these records, we know that the first person baptized at Grand Marais was Jean Atis Britto, who was born in 1791 but baptized on February 11, 1856, by Father Dominique Duranquet, at the age of sixty-five. This and other records were meticulously transcribed by Father Maurice of the Thunder Bay Catholic diocese. Each record has a birth name, the place and date of birth, the place and date of baptism, the parents' names, sponsors, the priest who performed the ceremony, and a place to record remarks about the event. For example, a twenty-year-old woman named Sabine Ogimakijigok was baptized in 1849 at the Pigeon River, where she was born. Her sponsors are listed as Marquerite Pecikwanebik and Joseph Morrison. Thumbing through the records, one finds many other familiar Cook County and Grand Portage names, including Phillison, Frost, Morrison, Kadonce, Addikonse, Cyrette, Naganab, Tawasige, Wishcop, Paro, LaPlante, Zimmerman, Maymashkawaush, Eshkwebi, Collins, Mercer, Gino-

Kids at Chippewa City. Courtesy of Cook County Historical Society.

jewabo, Katons (Kabegabaw), LeSage, Scott, Songakamik, Ajawigijib-
web, Anakwad, and many, many others.

The first Drouillard appears early on. Her name is Elisabeth Victo-
ria Drouillard, born on March 29, 1861, and baptized by Father Duranquet two days later. She is the daughter of Eliza Chauvin and Nelson
Drouillard and the younger sister of my great-grandfather John. Her
birth corresponds closely with Nelson's work as blacksmith at Grand
Portage. Beginning in 1856, two years after the treaty of 1854, there is
a gradual shift in the locations listed in the baptism records. As the
people of Grand Portage moved away from the reservation lands
to find work, the number of baptisms followed them. In fact, Joe
Morrison, the male sponsor listed in Sabine Ogimakijigok's baptism,
would soon be living in Chippewa City with his family, along with his
brother Jim Morrison, who is the father of Mike and George Morrison
and their sisters and brothers.

The number of births recorded at Grand Marais between 1856 and
1916 totals 155. It is likely that all of these baptisms took place at St.
Francis Xavier, as it was the only Catholic parish in service at Grand
Marais during that time period. Also, because this number includes
only the people baptized in the Catholic tradition, the total number
of births in Chippewa City is difficult to determine. According to her
great-grandson, Rick Anderson of Grand Portage, Katherine Boyer
Scott was the midwife for many of the births at Chippewa City, having
been taught that skill as a young girl by the nuns at the reserve con-
vent near Thunder Bay. She and her husband, Andrew Jackson (Jack)
Scott, are named as sponsors on many of the christening records in the
archives at the Catholic mission there. Because she delivered the baby,
it was common for the midwife to serve as a sponsor for the child.
Katherine and Jack's names also appear in the birth record for their
daughter, Anna Louise Scott, who was born on November 28, 1884,
and christened in March 1885 at Kimball Creek, "8 mi. N. of Grand
Marais," by Father Joseph Specht, S.J.[11]

In a photograph taken at the turn of the century, my great-aunt
Theresa Anakwad is sitting outside a home that was built in the style

of Frank Wishkop, the carpenter who built St. Francis Xavier. It's a chilly day with snow on the ground, either early spring or early fall. She holds a baby in her arms. This tiny baby is dressed all in white and is capped with a frilly bonnet on its head. It's baptism day, and though we have not yet identified the child, I'm certain that she or he is named and dated somewhere in the carefully documented records written in the cursive hand of Father Maurice.

Theresa Anakwad and child on baptism day. Courtesy of Patsy Drouillard Swanson Collection.

Joe Caribou on the path to his grandmother's house at Chippewa City, circa 1905.
Courtesy of Cook County Historical Society.

→ *Chapter 6* ←

NOKOMISAG MIINAWAA MISHOOMISAG

Grandmothers and Grandfathers

IN THE EARLY NINETEENTH CENTURY, the people were led by head-
men such as Espagnol, Maymashkawaush, Zhaganasheence in Grand
Portage and Ahkik and Addikonse in Grand Marais. These men were
the leaders of their respective clans and all of them are important to
the history of the Lake Superior Anishinaabeg. In the years following
the Allotment Act of 1887, when the land base was decimated at Grand
Portage and all across Ojibwe country, formal clan groups slowly dissolved with the division of the land base into smaller pieces. This
change brought the end to the totemic leadership system, at least in
terms of how tribal people functioned inside the political realm of the
U.S. government, which enforced the system of assigning leadership
titles or roles. When it came to land transactions, the French, British,
or U.S. government authorities were known often to install their own
tribal "chiefs" in order to ensure their desired outcome. It wouldn't be
until the Indian Reorganization Act was passed in 1934 that democrati-
cally elected "chiefs" would head the Lake Superior Anishinaabe bands.
The word *chief* is one of the most misleading words to be pulled from
the matrix of terminology associated with Native people. Say "Indian
Chief" and all kinds of Hollywood visuals and professional sports
stereotypes come to mind. But culturally, our modern Ojibwe leaders
are not defined by gender or age. You are just as likely to meet a woman
serving as tribal chair as you are to find a man with that title. Power, in
the Ojibwe worldview, stems from a more egalitarian society where

women and men share in the decision making, and where women are respected in their roles as mothers, aunts, grandmothers, and sisters having the innate power to lead their own families. The Ojibwe word that most resembles the word *chief* is *ogimaa*. If someone carries that title, it indicates that he or she is considered to be a "chief," a "boss," or, according to my Ojibwe dictionary, a *gichi-ogimaa* or "king." These meanings all carry an implied, masculine connotation, making the assumption that a chief is male, just like a king. The word for leader or chairman is *eshpabiitang*. It means that someone is high in status or holds high office. It can designate gender by adding *inini* (man) or *ikwe* (woman) to the end of the word: *eshpabiitang-ikwe* (chairwoman).

Jim Wipson lived with his grandmother in her log house in Chippewa City until he was ten years old. When asked who he thought the leaders were in the community, he replied:

> *I guess they looked up to certain people. We had chiefs and medicine men and I imagine my grandmother was looked up to at one time as a medicine woman. I guess a real elder, one that's real old, they might have looked up to him as somebody too. And of course, in my younger days all elders were looked up to. They were respected and so forth, as elders.*[1]

Many members of the tribe are considered to be leaders, both elected and otherwise. And all along, the Ojibwe people are led by our elders. The grandmas and grandpas, aunts and uncles are looked up to as the leaders of the community. Their role is not just to make leadership decisions but also to act as the keepers of Ojibwe tradition. Many of the Chippewa City descendants shared stories with me about their elders. When you listen to these stories, you hear about the fundamental values of family, relationships with others, and learning how to live in a way that honors the past, lives in the present, and prepares us for the future.

The elders whom I want to honor are the people who entrusted me with their stories and welcomed me into their past, present, and future: Jim Wipson, George Morrison, Mike Morrison, Mary Jane Hendrickson, Dorothy Johansen, Gladys Beckwith, Vivian Waltz, Milt Powell, my aunt Gloria Martineau, and my dad, Francis Drouillard. Thank you for allowing me to stroll beside you on the Old Road, and for giving me permission to ask you questions while we walked. Their voices are still with me, and I feel a great responsibility to tell their stories in a good way—to bear witness to their lives and honor their place in our shared history.

As is the nature of history, the story of Chippewa City and the Grand Marais Chippewa will continue to change and grow as new voices are added to the narrative. This story is given new life as it is listened to and shared by others. As a historian, I am constantly overwhelmed by the realization that each voice is important and each memory is worth recording. Some of those memories and voices are shared here, both in words and in pictures. This is not intended to be a comprehensive genealogy of those who lived in Chippewa City, but is offered as a touchstone, so that others might add their own recollections and family memories to the voices of those mentioned here.

The Caribous

We've already met Joe Caribou on the path to Chippewa City. A leader of the Caribou clan for many years, he is the grandson of Addikonse, the long-time chief at Grand Marais and the leader of the Caribou or Reindeer clan.[2] We know that Joe and his family lived in Chippewa City in 1905, because of a visit from the world-famous anthropologist Frances Densmore and her sister, Margaret. It was reported that he took his distinguished visitors to his grandmother's berry-picking camp.

Joe is also known as Iabedwaywaishking. Grand Portage Band member Dora Kasames explained that Joe Caribou and Elizabeth Blackstone Caribou are her grandparents, and their daughter—Dora's mother—was Louise Anna Caribou.[3] The Caribou clan is believed

Frances Densmore's photograph of Shingibbiss and his wife (*seated*). Mrs. William Howenstine and Joe Caribou stand to their right. Courtesy of the Minnesota Historical Society.

to have originally come to Grand Portage from the Winnipeg area, and have lived at Lac La Croix, and then Grand Portage, for many generations.[4] The Caribou family has a strong history of leadership, including community leaders Walter Caribou and Gilbert Caribou, who served the people of Grand Portage in the tradition of their ancestor Addikonse.

The Blackstone family name is traced to Lac La Croix, on the border between Canada and the United States. Ojibwe people with relatives at Lac La Croix often have family connections to the upper Gunflint Trail, Thunder Bay, Grand Portage, Red Lake, and Nett Lake, including Milt Powell and the Powell family, whose grandmother was related to Chief Blackstone (the first), a leader at Lac La Croix. Blackstone fought for the rights of his people during the time of the treaty of 1873 between the Ojibwe First Nations and the Canadian government. His son, Chief Blackstone (the second), was a legendary Kawa Bay headman who lived on Kanipi Lake, just north of Saganagons Lake. In the book *A Life in Two Worlds,* about Betty Powell

Skoog's life, Justine Kerfoot explained how "forty or more" Ojibwe families lived on the upper Gunflint Trail, including at Gunflint Lake, Saganaga, Saganagons, Kawnipi Lake, and at the mouth of the Kawawiagamuk River, or Kawa Bay, where Chief Blackstone (the second) once lived.[5] The story of Blackstone of Kawa Bay has a terrible end. He and his people were decimated by the influenza epidemic of 1918 and 1919. Only he and one of his wives were healthy enough to snowshoe to Jack Powell's cabin on Saganagons, in order to get help. On their journey home, Blackstone fell ill and died on the shore of Agnes Lake. The few people who survived the epidemic moved from Kawa Bay to Lac La Croix, to live on an Ojibwe reserve about two hundred kilometers west of Thunder Bay. Chief Blackstone's body was later retrieved by his people and buried at the site of his former village on the shore of Kawa Bay.[6]

Swamper Caribou, namesake of Swamper Lake on the Gunflint Trail, and Caribou Creek in Lutsen, where he used to set his trap line in the winter, is remembered by many who lived at Chippewa City and in Grand Marais. His Ojibwe name, Bazhidaywidang, identifies him on a number of church records as well as on the list of 1887 Grand Portage allotments. Swamper and Dave Caribou are brothers. Charles Johnson thought highly of the Caribous, offering that "they were very strong, good people; and my father was a very good friend of both of them."[7]

The two brothers were land scouts, hunting guides, trappers, and even served in local government. This story is from Will Raff's book *Pioneers in the Wilderness:*

> *During the Sugarbush season one spring, the William Ellquist family learned an impressive lesson on trustworthiness from Dave Caribou's brother, Swamper Caribou. One day the impressively tall Indian visited the farmer's home to borrow a supply of salt. Complying with the request, the Ellquists were pleasantly surprised later, when Swamper made the eight-mile-trip from town to return what he had borrowed.*[8]

Swamper Caribou and his wife at their home. Courtesy of Cook County Historical Society.

Lucy Caribou was a neighbor of the Drouillard family in Grand Marais whose home was located where the Grand Marais Free Church now stands. My aunt Gloria Martineau spent a lot of time at Lucy's house, where they helped her cut cloth into strips that she used to make rugs. They were also charged with feeding the dog that she kept tied up in her backyard:

Lucy had a nice, little, clean house. Katagon (Spot) was Lucy's dog. When we had to feed it—we had to just throw the food at it [laughs]. She would tell us, "Just throw it!" I guess Katagon even killed wolves.[9]

Both my aunt and my dad remember her house being filled to the brim with boxes and bags of rug-making materials. Aunt Gloria explained:

She hooked rugs. And she braided rugs too . . . She'd get rags from everywhere. She'd go up to the courthouse and get all those old rags, coats that were turned in that people didn't want. Some of her rugs were cotton. Some of them were pure wool. She'd cut them into strips and braided them. Some of them would be as big as this room! We were at Lucy's every day. And every time we'd walk past Lucy's house [giggles], she'd holler at us and want us to get her something from the store.[10]

Lucy's sister, Philomene (Evans) Caribou, lived in Grand Portage, just off of the highway in Mineral Center. She lived alone and would occasionally visit Grand Portage, though she rarely visited Grand Marais. Gloria recalled that the two sisters had very different life-styles: "I suppose Lucy was what we'd call a 'Citian' and Philomene lived up in the bush all by herself. There wasn't anyone around her. And she just lived up there and roughed it."[11]

My dad, Francis (Poot) Drouillard, spent two summers at Philomene's house when he was eight years old. Philomene, or Betawasinok, lived just off the old highway in Grand Portage, where she ran a souvenir stand at the border crossing just up the road from where she lived. Thinking back to his summers at Philomene's house, he got emotional, remembering the influence she had on his young life:

Philomene was a wonderful woman. She was kind. She spoke real quiet. She didn't have a mean bone in her body. I liked it there. She

*needed somebody there. She walked with a cane. She was pretty
limited to do a lot of things. She kind of made me feel needed.*[12]

He also credits her with teaching him a lot of important life skills:
"I consider myself a pretty good hunter and fisherman. I think some
of that I picked up from her. How to catch a brook trout. How to snare
rabbits. How to be quiet."

Betawasinok (Philomene Evans) at her souvenir stand on the old North Shore Drive,
1930s. Courtesy of Grand Portage National Monument.

He was eight or nine years old when he lived there—old enough to catch and release the tiny brook trout from the little stream that went by her house, but not quite old enough to be considered the "man" of the house.

One time we went out to check our snare line. And about a half mile from the house there was a bear, in the ditch. Oh man, did Philomene get excited! Well I was gonna shoot him. "I'm going to get him!" I said. She said, "No . . . no . . . no! Mazhan, mazhan! Wewiib, wewiib!" That means, hurry up, let's go [chuckles]. She wouldn't let me shoot that bear [laughing]. I remember that just like it was yesterday.[13]

Shingibbiss

Shingibbiss was born at Lake of the Woods in 1825 and was related to Chief Blackstone of Lac La Croix. The name Shingibbiss is the name for a diving duck, such as the mergansers that dive for baitfish in the Grand Marais harbor all summer long. His first wife was "Margaret" Shingibbiss, the daughter of Kenoshewaboo and mother of his two sons, Jim Gesick (White Sky) and Blue Sky. The family lived on the hillside in Grand Marais until Margaret's death. A widower for many years, Shingibbiss then had his home at Caribou Lake in Lutsen, where he lived with his son Blue Sky. White Sky Rock on Caribou Lake is named for Shingibbiss's grandson White Sky. White Sky's father, Jim O. Gesick, made a home for his family at the mouth of the Poplar River until 1885, when the land he and his family lived on— but did not have formal title to—was homesteaded to Charles Axel Nelson, who later built Lutsen Resort, a landmark resort for visitors to the North Shore.

There are several documented stories about Shingibbiss, as he was a well-known member of the community and served the people as a traditional healer. He was treated fondly by his non-Native neighbors and was described as "a very good man ... one of the best-liked Indian men" by a member of the Mayhew family.[14] He was known in the Grand Marais community as "a devoutly religious man, clinging to the old Indian religion and was never converted to the Christian faith as taught by the Catholics as were most of his native brethren."[15]

Shingibbiss. Courtesy of Cook County Historical Society.

Shingibbis made news long before the first newspaper was printed in Grand Marais—in 1853, he walked with the early settler Samuel Howenstine "along the Mesaba range to Vermilion Lake," where Howenstine hoped to secure a mineral claim in anticipation of the 1854 treaty signing. It took the men eleven days to reach the post at Vermilion, and the last three days were spent without food, "until just a few hours before reaching the lake they found a marten which had starved to death in a trap, the meat to them tasting sweet, indeed."[16]

Shingibbis and his wife lived in Grand Marais. According to Shingibbiss's great-great-granddaughter, Alta McQuatters, they "lived up the hill near the burying ground with other Indians."[17] A historian who has been doing the dedicated work of identifying and confirming the location of graves at Chippewa City for fifteen years, Alta speculated that the hill where the Shingibbiss family may have lived could be the site of the Birch Terrace, and that Margaret Shingibbiss may be one of the unidentified people who are buried there.

Catherine Jones, the wife of Dr. Henry Jones, mentions Shingibbiss and Mrs. Shingibbiss several times in her diary, including a visit on New Year's Day:

Sunday, Jan 1, 1899

New Years, cold and cloudy. First New Years' call in Grand Marais made us by Mr. and Mrs. Shingibbiss (Hell Diver). Walked in without knocking, shook hands and sat down. He could talk some but she could not speak English. Gave them each a package with popcorn candy and a cookie. They held it a few minutes then Mrs. Shingibbiss put it into a flour sack they carry to put in what is given them. We also gave them some magazines and he asked if we had any big pictures, "shoot-em-last-summer." He meant pictures of the war—so we gave him some.[18]

On a well-documented visit to Chippewa City in 1905, Francis Densmore's guide Joe Caribou brought her to the Shingibbiss home. The renowned anthropologist asked him to tell her about the use of "traditional Ojibwe hunting songs when out in the field." Shingibbiss's sense of humor is revealed in his response, which was simply, "We didn't sing then. We kept still."[19]

Weetch

Several of the people I interviewed remembered a woman known as "Weetch" who lived east of St. Francis Xavier—she appears in many stories but no one recalled her given name, as she was somewhat of a mystery. To some children, she was a caregiver; for others, she was seen as a frightening figure. According to Dora Kasames, who lived with Weetch for a time, the woman was a "half sister" to her father Joe Thomas:

> *She took care of me. And she had two grandchildren living with her. One was older and one was younger than me. She never worked. I don't know how she made her money, but she was always home. She was a homebody. She would go to church, but that's about all she would do. She never mingled with anybody or anything.*[20]

As a child, Gloria Martineau remembers being afraid of Weetch:

> *I remember Weetch. She used to come and visit Lucy Caribou. She had had cancer of the mouth and her lower lip would hang way down. And she chewed snus. And she always wanted to kiss us, and we didn't want to kiss her! But I think she did that on purpose, you know, because she knew us kids were scared of her.*[21]

Jim Wipson also could not recall Weetch's real name, but he did remember that she was at one time married to a soldier:

> *Well, Weetch lived in Chippewa City right down the bay there, not too far from us . . . I think she had a husband that was in World War I, because she took care of this man . . . See, the Germans gassed a lot of our soldiers . . . And a lot of them were dying like flies. They came back, all the soldiers. They were dying in Grand Marais. They would have the burials and it was really sad. And*

Weetch stands in the doorway at Sugarbush. Courtesy of Patsy Drouillard Swanson Collection.

Weetch took care of her husband until he died. And then after that she lived with her son, Antoine Anakwad.[22]

According to the baptism records of the Catholic church, Antoine Anakwad was born in Grand Marais in 1891 to Georges Anakwad and Marie Anne Wabibinens. They had a daughter, Teresa Anakwad, in 1893 and a second daughter, Dominique, in 1895. In Dominique's baptism record, the name "Weetch" is recorded in parenthesis next to the last name, Wabibinens.

The couple would have four more children: Marie Anne in 1897, Philomene in 1902, Eustache in 1903, and Paul in 1905. Corroborating Jim Wipson's memory of where they lived, Jim LaPlante recalled that the LaPlante house was close to Weetch's house, just east of what is now the Beckwith house.

The Morrison Family
⁓⚬

The Morrison family is one of the largest families to have lived at Chippewa City. According to grandsons Michael and George Morrison, their grandfather James (Jim) Morrison Sr. was a well-known singer at St. Francis Xavier who would sing Roman Catholic prayers as well as conduct the sermon in the Ojibwe language. The Morrisons would live in Chippewa City for most of their lives, as would many of their immediate family members. They were avid hunters and trappers. George recalled that when the trapping season was good, "the whole family—grandparents, aunts and uncles, and of course, the children—would move into four log cabins deep in the forest, where they stayed for the trapping season."[23]

James Sr.'s son Jim was also known as Basagee. Dorothy Johansen explained how Jim got this name from his brother, Joe:

> My mother (Margaret Morrison) told me the story that when Jim was a baby, Joe Morrison gave him a stick and said ba-sah-she-gun, meaning gun, and Jim said ba-sah-gee, so that's how he got that name.[24]

James (Jim) Jr. and his wife, Barbara (Mesaba), were the parents of twelve children, including Michael and his older brother, George Morrison. Mike was born in Chippewa City in 1919. His father, James Morrison, was also born there, but his mother, Barbara Mesaba, was originally from Fort Frances, Ontario. The Catholic priest in 1919 was Father LaMarche, S.J., who baptized Mike at St. Francis Xavier. He was born in his family's house in Chippewa City, which was just north of the church.

Michael was often matter-of-fact when he talked about his family and the challenges of raising a big family in Chippewa City:

> My mother used to bake bread. Sixteen loaves every other day! So, our family lived mostly on soup and bread. We would have supper

Antoine Anakwad (*left*) and Jim Morrison. Courtesy of Cook County Historical Society.

and it was a rough kind of life, you know? But no one complained. We all sat at the table, mother and father, six kids on each side of the table and it took a lot of bread. We were a happy family and we had concern for one another like we have even yet today.[25]

Mike's brother George would excel at school, showing particular aptitude for art and design. George left Chippewa City after high school to study at the Minneapolis College of Art. An extremely gifted and creative artist, George would go on to study in Paris and New York and would much later teach students at the Rhode Island School of Design, as well as other art schools. George referred to his father and his uncle Joe as "the old Indians" of Chippewa City. He described his experience like this:

There were good things about that atmosphere too. Being in a group together and sharing our own way of living. We were close with the neighbors and learned to play and get along. Through schooling I was encouraged by a few teachers who liked me and what I was doing.[26]

George Morrison (*right*) in shop class. Courtesy of Cook County Historical Society.

Dorothy Johansen had reached the status of elder when I interviewed her in 2001, and she remembered staying with her elderly grandmother, Teresa Morrison, who lived in Grand Portage:

> *Grandma Morrison was just a tiny little lady. She was an Elliot. She was Irish and Indian. She could speak English but she wouldn't do it. And of course, we had to stay with her whenever we couldn't get home because it was stormy. But we had to talk Indian, and I think that's why I didn't like to stay with her . . . But she was good to us. She was a no-nonsense lady.*[27]

The Anakwad Sisters: Kate Frost, Theresa Newton, and Elizabeth Drouillard

Jim Wipson loved his grandmother Kate (Anakwad) Frost and was very happy to share stories about her and her two younger sisters, who all lived in Chippewa City:

> *What it amounted to be was the three main sisters. They were originally Anakwads. There was my grandmother, Theresa Newton, and Elizabeth Drouillard. There were three sisters and then all the other people that were derived from them.*[28]

About his grandmother, Jim said: "She must have been born and raised in Chippewa City because she had to have lived there after her parents left or died. She carried on with their log house, so I surmise she was born in Chippewa City also."[29]

According to the 1880 federal census, the Anakwad family was living in Chippewa City in 1880. They are listed under the name "Cloud" and the family includes parents Martin and Theresa, their three daughters, Catherine, Isabel (Elizabeth), and Theresa, and three sons, George, Alexis, and Martin. The census record shows that Martin Anakwad was born in Wisconsin in 1836 and that his wife

Theresa was born in Canada in 1842. All six of their children are stated to have been born in Minnesota.

As adults in Chippewa City, the three sisters lived close to each other, shared the same maple sugar stand, and did what they could to help each other at a time when resources were scarce. Jim Wipson explained:

> *I was delivered by midwife. In them days, they didn't have the doctors they have now days, or the hospitals, so most people were born by midwife . . . It was my grandmother's sister, Theresa Newton. She's the one that helped deliver me.*[30]

Kate's younger sister, Theresa (Anakwad) Newton, lived up the hill. She had two children, Charlie and Hanna Newton. Mrs. Newton was the great-aunt to both Jim Wipson and Irene Sullivan. Irene said, "They called her Dahless, and I don't know how you would spell that. So, they were sisters; Kate and Dahless . . . and Grandma Elizabeth (Drouillard)."[31]

Great-Grandfather John Drouillard

In 1873, when my great-grandfather John Drouillard periodically left his wife Mary in Bayfield to work as an interpreter for the U.S. government payment agent, he would return to the North Shore, where he grew up and spent most of his childhood. After a year's absence, he returned to Bayfield, where he served somewhat notoriously as the assistant lighthouse keeper from 1874 to 1875. According to a series of letters written during that time, his fellow keeper, O. K. Hall, reported that John appears to have been ill suited to the work at hand:

Dear Sir:

*Last fall when I recommended John Drouillard, as an Assistant
Keeper, I did so under some reluctance, but men scarce with such
that ought to fill the place, and such a small salary as they give, it
was a hard matter to get the proper man for the place. Since then
I have found that he has a quick and violent temper and has no
control over himself whatever.*

*I have had a great deal of trouble with him, as he abuses me
with the most profane language a man can utter, from no cause or
provocation, and threatened to give me a thrashing. I caught him
asleep on his watch and since then he has lived in one part of the
house and I in the other.*

*During the fall he came to Bayfield, got whiskey (which I do
not use) and goods, saying I sent for it. They had their doubts
and questioned him close in regard to it. He is a man not to be
believed and has the reputation of it throughout Bayfield, not only
quarreled with me but his own family. I have lived in a perfect
hell. Therefore, I hope you will do all you can to get him removed
for they could not pay me enough to remain with him.*

*Since I have been in Bayfield, I have found a man whom
I think is capable of discharging the duties of an assistant, in the
person of Peter Ivery, being a good sailor and a hard-working,
industrious man. I recommend him as the man for the place.*

Yours truly,
O. K. Hall[32]

Indeed, John was "discharged" from his duties by the following
year. In 1876 he was listed as being on the Mayhew brothers' payroll,
helping to build the first dock in the Grand Marais harbor. Informal
family histories have made the claim that he married Elizabeth Anakwad that same year and they started a family soon after. Growing up, I
had always heard that great-grandmother and great-grandfather were

married. Doesn't everyone assume that their great-grandparents were married? And don't we also assume that our forebears adhered to the social expectations of the time, which did not allow for anything other than devout attention to religious and social norms? It turns out that this was a naive assumption, not necessarily supported by the historical record. Between 1877 and 1880, John spent his summers captaining a series of yachts. He was known after this as "Captain John," a title that would stay with him throughout his life. Although this required him to be away for long stretches of time, he is still known to have lived in Bayfield. For example, the 1880 Bayfield, Wisconsin, census lists John (last named misspelled as "Drawthorn"), his wife Mary, their two children Sebastian and Retta, and an eighteen-year-old girl named Cecile Balayia (thought to be Bellanger), who is described as being a "servant." Like searching for buried treasure, the tracking of family history can sometimes lead to unexpected places, and can put our own assumptions about the past into messy territory.

I looked to the Catholic baptism records from St. Francis Xavier for help in solving the mystery. The birth record for great-grandmother Elizabeth and great-grandfather John's eldest child, Josephine Drouillard, who was born in Grand Marais in 1884 and is proudly identified as the first person confirmed at the church, confirmed that the story was not quite what it seemed. Scrawled in the notes column, in a box on the far right of the page, it said, "Conditional baptism."[33]

I searched later baptism records for clues about what that phrase might mean. Three years later, the record for Josephine's brother Charles Drouillard, born in Grand Marais in 1887, with Mr. and Mrs. James Morrison as sponsors, states clearly in the notes column: "Condit. baptism. Parents not married."[34]

It turns out that the papers for all twelve of their children are marked as "conditional baptisms" in the records transcribed by Father Maurice of the Thunder Bay Catholic diocese. And on Rose Drouillard's baptism recorded in 1903, it clearly says: "Parents not married. Father refused to recognize child as his."[35]

Between the time that their eldest daughter Josephine was born in

1884 and when their youngest son, Fred Drouillard, my grandfather, was born in 1906, John Drouillard worked a multitude of colorful jobs, including for the Pittsfield Iron Company doing mineral prospecting on Gunflint Lake and Whitefish Lake. He was in charge of the North Shore Mining Company packers between 1890 and 1891.

John's brother James E. Drouillard was also living on the North Shore during this period. He was known as a "mining captain" of the Charleston Mining Company and did extensive mineral prospecting on the Iron Range and on the North Shore, primarily between Gunflint Lake and Whitefish Lake. James E. Drouillard's heroic trek from Grand Marais to Two Harbors on snowshoes made news in Bayfield, the Drouillard family's hometown and where their father Nelson served as sheriff of Bayfield County:

A well-known explorer's journey of two months on the north shore is completed. J. E. Drouillard . . . is back from a two-months trip from that region. He came up from Grand Marais to Two Harbors on snowshoes and reports from two to three feet of snow on the level entire distance; although in places it is badly drifted . . . Between Beaver Bay and Two Harbors the storm had abated so that the traveling was comparatively easy, but by the time he reached Two Harbors his feet were in a pitiable condition from the chafing of the snowshoes. Mr. Drouillard says that John Beargrease, the intrepid mail carrier, is making a good record this winter, and has carried the mail all the season, losing only one trip. The last six weeks Beargrease has taken the mail overland, because of the extreme cold on Lake and floating ice, which made the water route doubly dangerous. The Grand Marais people, Mr. Drouillard says, are all well, but late last year there was little typhoid fever which has since disappeared . . . Mr. Drouillard will return to Cook County on the first boat from Duluth.[36]

The two brothers had more in common than just wilderness prowess. James Drouillard married Elizabeth Anakwad's sister, Catherine

(Kate), making the two brothers and two sisters an extended family of interlocking relations. James and Kate had two sons, James Jr. and Martin. Their marriage was not permanent. James reportedly married a woman named Olive Genery in 1898, in Ashland, Wisconsin. And Kate married Joe Frost, from Bad River. She and Mr. Frost had a daughter, Ida, who is Jim Wipson's mother. This tangle of relations, both near and far, explains why it's difficult to follow the Drouillard family tree, in which sisters married brothers and named their children after each other.

James and John Drouillard were kindred spirits, their bravado and wilderness skill serving them well in a number of trades, including logging, blacksmithing, carpentry, and road building. While James was prospecting on the Iron Range, John stayed closer to Cook County where he worked for Charles Johnson as an interpreter for timber sales on the reservation and at Sugar Loaf Cove in Lutsen, as well as running the mess hall at Johnson's cedar shingle mill on Good Harbor Bay just west of Grand Marais. He was also instrumental in establishing the Hovland Township and was known to be living in Hovland in 1894 when he served as the first Hovland chairman of the board of supervisors. In 1900, he was working with a crew of men to fix and build roads in the vicinity of the Gunflint Trail as part of the widespread effort to accommodate increased interest in metal mining and exploration.

Captain John was known for being able to spend long periods alone in the wilderness and in one particularly heroic account,

> spent 184 days in the woods alone, moving from place to place, and sleeping in a tent all the time. He says he liked it and would be willing to do it now, as, according to his telling, he got fat eating food of his own cooking. The deer were his pets, never killing any of them, depending on rabbits and partridges for meat. He says he has spent more time in the woods than any other man in Cook County, and never had wolves, a bear, or moose, chase him up a tree. He thinks all wolf, moose and bear stories are fakes. "Leave

them alone," he says, "and they will leave you alone." He has been
with the Indians since he was seven years old, and has never heard
of one being chased up a tree by any animal.[37]

Because John's work record and land ownership history after 1881
are well documented, it can be surmised that he never returned to
his family in Bayfield. It's not clear, however, what formal or informal
living arrangements were made with his North Shore family, who had
grown to twelve by the time his youngest son, my grandfather Fred
Drouillard, was born in 1906.

Great-Grandmother Elizabeth Anakwad

Elizabeth Anakwad was the mother of twelve children, all of whom
claimed John as their father. I don't know if she ever knew about his
other children in Bayfield, although, given that the Catholic priests
did not view the couple as being married in the eyes of the church,
it could be surmised that she did know about his first wife, Mary
Bachand. It's almost certain that Mary and John were never officially
divorced owing to the Catholic church's opinion on the matter; divorce was strictly forbidden. To further deepen the mystery, Elizabeth
and John are listed as a married couple on the Grand Marais census,
recorded in 1900. According to that document, they were married in
1882, having stayed together for eighteen years. But I've not found the
marriage record to corroborate that, nor have I been able to explain
why their children were given conditional baptisms, and in some cases
fatherhood was contested. It's also relevant that John Drouillard, as
researched in Will Raff's history, was living in a cabin in Hovland in
1894 that he shared with a man named Adolph Carlson, Hovland's first
town clerk. John and Elizabeth's daughter Mathilde was born in 1895
and was baptized at St. Francis Xavier church in Chippewa City. At
that time, there were no easily navigable roads to and from Hovland,
and because all of their children were recorded as living in Chippewa

City it can be assumed with some accuracy that great-grandmother Elizabeth and great-grandfather John lived in separate houses and that she, with help from her extended family at Chippewa City, mostly raised the children on her own.

In order to unravel our murky family past, where only half of the story is well documented, some conjecture about their cultural differences and cultural convergences might be enlightening. We do know that John came from a devout Catholic family tradition that would not have allowed for divorce or bigamy. If they were indeed married in 1882, as stated in the 1900 census, then why did he live apart from his wife and children ten years after their first child was born? And if John was a practicing Catholic, what were Elizabeth Anakwad's religious beliefs? Did she choose to live and raise their children on her own or did they live apart because of John's need to financially support his growing family? Or perhaps because of John's lifelong connection to the Ojibwe people of the North Shore, his own religious ideology wasn't quite as conservative as we thought. Unfortunately, there are no written records of traditional Ojibwe marriage ceremonies that took place alongside the written records kept by the church. And on each of the birth records for their children, my great-grandmother is always listed by her maiden name only—Elizabeth Anakwad. Jim Wipson provides some insight into the marriage question and the cultural divergence between traditional Ojibwe marriage and marriages performed by the Catholic church:

> Well, in them days . . . the Indians, I guess they just lived together and then they considered themselves married, I guess. I don't know if they had ceremonies like they do nowadays . . . but I think there was a lot of that going on in the olden days . . . they live together so many years and then pretty soon they're considered married. Common law.[38]

Very little is known about great-grandmother Elizabeth and how she lived her day-to-day life, raising twelve kids fathered by a renowned woodsman who did not live with his family on a regular basis. But her sisters Kate and Theresa, and her brothers Martin and Alexander, all lived close to one another in Chippewa City. And in her later years, when she had moved to a house between Chippewa City and Grand Marais, many of her grandchildren lived close by and do remember some things about her. First cousins Vivian Waltz, Dorothy Johansen, and Gladys Beckwith all shared memories of growing up with their grandmother, Elizabeth, or "Chi'za-bet"[39] to her neighbors. Said Vivian:

When [my grandmother] moved to Grand Marais, she lived not too far from my mother's house. We'd go on the back porch and we could see her house. I used to go over there and clean for her and stuff like that. She didn't talk English, you know, and I didn't understand Indian. Mother would send us over with food to give her and we'd try to make her understand what it was.[40]

Dorothy had this to say about her grandmother:

I barely remember Grandma Drouillard. It seemed to me that she was always smiling and probably giving us hugs or something. We used to stop there a lot when we went into town. We would stop and see Grandma.[41]

Sue Zimmerman, a Drouillard cousin, recalled hearing that when great-grandmother visited a friend in Grand Portage, "she used to laugh a lot, she loved to laugh and tell stories."[42] Sue's aunt, Gladys Beckwith, was able to identify the former location of her house, along with some living and blooming evidence of her life there:

You know where the motel is down here . . . down on the highway? The one that's over a little bit? There's a road that goes down to the Federal Credit Union, and that was the end of my mother's land. That's her rose bushes and her lilac bushes that are there. And my grandmother Drouillard lived over where the big hotel is.[43]

Great-grandmother Elizabeth's lilac bush is still there, and it still blooms every summer. To think of that, and think about her life there, where people from all over the world now come to visit, makes me very proud. She lived where honeymooners now sleep, where families pick rocks, and where tourists taunt the seagulls with their picnic lunch, just down the beach from where her front porch used to be. Knowing this gives me the grounding that I need to tell the story of this place. Of home. And how we, just like the lilacs, draw strength from the earth beneath us. Stored in our roots, we are nourished by the memory of the people who came before us. Who, like the hearty perennials of early summer, are not afraid to show the world who we are. And most important, that we are still here.

Great-grandma Anakwad's lilac bush in bloom today. Photograph by the author.

Jim Morrison (*second row, center*), Joe Morrison (*far right*), Martin Drouillard (*front right*), Charlie Drouillard (*front left*), Swamper Caribou (*far left, with pipe*), and others. Courtesy of Michael Morrison.

→ Chapter 7 ←

INDIAN MAIDENS AND PLASTIC TOMAHAWKS

How to Make a Living

WHETHER YOUR ANCESTORS are Scandinavian or Ojibwe, life along the North Shore was never easy. However, the people I've spoken to who were born and raised in Chippewa City rarely portray their lives there as being particularly difficult or harsh—they simply describe it as what life was like for them. They most often shared stories and memories of a village made up of close-knit friends and relatives who shared whatever skills and resources they had with the greater community. Sharing what one had with others was often the difference between surviving in the wilderness or going hungry—a fact that Jim Anderson, a first cousin to my dad, attests to in his story about working as a logger when he was a teenager, where he learned an important lesson from my great-uncle Charlie Drouillard:

> *Some old timers here will remember Victor Johnson and Charlie Drouillard for that's who they were sure enough. One buggy evening after an easy day in the swamp with saw, ace and bugs, Charlie D. came over to our tent to see if we had starved out and bunched it. Think he was sorry to see us ragged, dirty and hungry all the time (tho' we jumped in the lake every day we never thought to wash clothes all summer).*
>
> *Now Vic and Charlie were used to roughing it I said, any time of the year and could see we weren't doin' so hot. "Come on over to my teepee," says old quiet Indian Charlie, "I got something for*

*you boys." There he gave us freshly made donuts, hot, sweet all we
could eat, cooked fine brown in a black kettle of smoking hot bear
grease. Never before or since have I eaten anything to compare to
that tasty treat.*

    *Even after that we thought C. D. was a good man to know.
He may have seemed sorta reclusive to some people but I know he
also could be good, for he was real kind to brother and me, and
he shared what little he had with us, that long time ago day in
the pulp swamp. Two teenage boys and one old Indian, we're all
brothers you know.*[1]

On the North Shore, there's no great equalizer like a batch of fresh
donuts. In order to make a living, everyone had to work hard and work
together. It is because of the hard work and fortitude of the people
who came before us that the North Shore is the culturally rich place
that it is today.

Relying on the Old Ways

The 1885 Grand Portage census recorded that of the three hundred
enrollees at Grand Portage, 30 percent of tribal members were employed by others, with 65 percent subsisting on hunting and 5 percent
subsisting on government rations alone. Just four years later, the 1889
census reported that half of tribal members were now employed
by others and the other half were self-supporting by hunting. That
same year, of the total number of enrollees, 25 percent reported receiving government rations in addition to their primary means of
making a living.[2] The people living on the reservation were growing
increasingly dependent on government annuities, as job opportunities decreased for people living on the reservation. They still relied
on the old, traditional ways of getting by, but were also forced to live
within the European parameters that dictated the way commerce was
conducted.

Those who moved off reservation seeking work are in the category "employed by others," which refers to employment as a builder or laborer on one of the many construction projects in Grand Marais or clearing trees for local lumber companies. This work would require cooperation with the fledgling European industrialists at Grand Marais: Charles Johnson, Henry Mayhew, Ted Wakelin, and Sam Howenstine, who headed up many of the building, logging, and infrastructure projects on the North Shore in the late 1800s.

Whether they lived on or off the reservation, many used their knowledge of traditional life skills to subsist, relying on hunting, trapping, and fishing to make a living. James (Jim) Morrison Sr. was a commercial fisherman out of Chippewa City, as was Bill (Willie) Drouillard. The fishing tradition on the North Shore began with the hard work of Jim, Bill, and many other Anishinaabe fisherman who based their operations at Grand Portage, Hovland, Colvill, Chippewa City, Grand Marais, Good Harbor Bay, and all points southwest along the shore. Jim LaPlante remembers eating a lot of fish caught by his uncle:

My Uncle Bill was a commercial fisherman, in the fall of the year especially, he'd go out for herring. And mother would tell me, "take that bucket there down to your Uncle Bill and see if he's got some fish." He'd have a whole boat-load full and I'd fill up that bucket and take it home.[3]

Occasionally, Bill would deliver fish to his Chippewa City neighbors Kate Frost and her grandson Jim, as Jim shared with me:

He pretty well seen to it that my grandmother could have all the fish she wanted. He used to come by the house there, real early in the morning and holler, "Katie, you need some fish?" And my grandma would say, "Oh yes, we could use some fish." Then he'd say, "Come to the door there, send your son there!" That meant me. And I'd go to the door and he'd have maybe two or three dozen fish. And we'd eat fish for a while.[4]

Bill Drouillard with Elizabeth Anakwad, 1930s. Courtesy of Dorothy Johansen.

It seems everyone on the North Shore wanted to fish. In 1889, Grand Portage band members made a formal complaint to the government to protest the presence of Scandinavian fishermen "camped out" on the Susie Islands and just outside Wauswaugoning Bay with nets so large the Anishinaabe fisherman were not able to compete with their fish harvest—a grave situation when fishing was one of the few sustainable industries remaining on the reservation.[5] Fishing as a way to make a living would work well for some, including a French-Canadian fisherman named Pete Gagnon, who built a dock, a hotel, and a store on Grand Portage Island and was able to hire fishermen from the area. Gagnon was backed by A. Booth and Company out of Duluth, and the fish caught at Grand Portage were shipped all over the Lake Superior region.

The commercial fishing economy, like other industries, began to decline, leading up to the Great Depression. But because the North Shore Anishinaabe did not lose their close connection to the lakes, rivers, and woods, even when times were hard, they retained the skills they were taught over the years. Knowing how to fish meant the difference between starving or feeding one's family.

Joseph Milton Powell was raised far inland on Saganaga Lake, on the Canadian side, until he moved with his family into Grand Marais in 1939. The economics of the time required many to move periodically to another place to follow work opportunities. Milt explained why his family then moved from Grand Marais to Grand Portage in 1943:

> *We moved to Grand Portage for three years, because my dad . . .*
> *they offered him a job commercial fishing. It was bad. They'd get*
> *a nice catch and then the price would go down. So, at that time*
> *in Grand Portage it was really sad. The people, they were limited.*
> *They only made so much money and that was it. It was tough*
> *making it.*[6]

Milt's dad was also a hunting and fishing guide and a Quetico Park ranger. He, like my Grandpa Fred, managed to keep their families fed utilizing the wilderness skills they were taught as children. Grandpa Fred spent every summer for many years working as a fishing and hunting guide at Chik Wauk Lodge on Saganaga Lake. He was an in-demand guide with a number of repeat customers, including a wealthy doctor from Chicago who would visit every year and request

Fred Drouillard at work on Saganaga Lake. Courtesy of Gloria Martineau.

his skilled guide services. Grandpa's ability to catch fish was legendary and my dad has often boasted about how his dad was often the only guide to come back at the end of the day with fish. There is a family photograph of him, crouched next to a fire, cooking a "shore lunch" of freshly caught fish, potatoes, and onions, all fried in bacon grease— just another day's work on mighty Saganaga Lake.

A Brand-New Model T Ford

Many people who lived in Chippewa City also brought in money by selling furs in Grand Marais, Thunder Bay, or Duluth. Catherine Jones noted that on Sunday, January 8, 1898, "An Indian brought to the store a silver-gray fox skin for which he received (we heard) $65.00."[7]

Chippewa City brothers Jim and Joe Morrison were well-known trappers, as was an associate, Joe Thomas. Joe's daughter Dora Kasames remembers the impact the fur trade had on her life when she was a child:

> He'd go up to Swamper Lake, also called the 22 Mile Post, and he'd go up there and live for the winter. In the spring, he'd bring all his furs down and then we'd all come to Duluth to sell them. And we'd have a brand-new Model T Ford going home.[8]

George Morrison recalled that there were "a couple of buyers" in Grand Marais, including Charles Johnson.[9] According to Will Raff, by the mid-1890s, Charles Johnson "had acquired an extraordinary reputation as banker and merchant, for honesty and fair dealing." He also noted that, "Beginning in the mid-1890's, Johnson made regular late-winter buying trips by dog train up the Gunflint Wagon Road to the Indian camp on Saganaga, then east through Gunflint and Rose Lakes."[10]

Michael Morrison remembers that "the trapping season was for furs that were sold to fur buyers," and that once the pelts were sold to

Johnson Trading Post with furs, 1945. Courtesy of the Minnesota Historical Society.

the buyers, his family would often subsist all winter on beaver, deer, and moose meat that his mother canned from the animals his father and uncle Joe had trapped during the fall and winter.[11]

Even though the days of the fur trade had long passed, the demand for wild furs was enough to sustain several area Native families during the wintertime. My grandfather Fred was known to leave the family in Grand Marais for several days at a time to tend his trap line. The Powell family, while living on Saganaga, also made a living by trapping animals whose hide was in demand in other parts of the world. Milt shared this story about his dad's dog team:

> *My father, when he was trapping, he snared a wolf. A female wolf and she had five pups. And he drove the five pups as a dog team. He'd go from Saganaga to Gunflint nonstop . . . He was the only one who could go around them. Us children were never allowed to go up and play with the work animals . . . We could feed 'em but not play with them as pets.*

I asked him if it was because they were wild. He clarified: "If you played with them, they wouldn't behave like they were supposed to." Milt's father would be gone for two or three days, and would usually come home with a sled full of furs:

When he was trapping, he would maybe get fifty to sixty beaver, and then he would get the same amount of mink, and a few fisher and a few otter and he got one wolverine . . . that was his winter kill.

I asked Milt if he ever joined his dad on his trapping trips. He said:

I was with him a couple of times. But I froze out. And when I'd start getting cold, he'd have to shorten his trip. So, that only happened about twice. After that I'd stay home where it was warm.[12]

Sophie and Mike Powell, with Milt Powell in rabbit-skin coat, sister Vera, and dog Spot, on Saganaga Lake around 1935. Courtesy of Alice Powell.

Berry Hunters

The children of the community also did their share to contribute, utilizing the natural resources that were available to them. Gladys (Zimmerman) Beckwith recalled the importance of wild berries to the local economy, which was growing more and more dependent on visitors and locals who patronized the local restaurants:

> *We had to pick blueberries and raspberries and take them downtown and sell them at the back door of the restaurants. And they'd probably give you five or ten cents a quart. And I always said, "When I get married, I'm never going to pick another berry again." Well, I had seven kids, and I picked berries!*[13]

Mike Morrison and all of his siblings worked hard for their family, including long stints picking berries that they would later sell in town:

> *When I was a boy, the blueberries and raspberries we picked in the summertime brought in a lot of income to our family. My dad made crates for the berries out of wood. Each crate held thirty-two quarts, and we would take these out to the berry patch and fill them up. We didn't have a car, so my dad would hire somebody to drive us out there. He'd tell them to pick us up in five days. Then they would leave us there, and since we didn't have tents or anything to sleep in, we lived right out in the open, eating the berries we picked, the rabbits we snared, and the bannock we cooked. All we brought with us was the bare necessities. And we picked a lot. Figure it out—there were four of us kids who were old enough to pick, plus my dad. Each of us had a crate. So, there were five crates, each with thirty-two quarts. That's 164 quarts in all. Although I don't pick berries anymore—I guess I've been spoiled by the white man's ways—whenever I buy blueberries or raspberries now it reminds me of those days. And they were happy days.*[14]

Harvesting on Good Harbor Hill and Maple Hill

Although the North Shore is not prime agricultural land, the people did utilize the fertile hills north and west of Grand Marais in a limited way. Mike Morrison recalled working for some of the farmers on Good Harbor Hill in exchange for fresh fruits and vegetables.[15] The Morrison family is still remembered fondly by members of the Matt Johnson family, Norwegian settlers who first arrived in 1887. When Mathias (Matt) Johanasen (Johnson) and his wife Christina moved to Cook County, they were stranded in Grand Marais by a storm on the lake that prevented them from reaching their land claim—a piece of property they had chosen sight unseen from the Duluth Land Office map. The land was located on a steep hillside seven miles west of Grand Marais, now known as Good Harbor Hill. When they arrived in Grand Marais on the *Dixon,* a steamer servicing the North Shore, all of the hotel rooms were full, but they were graciously invited to stay at the home of John Morrison, who was the county surveyor.[16] Soon after, Johnson built his first cabin on Good Harbor Hill, but accidentally built it outside of his homestead lines. The error was discovered by their surveyor friend John Morrison, and as a result the Johnsons had to build their cabin again, this time within the boundaries of their property line.

This family connection was never forgotten by the members of the Matt Johnson family, who years later would give John Morrison's great-nephew Mike Morrison soup bones and other groceries as a gesture of goodwill between the two families. Mark Johnson, the current owner of the Johnson family grocery business, shared that his family had warm memories of Mike and the entire Morrison family, because of the early connection that their elders had to each other, back when times were tough and you needed the help of your neighbors to survive.[17]

There were some farms on Maple Hill built by early dairy farmers on land that is still farmed by the same families today. And Jim LaPlante recalled that at least one cow lived in Chippewa City. It was owned by Ernie Savor, who, according to Jim, lived in the house that used to belong to fisherman Claus Monker: "We used to go down and watch him milk that cow. He would say 'open your mouth,' and we'd open our mouths and he'd squirt that old milk in our mouths."[18]

Jim also shared a story that was passed along to him by his mother, Alice Drouillard LaPlante, about how Great-grandmother Elizabeth Anakwad carried on the tradition of the sugar bush, tapping the trees at one of the tree stands on Maple Hill:

> One time, Grandpa Drouillard told my grandmother, "Don't you take those kids up there today. There's going to be a storm." My grandma was pretty bullheaded, and she had made up her mind that she was going up to the sugar bush. She packed up all the kids and took them up even though it was snowing and blowing and miserable as hell . . . she was having to drive those kids through the snowbanks and everything. When old John Drouillard came home to an empty house, he figured that they had gone up the hill anyway, so he went up to the sugar bush. Sure enough, they were all along the trail, and he gathered up the kids and his wife and took them home. Good thing, too, because they probably would have frozen to death up there.[19]

It seems that regardless of whether the people lived in Grand Portage, Chippewa City, or Grand Marais, the pull of the seasonal lifestyle remained strong, regardless of how much time had passed or what the conditions were. Like the Grand Portage families of the children who, in 1856, believed that going to sugar bush was more important than going to school, Great-grandmother Anakwad was doing her part to keep Anishinaabe tradition strong, even when it appeared to others that it was at her own peril.

Going to Sugar Bush with Grandmother Kate
~❀

Gathering maple syrup in the spring is what is known as "going to sugar bush" and is a long-standing tradition among Chippewa people. The Grand Marais and Chippewa City people made camp in the spring and would stay in the woods until the sap stopped running, a process that might take several weeks. The sugar bushes nearest to Grand Marais were located about ten miles north, on Maple Hill, stretching eastward to the maple woods east of Durfee Creek, north of Croftville. Chief Espagnol was known to have maple-sugared near Croftville, which made sense, especially if he and his people had over-wintered at Kitchi-bitobig, Grand Marais.[20]

Bill Amyotte recalled that this northeasterly maple stand was a place they called "Cornwall's,"[21] a name corroborated by Grand Marais resident Cac Hussey:

> *[The Indians] had a sugar bush up by the Five Mile Rock road . . . Cornwell's they called it. There was five or six wigwams up there. They'd live out there in the spring of the year, snow on the ground, colder than all billy-heck, makin' maple sugar.[22]*

Jim Wipson remembers the sugar bush in detail, even though it was more than eighty years ago that he last visited:

> *I've been to sugar bush with my grandmother. We used to go from Chippewa City. Well, she'd always hire somebody from Grand Marais with a car to take us up to some of these roads that go way up in the woods. You know, you'd come down past Croftville. It would be an old road going up there and that car would take us up there, far as they could go on that road, maybe they'd go two to three miles up in the woods. And from there I'd have a little pack-sack, my grandma would put a packsack on me and she'd have a packsack. We'd take our necessities up there, you know, to cook.*

Kate Frost and family at their spring sugar bush, early 1920s. Jim Wipson waves in the front row. Courtesy of Patsy Drouillard Swanson Collection.

And we'd go up and all the Indians had designated areas where they made teepees.

My grandmother had a place where she had a birch-bark teepee, and her sisters had teepees down the road aways, maybe one-quarter mile down one side and the other one maybe one-half mile the other way. And what happened is they'd make it just like a community while we were up there. They'd visit each other at night. Maybe we'd walk over to my grandmother's sister or maybe her cousins and we'd visit. They'd all get around the bonfire and the teepee, and they'd sit and talk and have a little tea or maybe a little homemade wine or something, and it was just enjoyable. I was a little boy and I used to enjoy that, just sitting around that fire. It would feel so good, and to be in the teepee.

And then my grandmother would go out and she'd take a hatchet, and I'd go with her, and she'd tap these trees. She'd angle

*a hatchet against a maple tree a certain way and hit it with a
hammer or something, and make a notch in there, only so far on
this maple tree. And then she made wedges out of wood, I don't
know, I think she made them ahead of time and had them in her
teepee, and she'd knock, pound these wedges into that maple tree
and that's where the sap would drip. And then she'd make birch-
bark containers . . . made out of birch bark, and set them down
below that tap.*

*So, each day in the evening I'd go with her, and we'd take
little buckets, and we'd go to each tree and pour that sap into this
bucket. When they'd get full we'd carry them over to the teepee
and put 'em in a big cast-iron container, usually by a bonfire.
When we got the cast-iron container, I don't know if they have
them old-fashioned cast-iron containers anymore. It'd get about
three-quarters full and then she'd start cooking it on the bonfire,
and she'd know just how to do it . . . a certain length of time, when
that sap got to a certain frequency—that would be the syrup. And
after she'd got so many jars of syrup, she'd keep cooking it again,
and then start making taffy candy. And boy, them taffies used to
be delicious. [smiling] She'd give me one of them and I'd suck on
that thing. And then after that you'd make hard candy and brown
sugar. You could make so many things out of that maple syrup.
Boy, I used to love that candy.*[23]

Bootlegging
~ঙ

Several people recalled the making of liquor or beer. Jim Wipson said
that his grandmother would make homemade wine or beer as part of
the New Year celebration. In some instances, however, homemade
liquor was a way to make a living. Up until the late 1930s, it was illegal
in Grand Marais or Grand Portage to sell alcohol to Indian people. Jim
Wipson explained how people got around the law:

Well, the Indians, you know, made their own drinks. They made home brew and they couldn't stop them from getting the ingredients to make it. There was no law against them buying malt or raisins or sugar. And they just put everything in the home brew. They'd even cut up potatoes. And I tell you, some of that home brew is a lot better than the beer they serve nowdays. It was really good.[24]

As a way to make a living, bootlegging was the difference between going hungry and having plenty to eat in a time when money was scarce for most families. However, it was a risky way to make ends meet, as Jim LaPlante related in an interview about his mother's (Alice LaPlante) bootleg business, which she shared with her brother, my grandpa Fred Drouillard:

That home-brew she made for fifty-cents a quart, and boy we ate good for a while, when she was selling that stuff, she made good money. She was answering the door all night long, the boozers coming for their bottle.[25]

Jim explained how his mother eventually got caught:

[My uncle Fred] would come down from the woods. He used to guide up at Saganaga all the time. And he come down and he brought this guy over to the house and my mother said, "no, he don't look right," and she was right, 'cause she went to jail for it.[26]

This is not the first time that Grandpa Fred ran into trouble involving alcohol. The following was reported in the *Cook County News Herald* on December 13, 1923:

Fred and Charles Drouillard, Sam Wiggins and Chas. Gerken, the latter living at the Cornwall farm, were arrested Saturday night by Sheriff Lien for being drunk and disorderly. They were taken

before Justice Larson and altogether they were fined $89. During
the brawl, a window was broken in the Nylund Barber Shop and
another in the People's Supply Company Store. The wire screen on
the bakery door was torn.[27]

It's not a secret that drinking was a part of our family history. It would
be dishonest not to acknowledge that Grandpa Fred struggled with
alcoholism and that it affected the daily lives of his family. The role of
alcohol in the history of colonization, land acquisition, and cultural
assimilation in Native American history in the United States is multi-
faceted and complicated. It's a dark reality of history, in my family
and in many others, that has affected the ways that we view the past.
For everyone, it's a difficult road to follow. As Aunt Doreen used
to say, "Don't judge someone until you have walked a mile in their
moccasins."

Chores

The people in Chippewa City and many of those in Grand Marais did
not have running water or electricity until the 1940s. Although some
homes in Grand Marais did have these amenities, the Indian people
in the area lived without. My aunt, Gloria Martineau, shared that our
family got electricity in 1943 when she was eleven years old.[28]

Many people remember having to carry water from the lake or
help their parents with the housework. Jim Wipson remembers carrying water from Thunder Hook Point to his grandmother's house
onshore:

When I was a little boy, I had a little bucket. I walked down this
cliff, it was like a rocky cliff, and then I would go down there and
dip the bucket in and carry the water up to the house. Oh, maybe
you're talking about a block and half from the house down to the
cliff and then down to the lake.[29]

Michael Morrison recalls washing his own clothing as a way to help his mother:

The main job was to wash clothes because we didn't have a wash system. We had to haul water from the lake. So, we took all the clothing and baskets and hauled them down to the lake and took our tubs down there, and we built a fire and heated the water and scrubbed our clothes with a washboard. Each one of us kids had a washboard and we each had a tub of water. And we had plenty of water for rinsing because we got it from the lake. And after we had washed, my mother used to inspect our clothes to see if we had washed clean enough.[30]

Dorothy Johansen described what a typical day was like for her in Chippewa City:

Well, we had to get up in the morning. And get all cleaned up and everything and have our breakfast, go to school. And after school we'd come home, and we had our chores to do. The worst chore was to clean the kerosene lamps—to wash the chimney, and my mother was very, very fussy about the chimney, it had to be sparkling clean, had to trim the wicks. That was the worst job. And I tried to help cook supper and set the table and wash dishes and stuff and then I could go out and walk around with my friends, or play or something after I did my schoolwork or whatever I had to do.[31]

Making a living was not easy for the people who lived in Chippewa City. The community shared resources and people contributed what they could to the community. Sharing what you have with others is another example of how traditional Anishinaabe ways were integrated into Chippewa City life. As Dora Kasames explained, "Chippewa City used to be a nice place when I was a kid. Everybody was the same, this family didn't have any more than the next family and they would share."[32]

Dora Kasames with her mother, Anne (Anna) Caribou, in Chippewa City, mid-1920s.
Courtesy of Lani Blackdeer.

Robert Drouillard told this story about his boyhood in Chippewa
City:

> Well, one time Antoine Anakwad hollered to me, "Bizhan!
> Bizhan!" (Hurry! Hurry!) So, I went. The dog had chased a deer
> out in Lake Superior . . . so we jumped in the boat, one set of
> oars, took off after this deer. We were out about there about three-
> quarters of a mile. Old Antoine took the anchor rope off the front
> of the boat, grabbed the deer around the neck with it. He said,
> "Grab ahold of his legs" in Chippewa. So—we finally got the deer
> in the boat. And no gun, no knife, no nothing. Antoine took his

*oar, I'll never forget it, he jabbed and jabbed, I said, "You'll punch
a hole in the boat!" I had a hard time hanging on to him. I had his
back legs. He finally murdered that poor deer. We got the boat back
to the land and everybody was watching in Chippewa [City], they
all came down. Cut the deer up, divided it up, so everyone had a
piece of venison.*[33]

Jim Wipson explained how he and his grandmother got by with
the help of their neighbors and each other:

*We didn't have nothing. Just had a few means, and most of the
food we ate came from the wildlife. She would snare rabbits down
at the point, and some of the Indians would go and kill a deer. They
were pretty good about that and they would share their meat.*[34]

Jim also recalled going to Canada with his grandmother to visit
the Fort William Reserve just across the border, or occasionally as far
north as Nipigon, where she would sell her homemade medicines to
the people she knew on the Canadian Reserves:

*In them days we didn't have much money, and mostly they would
give to her in trade, stuff for her medicines, like beadwork, birch
bark, canoes and rugs. In turn, she could take that and sell it when
we got back here and she would get a little of her money back.*[35]

In contrast, transactions between the Ojibwe and white settlers
most often included the exchange of goods for money or specific services. For example, Catherine Jones writes of buying "twelve pounds of
moose meat from Weetch's husband George Anakwad."[36] It is doubtful
that Mr. Anakwad would have asked one of his Chippewa City neighbors to buy the moose meat, but would instead have traded for fish or
some other commodity. More than a hundred years later, the people
of Chippewa City still upheld a traditional way of commerce with one
another, but not with others from outside of that cultural tradition—

just as their relatives on the Granite River did when they sold fish and *manoomin* to Alexander Henry in exchange for money instead of offering him a trade. This cultural divide between the two communities would eventually grow into a wide chasm between the Ojibwe families in Chippewa City and their non-Native neighbors.

Indian Maidens and Plastic Tomahawks

The quiet beauty and surrounding wilderness made Grand Marais an early tourist destination. As roads and communication systems improved, the community became more and more accessible to the outside world. Touted as a "quiet, inexpensive place for an outing," the North Shore became a haven for visitors from Chicago and other large cities accessible by ship.[37] The fresh air, clean water, and ruggedness of the area were sold in advertisements throughout the Great Lakes region, as evidenced by this statement from the 1903 *Cook County Herald:*

> *Travelers and cruisers are in praise of our climate and golden weather of the North Shore. They say it invigorates the whole system, gives life and strength to the body and energy and renewed activities to the inner man.*[38]

The white businesspeople who claimed the North Shore for their own interests were not above exploiting the area Native population as an exotic draw for people from out of town. In one advertisement sponsored by the Grand Marais Business Men's Club, the town is said to offer a variety of natural beauty and scenic opportunities, including "Indian Maids," a proclamation made in an advertisement for the Grand Marais Gentleman's Club in the 1920s.[39]

When the exclusive "Naniboujou Club" was founded at the mouth of the Brule River in 1928, the club officers lured in new members with an offer to "belong to the tribe." Their elegantly typeset recruitment

Advertisement for The Business Men's Club of Grand Marais.

literature stated, "*And if you belong to the tribe, the answer will surely come back faintly as from a distance, 'Bou jou.'*" *Boozhoo* is an informal way to say "hello" in Ojibwemowin. Club membership also promised:

> *If you belong, you throw a pinch of tobacco in the stream before you wet your line. Then Naniboujou will be pleased; the brook trout will rise, the lake trout will respond to the glittering spoon, the great northern pike or the landlocked salmon will be lured from the depth of the inland lake. Make friends with Naniboujou and the country is yours.*

It's important to know that Naniboujou as a figure in Ojibwe lore is akin to Jesus' role as a figurehead in Christian stories. In the stories passed down by elders for one thousand years or more, Naniboujou is credited with creating Lake Superior, naming the animals, and teaching the Anishinaabe the most important lessons about the natural world, living with others, and being human. Ojibwe artist, teacher, and astrologist Carl Gawboy put it this way:

Naniboujou, who is the embodiment of early ancestral peoples, went about making the world a safer place for humans.[40]

Co-opting the name Naniboujou and climbing inside the mythology and worldview of the Anishinaabe in order to sell membership to an exclusive, white club delivers a one-two punch to Anishinaabe people by both exploiting Native culture for profit and firmly placing the Indigenous people of the North Shore into a romantic past accessible only to those who pay to belong.

By the 1920s, natural resources on the North Shore were becoming depleted. With timber resources growing thin, traditional hunting and trapping grounds becoming smaller, and having to compete with Scandinavian fishermen for herring and trout, many Anishinaabe people, both on and off the reservation, had to turn to the growing tourist industry to make a living.

Some people made homemade crafts to sell at the Johnson trading post or in stands at Mineral Center or along Highway 61, and many others worked in the local hotels or restaurants that served tourists. Jim Wipson described how his grandmother made a living trading her homemade crafts:

She did a lot of beadwork and she made baskets. And all of that stuff she made, she'd sell it. In those days, there wasn't much money to transact. People would give her groceries for maybe a few baskets . . . We had a lady coming from Duluth—and she used to come down there and buy a bunch of this stuff for souvenirs and

*take 'em to Duluth. And she'd probably sell it to tourists or sell 'em
to . . . who knows, but around the community itself everything was
traded in goods.*[41]

Gloria Martineau described how her Grand Marais neighbor,
Lucy Caribou, made a living:

*Lucy hooked rugs and braided rugs . . . And her rugs were abso-
lutely gorgeous. Her whole kitchen was filled with boxes of rags
that she cut up. She had a great big loom on her table all the
time . . . I mean people from all over the country had Lucy's rugs.
And she braided rugs too. She made a picture on the rugs. And
there would be, like, an oval in the center, and there would be two
deer, or something. And then on the edge it would be like, black,
but then she would make all of these beautiful flowers all around
the edge . . . And people from all over, once they found Lucy's rugs
at Philomene's, then she made a living that way.*[42]

I asked her what kind of price Lucy would get for a large, hand-braided
or hooked rug. After thinking for a moment, she said, "Twenty-five
dollars . . . thirty dollars . . . something like that. Back then it was a lot
of money, I guess."[43]

A hooked rug made by Lucy Caribou in the 1920s or 1930s. Courtesy of Diane Johnson.

Michael Morrison described how he and his siblings would make things to sell as souvenirs to tourists: "We made handmade things. Woodwork canoes, paddles made of wood. So, we got a lot of money from that. And we made tomahawks, wood and bone with hide and sold them."[44]

Ironically, as the Ojibwe tradition and way of life was gradually overtaken by European ways, Ojibwe culture would become increasingly in demand by the growing numbers of visitors to the area, who were excited to experience what was being sold as authentic "Indian" culture. Henry Mayhew's daughter, Edith (Mayhew) Strom, describes the arrival of a passenger ship to Grand Marais harbor:

> Now when these passenger boats would come in, why, you could hear them from Lutsen. And when this whistle was heard, the Indians started from Chippewa Village and came up in single file. Some of them had papooses on their backs and some of them had these rolls of mats and they had their baskets. They all went down on the dock and waited for the passengers to come off and they'd buy their baskets and moccasins and other beaded objects that they might have.[45]

Great-grandmother Elizabeth made her living by making things out of birch bark and selling them. My dad remembers that her house was full of wood and bark—and that she made beautiful makuks (containers) or quilled picture frames, and miniature canoes that she sold to tourists. The Native people who lived in Grand Marais and Grand Portage between 1900 and 1930 experienced the transition between an economy that was reliant on their traditional skills and knowledge of the area to support their families to an economy of exploitation, where it was believed that Native culture was something that could be bought in a store. From the 1930s through the 1950s, handmade goods were edged out by mass-marketed versions of "trading post" curios that depicted Native Americans and Native culture in a cartoonish or exaggerated way. When these inauthentic knickknacks were brought

Elizabeth Anakwad's quilled *makuk* and awl, likely made in the 1920s. Courtesy of Susan Zimmerman.

in wholesale, there was less demand for the more authentic, hand-made souvenirs that many people relied on to make a living.

Sadly, the blatant marketing of Native culture continues to show its ugly face in some modern downtown establishments and curio shops. You can still find plastic tomahawks or gaudy beaded key chains with fringe that proclaim they are from "Grand Marais"— except now those tomahawks and key chains were not made by the hands of actual Ojibwe people but by machines that spit them out of factory molds in sweat-shops far across the ocean. The people profiting from "Native" culture now have probably never met a real live Native American in person and have certainly never been to Grand Marais.

Grand Marais calendar. Courtesy of Dan Helmerson and Cook County Historical Society.

Because of the overt attempts by non-Native people to sell Grand Marais as an "Indian Village," many visitors to the area had certain expectations of what it means to be an "Indian" and how they thought an "Indian" was supposed to act. Grand Portage band member Vivian Waltz shared this personal encounter she had with visitors to Grand Marais in the 1930s:

> *Well, I think most of the tourists that came up that way thought that the Indians lived in tepees and mud houses. I used to work at Mabel's Café, and one morning there was about three or four ladies that came in there. They had gone up to Chippewa City and Grand Portage and on their way back they said to me, "In Grand Portage and Chippewa City too, we were surprised that there were houses." Then [another woman] said to me, "Do you see very many Indians?"*

Vivian paused, gave me a sly smile, and continued: "I said to her, 'Every morning when I look in the mirror!'" We both burst out laughing at her kitchen table. She tapped my arm in a playful way and said, "I think I could have bought her for two cents!"[46]

Mabel's Café, circa 1938. Courtesy of Cook County Historical Society.

Powwow in Grand Marais on the Fourth of July, 1920s.
Courtesy of Cook County Historical Society.

→ Chapter 8 ←

A CALL FROM LONGBODY

North Woods Neighbors

THERE ARE MANY WRITTEN ACCOUNTS from settlers new to the North Shore that offer insight into how the two worlds, that of the traditional Ojibwe and that of the European settler, coalesced. Together the two cultures developed into a somewhat symbiotic, yet very diverse, community that, despite their varied histories and cultural beliefs, shared the common boundaries of space and the need to maintain their home communities. Ella Mayhew, the daughter of early settlers Joseph and Carrie Mayhew, observed:

In the school, there were only four white children—my two brothers, my sister and I. My mother was the only white woman up in this part of the country for many, many years ... It seems to be an inherited tradition in my family to get along with the Indians and to like them. We all seemed to be inclined to be pioneer people.[1]

Many of the Chippewa City residents played important roles in the larger community. For example, the Morrison brothers served as surveyors and road overseers in the early days of Cook County. Many logging operations and building projects relied on the hard work of laborers from Chippewa City. The relationship between the two communities was described by historian Will Raff as one of mutual participation, on the one hand, and, on the other, what he describes as a kind of paternalistic self-sacrifice on the part of Ojibwe women, who he says generously offered themselves as a kind of welcoming committee to the lonely, single European men who were seeking their fortunes on the North Shore:

> *As guides and explorers, prospecting in their own interests, as trappers, acting as land locators, as mail carriers, even in providing brides for the early, lonely, settlers, and children for some of the first families, [the Chippewa] were and remained an important element of the general community.*[2]

The starkness of this characterization is stunning. It implies that Native women "served" as brides and as "providers" of children for the good European settlers to the area, acting as a welcome wagon for new arrivals for the benefit of the changing community. There is no attempt to explain the complicated history of the time, which included widespread economic disparities and government actions designed to undermine tribal societies, or any attempt to acknowledge the local priorities at the turn of the twentieth century, which were often driven by an unapologetic form of violence known as Frontierism. The term "Frontierism" is just another way to say Manifest Destiny—or claiming that it was "God's will" to tame the savage lands west of the Mississippi. For the purpose of his local history book, Raff prefers to call them "Pioneers." But by any name, the opportunistic overtaking of resources and tribal lands was happening all across North America, including on the North Shore. It was a brand of national priorities that put the will of a Christian God at the forefront, and viewed everyone else as objects to be disposed of, moved out of the way, or assimilated.

By the turn of the twentieth century, Grand Marais and Chippewa City had developed somewhat of a convenient reliance on each other. The people of Chippewa City relied on sporadic employment, the medical services (as in the case of Dr. Henry Jones), and the "modern" conveniences found in Grand Marais. In turn, the businesspeople of Grand Marais relied on the abundant labor force and the wilderness familiarity of their Chippewa City neighbors to be successful in their business pursuits.

Catherine Jones and others picnic at Grand Marais, 1898–99. Courtesy of Cook County
Historical Society.

The Chippewa City residents and the Grand Marais residents,
despite their reliance on each other out of necessity, remained very
much distant from each other because of their physical segregation.
Another factor that contributed to the mutually beneficial relationship was the population ratio, which was approximately one white
person to every fifteen Ojibwe.[3] This imbalance made Europeans very
much a minority on the North Shore until after 1900. However, those
rugged Europeans, who were the first to arrive after 1854, managed to
maintain a certain degree of "civilization" within the vast wilderness of
northern Minnesota. A fine example of this Old World European sen-
sibility is found in the diary of Catherine Jones, the wife of Dr. Henry
Jones, an early medical doctor in Grand Marais:

> *Saturday March 11, 1899*
> *In the evening, the Cook County Social Club gave an enter-
> tainment at the courthouse. Dr. made the opening address and
> Kirby with the leading part in the drama. For dinner, we gave
> them venison croquettes with cranberry sauce, creamed potatoes,
> hot biscuits, and suet pudding. Coffee.*[4]

Two days later she captured this telling juxtaposition between the civilized and the lawless ways of life in Grand Marais:

> *Monday March 13*
> *Snowed some. Ice again forming in the bay. Indian dogs got*
> *our box of meat and carried off a ham.*[5]

Although it's true that a few European settlers married Ojibwe women and started families, in most cases they married women of their own ethnicity, and Ojibwe people married other people with varying degrees of Ojibwe heritage or Ojibwe people from other places. There were, of course, exceptions to this, but for the most part, the non-Native people living in Grand Marais and the Ojibwe people living in Chippewa City and Grand Portage were growing increasingly disparate in terms of their cultural worldview. It was also during this time period that many Ojibwe people struggled to find their economic foothold in the changing local economy.

Visits to Chippewa City

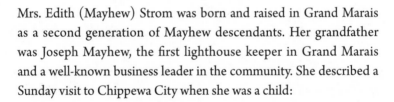

Mrs. Edith (Mayhew) Strom was born and raised in Grand Marais as a second generation of Mayhew descendants. Her grandfather was Joseph Mayhew, the first lighthouse keeper in Grand Marais and a well-known business leader in the community. She described a Sunday visit to Chippewa City when she was a child:

> *I remember one time my father put on his gray and white trousers*
> *and black coat with the tails in back and when I saw that I knew*
> *somethin' special was gonna happen. So it was a beautiful sunny*
> *day and he took me by the hand and we walked down to church*
> *in Chippewa Village. The Indians didn't expect us and they were*
> *very, very cordial. We were bowed in and bowed out and I was sur-*

*prised to see they had a choir loft there. They sang very well. A man
by the name of Jim Morrison passed a collection plate. The sermon
was in Chippewa and after it was all over we said our good-byes
and everyone was so cordial and came home again.*[6]

As a member of one of the most prominent families to the area,
Mrs. Strom speaks with pride about her family history and the success
that they enjoyed as a successful "pioneer" family of the wilderness.
This success included a "great deal of land" that the Mayhews acquired
for "$1.50 an acre" in the late 1800s, as well as owning several busi-
nesses and being extensively involved in local politics.

Jim Wipson gave his own perspective on visitors to the Chippewa
church:

*I guess they were more or less inquisitive to see what was going on
in this traditional Indian Catholic church. A few of 'em would come
and some of them enjoyed it. They like to hear the Indian hymns
they were singing and some of them just came there to enjoy the
singing and see what the Indians were doing. Well, some of them
were real friendly, and actually they were friends with the Indians. But, traditionally I don't think all the white people in Grand
Marais came there. Some of them never did come at all, I guess.
I think a lot of times, when I think about it, it was mostly businesspeople that came. Why, I don't know. Maybe to increase their
business! [Laughs] The storekeepers would come once in a while
and their wives and their children and a few of them would come.*[7]

Catherine Jones writes of many personal visits to Chippewa City.
Her son Kirby was a photographer who is responsible for many of the
early photographs of people in Chippewa City. In this telling passage,
Mrs. Jones hints at the role of her Chippewa neighbors in her new
north-woods life:

Saturday April 8th
  Bright all day. We all went to "Chippewa" with Dr. Mayhew.
While the doctors called on the sick, Kirby and I amused ourselves
taking pictures of the Indians and their surroundings. One of the
chief and his mother. She was making baskets. Two of a baby in a
tikanoggan and several others and one of the rig we went in.[8]

Again, in this journal entry, Mrs. Jones reveals her own social and
racial constructions that are in juxtaposition with her Chippewa City
neighbors. She speaks to us from the safe, domestic sphere of "venison
croquettes and suet pudding" in Grand Marais, as someone who is
peering into the wilderness of the Chippewa village from a distance.
From this vantage point, she remains safe behind the subjective eye of
her son's camera. When you are sensitive to the history of a place, and
if you are willing to examine the words of our historical predecessors
as a way of seeing the past, you only need to listen for the pronouns

Mother and baby in *tikanoggan*. Photograph by Kirby
Jones. Courtesy of Cook County Historical Society.

that separate "us" from "them." Mrs. Jones, who is using the privacy
and candor of a diary to describe her life, has nowhere to hide. She
writes about "the Indians" and "their home" and "their surroundings."
"They" are a curiosity to her, mostly devoid of human qualities, cultural relativity, or spiritual life. This homogenizing of the "other" is a
common element in colonialism and serves to create a clear distinction between those who colonize and those who become colonized.
It is the product of a culture that names majestic mountains after a
person instead of honoring the mountain with a spirit and a voice of
its own. It is also the force that continues to threaten tribal people and
lands all over the world, including in the United States, where Native
nations continue to fight for treaty rights, land rights, and civil rights.
This part of the story is particularly hard to tell, because it's the part
where we have to admit that our local history isn't that different from
that of other places, and that our modern age was built on top of the
bones and the people who lived here, long before golf courses and
art festivals. It's also the part of the story that is the most important,
because the fate of Native people is equivalent to the fate of the natural world. And the words that we all use to interact and negotiate our
collective history will set the stage for what is to come.

A Call from Longbody

Wednesday 12 April.

*An old Indian (a pagan) Cognoshwa or Longbody called on
us. His hair is long and black and he is a pure type of Indian. He
lost his wife and buried her near their wigwam and for a year or
more he spent the greater portion of his time by her grave com-
muning with her spirit. He is a favorite among the whites and
they all help him. We gave him a pair of glasses and he was greatly
delighted that he could see pictures. Then he asked for a needle and
thread and showed he could thread it now—but could not before.
He can't speak English so had to make us understand by motions.*[9]

Cognoshowa (also known as Longbody) and Catherine Jones.
Courtesy of Cook County Historical Society.

Mrs. Jones's visit from Longbody does a few remarkable things.
It sheds light on the period in American history when the traditional
Anishinaabe people were gradually becoming more and more assimilated. Like previous journal entries by non-Native people describ-
ing their Ojibwe neighbors, Mrs. Jones makes a judgment about Mr.
Longbody based on her own perceptions of tribal ethnicity. By denot-
ing that her visitor is a "pure type of Indian," she is, in a sense, intro-
ducing us to others like him, who are "purely" Indian, as opposed to
those of us who are "nonpure" or mixed-blood people of Anishinaabe
descent. In a Cook County Historical Society interview, Lloyd K.
Johnson, the son of Scandinavian entrepreneur Charles Johnson, took
the definition of "mixed-blood" one step further, inferring that people
of mixed heritage were heavy drinkers, not suited for marriage, and
couldn't be trusted:

> My dad said that the pure-blood Indians—their word was bond
> and very reliable and dependable. But heavier drinkers would

want to get married and the only girls who would marry them
were the Indian girls and their children were as undependable as
could be.[10]

Given the changing demographics of the Grand Marais area, the
Chippewa people were experiencing an intensified dependence on
their white neighbors, who were growing in number and also starting
to accumulate wealth. This is an important turning point in the history
of Chippewa City, and Native American history in a broader context. This is the point when acculturation takes hold, and the people
begin to suffer a growing dependence on the European way of life.
Not coincidentally, Longbody's visits to the Jones household become
somewhat regular occurrences and are directly related to the economic hardships the people were suffering as a result of their growing
dependence on U.S. government rations.

The next four diary entries illuminate the desperate circumstances
of Mrs. Jones's neighbors, as well as her growing cognizance of their
situation:

Friday [May] 26
  Cloudy. Rained some all day. Cognoshwa called. I gave him
lunch as usual. They tell me the Indians will take advantage and
come too often but they haven't yet. I nearly always feed them and
our coffers still hold out.

Monday [June] 19
  Cognoshawa called and I gave him lunch. Susanna came with
two of her grandchildren. I bought two baskets from her—a good
sized one and a small round one with birchbark worked in with
porcupine quills.

Thursday [June] 29
  Dozens of Indians are waiting here to receive government
supplies from the boat.

Saturday July 1st.

The government sent supplies for the Indians and they have been going by all day each family with a new broom, a hammer, axe, rake, pan and nails, teapot and flour. Most of the men used their hats to take home the nails and went bareheaded.

A few weeks later, in a show of reciprocity, Longbody delivers a gift to Mrs. Jones:

Saturday July 15, 1899
 Mr. Cognoshawa gave me a bead bag.

By the end of that month, she and Longbody seem to have struck up a friendship that now included relaxed and personal visits to Chippewa City:

Sunday [July] 30th
 Very pleasant. Dr. and I went out for a walk in the afternoon. Called at the five wigwams. Went to Cognoshwa's wife's grave.[11]

At the time Catherine Jones was developing a friendship with Cognoshwa, the United States had entered the "forced assimilation" era of Native history. All across the United States, Indigenous people were experiencing the repercussions of the Dawes and Nelson acts. It was illegal to practice traditional Indian medicine and religion, children were sent to boarding schools away from their homes and families, farming was encouraged as a way to gain self-sufficiency; and all tribal decisions made by local governments regarding land title, mineral rights, and other issues had to be reviewed by the secretary of the interior.

When Catherine Jones made her last entry in the diary on November 14, 1900, the Anishinaabe of Grand Portage and Chippewa City were very much wards of the government. The population at Grand Portage was 108 and the estimated Ojibwe population in Grand

Marais was about 200. In comparison, white settlement in Cook County had grown from 98 people in 1890 to 810 in 1900.[12]

Visiting Relatives in Grand Portage
~&

Like all of Indian country, the people of Chippewa City were either blood relations or related to each other through marriage. In most cases, even if someone was not related to you, you knew them well and treated them as if they were your relatives, a tradition that continues today. Most of the Chippewa City residents kept ties to their friends and relatives in Grand Portage. However, travel to the reservation was rare, owing to the lack of automobiles and public transportation.

The connection between Chippewa City and Grand Portage is described by some as an "extension" of the reservation. The early village of Chippewa City included families who never lived at Grand Portage but were often related to the people there or at other Chippewa settlements. Many people who lived in Chippewa City and Grand Marais would occasionally visit the reservation for powwows, funerals, or other events, which is how Jim Wipson remembered it:

> *I think they might have put on a powwow once in a while in Grand Marais. But I can't remember them having any powwows right in Chippewa City. They had powwows in Grand Portage. In fact, my grandmother used to come to some of the powwows they had.*[13]

Dora Kasames was raised in Chippewa City and recalled visiting Grand Portage relatives as a child. She said, "We got to stay the night over there, because we couldn't make it back [to Grand Marais] in one day."[14] Gloria Martineau shared this story about visiting cousins in Grand Portage in the 1940s:

> *I would take the school bus up to stay with Dorothy [Drouillard] for the weekend. Grand Portage was a lot bigger. It was good sized.*

But it was pitch black—no street lights or anything. One time these wild horses chased us. We were going to walk up to the store and those horses came out after us. We jumped in a ditch to get away from the horses. And I'll never forget, Theodore Deschampe come and got us out.[15]

Visits to Grand Marais
⌒ჱ

A number of businesses in Grand Marais were patronized by the residents of Chippewa City. It was where you could buy grocery staples like flour, milk, sugar, and domestic meat. Because the town was small, a number of businesses served a multitude of purposes; they included Johnson's Trading Post, Mabel's Café, and Jackson's Café, which also had a tavern in the back. This business served as the first bus stop in town and as the early department of motor vehicles.

Dorothy Johansen remembers Grand Marais as being a source of provisions for her family in Chippewa City, who relied on income from her dad's fishing business:

I didn't have a hungry day in my life because my dad [Bill Drouillard] had shares in the North Shore Fishing Company, so he'd go up to Grand Marais and he would buy cases of food. He'd buy a case of tomatoes, a case of milk, maybe a half case of peas and corn and probably a hundred pounds of potatoes.[16]

Besides visiting Grand Marais for supplies, the people of Chippewa City and Grand Portage would also visit the town for special events and holidays. Dora Kasames remembered: "On the Fourth of July, the whole town would come into Grand Marais. They would have a big celebration and pow-wow. Everything happened in Grand Marais."[17]

Richard Anderson describes an early version of the infamous Grand Marais summer festival called "Fisherman's Picnic":

The people from Grand Portage and other places would come in and set up their tipis. Down on the point or where the Payne Hotel was at one time, right on the lakeshore, by the Lake Superior Trading Post. They would come in and do their pow-wows and so forth. It was just an old-fashioned get together.[18]

Mrs. Tamarack of Chippewa City and Grand Portage, outside Jackson's Café in downtown Grand Marais. Courtesy of Cook County Historical Society.

Local Sports and Cowboys and Indians

Getting to know what everyday life was like in Chippewa City means learning about what the people did for work and what they did for play. This recollection about her mother Mary Morrison Dahmen comes from Barb Dahmen, writing for the Grand Portage *Moccasin Telegraph:*

> *She said when she was little, about nine or ten years old, and lived in Chippewa City, she used to play Cowboys and Indians with the Drouillards. She used to push her baby brother around in a buggy which was supposed to be the covered wagon, and the Drouillards would hide in the woods and pretend to shoot at them. I said, "If you had the covered wagon, you must have been the Cowboy, and the Drouillards must have been the Indians." She looked at me aghast and said, "I was the horse!"*[19]

In July 1899, Catherine Jones related that a group of visitors from Two Harbors were invited to dinner, where they were treated to a bit of local culture:

> *After supper, the Indians got together and gave a little outdoor entertainment of games. One was LaCrosse and another a moccasin game, which was quite novel. In the evening, a party of us were at Chas Johnsons where we had some good music.*[20]

The games Mrs. Jones referred to are the traditional lacrosse game, in which a ball is tossed with a racket made from a bent sapling. This is a team game using a ball covered with deerskin or moose hide. Frances Densmore documented this game in her writings about Chippewa culture. She also documents the moccasin game. This game of chance involves hiding four bullets under four moccasins. One of the bullets is marked apart from the others. Players take turns guessing the location of the marked bullet.[21] Both of these games have modern trans-

Chippewa City football (soccer) team, 1901. Courtesy of Cook County Historical Society.

lations. A version of lacrosse is still played in arenas and backyards everywhere, and a variation of the moccasin game can be seen on *The Price Is Right*, except it's now known as the "shell game."

Both Grand Marais and Chippewa City had their own soccer teams. From the sports section of the *Cook County News Herald*, September 28, 1901:

> *Local Foot Ball—Last Sunday afternoon the second series of games between the two football teams which have been organized here was played on the Howenstine field. The two teams which are called Grand Marais and Chippewa City have a decided feeling of rivalry which was displayed at all stages of the game. The running ability of both teams would astonish Dr. Williams if he were here. This was especially noticeable among those who have played the game at Fort William.*

The game resulted in a tied score, Chippewa City getting the first goal in 35 minutes, the second one in 15 minutes and then Grand Marais getting two goals in quick succession. After playing until dark with neither side scoring again it was decided to call the game a draw. Another game will be played Sunday afternoon which will no doubt be worth seeing.

The teams lined up as follows: Grand Marais—Captain Alex LeGarde; Geo. Zimmerman, Earl Miller, Paul LeGarde, Leonce Zimmerman, Chas Howenstine, Joe Messabi, Half Sky, Wabane Geezis. Chippewa City—Captain Weyweska, John Zimmerman, Peter LaPlante, William LaPlante, Frank Frost, Peter Stevens, Leonce Mejansin, Chas. Bessau and Vincent Louis.[22]

Because of this excellent local sports coverage, we can identify all of the Chippewa City players who posed for a team photograph. This is such a gift to local history and to anyone searching for a Chippewa City relative who played in the game that day.

Happy New Year-ing

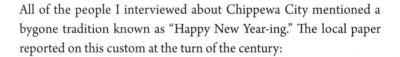

All of the people I interviewed about Chippewa City mentioned a bygone tradition known as "Happy New Year-ing." The local paper reported on this custom at the turn of the century:

January 6, 1900—New Years Day, which is the most important holiday in the year at this place, was observed and thoroughly enjoyed by everyone. The custom of the Indians to visit everyone in the neighborhood has grown so that it includes the white people. At each house preparations had been made and everyone, big and little, was presented with a package of choice eatables. This custom helps to promote a feeling of good fellowship and is one that will not die out here. In the evening, there were two dances, one at the Court House and one at Anaquet Hall. Those who attended report a good time.[23]

As kids growing up in Grand Marais, we knew nothing about this tradition and never experienced it. And then Mary Jane Hendrickson came to my parents' house in Grand Portage eager to talk about history. She was a fearless interview subject, divulging a lot of family gossip along with her thoughts about the past. She lived the Happy New Year tradition in Grand Portage, as well as in Chippewa City, and when she described it, her voice bubbled with enthusiasm remembering what that day was like for her when she was young:

> *On the first of January, everybody went from house to house, shook hands, and you had a plate of cookies. Us kids just waited for that. Sugar and flour came in rag bags, and our mothers would wash them up and that's what we'd carry it all in. We'd go from house to house and I think it was Vivian [Waltz] that told me that their dad would hitch up their two dogs and they'd come by sleigh to Chippewa City and go around Happy New Year-ing everybody. That was a big thing!*[24]

This tradition is believed to have started when the first government payment was issued to Grand Portage band members on New Year's Day 1856, as part of the 1854 treaty. The area Anishinaabe celebrated the event by visiting each and every household, exchanging homemade treats and shooting their guns in the air. The Happy New Year tradition was practiced by everyone—the people of Chippewa City, Grand Portage, and Grand Marais. The people would begin visiting their close neighbors and then fan out into the neighboring villages, including the homes of their non-Indian neighbors, such as Catherine Jones, who described a New Year's Day visit in her diary:

> *January 2nd, Snowing.*
> *This is the Indian's day to make calls. It snowed all day but did not prevent 144 Indians calling on us. Kirby was not well enough to have them come into the house so we let them come into the hall and they shook hands all around and those who could*

*speak English wished us a happy New Year and we gave them
each (children and all) a package containing candy, popcorn,
cookies and dates and they all shook hands again. After putting
the packages into bags or flour sacks they brought for that purpose,
and then went on to the next house until they had visited all the
white people who could receive them. They were cleanly and neatly
dressed. Each one seemed to make a point to have a new pair of
moccasins for the New Year.*[25]

According to grandson Jim Wipson, Kate Frost would spend days
preparing for New Year's Day visitors in Chippewa City:

*My grandmother always made a big deal out of New Year's. She'd
stay up all night baking. She'd bake pies, cookies, she even had
homemade wines. Then the next day the people started coming
and they'd greet each other, and then they'd visit awhile, and then*

New Year's Day visitors in Chippewa City, late 1800s. Courtesy of Cook County
Historical Society.

they'd have lunch and they'd talk. The tradition was, when the
day was over with, the last house would be designated as a dance.
Boy, I tell you, New Year's was a tremendous deal around there,
amongst the Indians anyway.[26]

Gladys Beckwith and her sister, Vivian Waltz, both shared memories of Happy New Year and traveling from their home on the east bay in Grand Marais to visit their friends and neighbors in Chippewa City. Vivian said, "We'd take our pillowcases and go to all the houses and they would come in to Grand Marais too."[27]

In her own description of Happy New Year, Gladys smiled and added, "You always had to kiss the boys. Always. And you always had to shake everyone's hand when you were coming and going." And then she added with a scratchy laugh, "Going is when you usually got the kiss!"[28]

It's fun to imagine it: all of the people bundled up against the cold and making their way from house to house for a day of celebration and neighborliness. And then to picture them all, kids and parents and aunts and uncles and grandparents, meeting at "Anaquet Hall" in Chippewa City for food and dancing, with a warm fire burning in the stove, and welcoming in the New Year together—it's a nice place to return to.

Dancing to Beat Heck

While Charles Johnson was throwing lavish parties for out-of-town visitors and associates at his home in Grand Marais, just a mile away the people of Chippewa City were creating their own fun. Jim Wipson explained:

The dances were tremendous. In them days they had a lot of tal-
ented musicians. They'd know how to play guitar and a violin
and, boy, they'd just play away and have a good time. Everybody'd

be just dancing! When I was a young boy, I used to sit there and watch my grandmother get out there and dance to beat heck. And all the old people too. And then they'd have circle dances and everybody just had a real good time.[29]

Despite the business of each day, many people shared stories of playing with other kids in Chippewa City or, as Gloria Martineau recalled, walking to Chippewa City several times a day to play with her friends Leona Morrison or Loretta LaPlante.[30] The one-mile walk to Chippewa City didn't mean anything to the young people, who were used to walking to and from school or to a distant neighbor's house to visit for the day.

Jim LaPlante recalled playing with toy trucks and cars and riding his bicycle on the trails of Chippewa City. George Morrison remembers playing near Thunder Hook, which he knew as "Katie's Point," where Kate Frost and Jim Wipson lived.

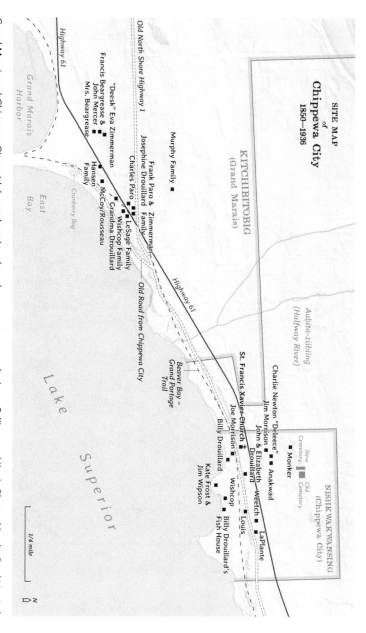

SITE MAP
of
Chippewa City
1850–1936

KITCHIBITOBIG
(Grand Marais)

Aabita-ziibiing
(Halfway River)

NISHKWAKWANSING
(Chippewa City)

New
Cemetery
Old
Cemetery

■ Monker

Charlie Newton "Deleece"
Jim Morrison ■ ■ Anakwad
John & Elizabeth — weetch
Drouillard
■ Louis ■ LaPlante

Joe Morrison ■

St. Francis Xavier Church ✝

Billy Drouillard ■
Kate Frost & ■ ■ Wishcop
Jim Wipson ■ Billy Drouillard's
Fish House

Beaver Bay –
Grand Portage
Trail

Highway 61

Old Road from Chippewa City

Murphy Family ■

Frank Paro & ■ Zimmerman
Josephine Drouillard Family
Charles Paro ■ ■
■ Wishcop Family
"Deesk" Eva Zimmerman ■ ■ Grandma Drouillard
Francis Beargrease & ■ ■ McCoy/Rousseau
John Mercer ■ Hansen
Mrs. Beargrease ■ Family

Old North Shore Highway 1

Highway 61

Grand Marais
Harbor

Grand
Marais
Bay

East
Bay

Cranberry Bay

Lake   Superior

1/4 mile

N

Grand Marais and Chippewa City, with house locations based on memory maps by Irene Sullivan and Jim LaPlante. Map by Brad Herried.

Cross on the old side of the cemetery, 1991. Photograph by the author.

-→ *Chapter 9* ←-

WE ARE BURIED HERE

The Old Cemetery

THERE ARE MAPLE WOODS just up the hill from the house that I live in on Good Harbor Hill. Our neighbors have tapped these trees for many years, setting up a semipermanent sugar-bush cabin specifically designed for the long days of gathering sap and boiling it down into syrup, and taking it one step further into maple sugar. We've walked under these trees so many times, and in so many conditions, that I felt that I knew almost everything about them and that they held no more surprises. Of course, I knew that these trees were tapped many years before our neighbors did. And I knew that the area had served Anishinaabe people generously over the course of history—not only because of the maple stands, but also because of the natural spring located on the ridgeline where the water comes to the surface, providing a drink to any thirsty person or creature in the maple stand. Whitetail deer and moose migrate through these woods in the spring and fall, moving closer to the lake to avoid the heavy snows of the higher terrain. At the base of the hill, Lake Superior forms a beautiful bay where you can fish for trout in the summer or steelhead in the spring. For all of these reasons, it is easy to see why the Ojibwe people frequented these woods to help feed their families, why Mathias Johnson's family built their homestead here on Good Harbor Hill (twice), and why other families now make their homes here, including mine.

I learned only recently about Shingibbiss and his last day on earth, which was spent tapping the maple trees on the hill just behind our house. His obituary read:

Shingibbiss died at the sugar bush at Good Harbor Hill Friday, aged about 80 years, leaving a wife. He was well known and much loved. His body was interred at the cemetery at Chippewa City Monday—May 2, 1907[1]

Shingibbiss left this earth fiercely practicing his right to gather maple syrup from the homelands of his people. Like the families in Grand Portage who pulled their children out of school when the sap started to run, like Jim Wipson who learned the craft of tapping trees when he was a young boy with his grandmother Kate, and like Great-grandmother Anakwad who marched into the late spring storm to fill her buckets with maple syrup, Shingibbiss did what he was taught to do, because the continued survival of his family and his culture depended on it.

Some of the older maple trees on the hill where he spent his last sugar bush are still there. The old scars where taps were hammered into the bark of the trees have long since healed over, but sap still runs every spring. The maple woods that stretch all along the North Shore, from Tofte and Lutsen to Croftville and Grand Portage, are still growing and producing syrup and have created a modest industry for a few small, local companies. Our relationship to the trees is not short-lived, nor is it superficial or easy. To work the trees and make sugar into syrup requires knowledge, time, and patience. These hills are steep and the spring weather is often frigid and uncompromising, but still there is an important amount of labor that needs to be done. Regardless of age and the weariness of their backs, the Ojibwe people of the North Shore knowingly wait for the warm days and cold nights of late winter to return, and then head out to sugar bush.

They'd Have a Great Big Feast
~&

Part of the complete, living story of the Anishinaabe includes cultural traditions like going to sugar bush, as well as what happens when it's time to put someone to rest. Many written histories describe St. Francis Xavier and the role of the church when someone in the community died. When Catherine Jones wrote this observation in 1889, the people of Chippewa City were steeped in the ways of Catholic tradition:

> *Weather cold but clear. They made the coffin for Mr. Caribou down at a little carpenter's shop, covered it with black cloth and a long cross of wood and drew it by here on a sled. His funeral is to be tomorrow at the little Catholic church at Chippewa City.*[2]

While almost everyone who remembers attending church services and funerals at Chippewa City identifies as Catholic, most of the people interviewed recall a funeral tradition that is unique to the Chippewa people. Although the event could not be described as "traditional" in the way of the Midewiwin, the practice of medicinal healing and spiritual ceremony, it could not be described as wholly Catholic either. Dora Kasames shared this vivid memory of the three-day event from her childhood:

> *There was crying . . . and other people would come in and visit for a while, or they would bring food. They sang in Indian hymns, and there was one song I always remembered, it was such a pretty song. In Indian it's called Geebiawictic. It means crucifix. And it was always one leader and then they would all come in and sing. And then the third day they would take the body out of the house and close the casket and go to the church and have a funeral and buried them. Of course, we were poor back then, we didn't have the caskets they have now. They had wooden caskets.*[3]

Mary Jane Hendrickson shared this memory of her parents, Mr. and Mrs. John Rousseau:

> *My mother and dad were singers, you know. Oh yeah. They'd sing all of these church hymns when somebody died in Grand*

Grave on the new side of the cemetery. Photograph by the author.

Marais—the last time I went there was when Steve Zimmerman died. They would sing those songs all night! At midnight, they'd cook this big meal and everybody sitting in there would eat . . . I know some of them songs . . . and I never want to forget them.[4]

Michael Morrison described how the community came together for a funeral:

I would say 5 percent of the people were active in a lot of ways, such as whenever a person passed away, everybody was active in supplying food for a wake—helping out the family who had lost their loved ones.[5]

Jim Wipson shared this about the tradition of having a community feast when someone passed on:

*To put a little humor in it—when I was a little boy I would always
wait for somebody to die to have a good feast. [laughs] You're just
a child, you don't realize how serious it is. But every time somebody died they'd have a great big feast and everybody would bring
food. The coffin would be in the living room, and in the kitchen
everybody would have a feast.*[6]

Dorothy Johansen recalled that her father, Bill (Willie) Drouillard, would often toll the church bell when a friend or neighbor passed
away.[7] Jim Wipson remembers hearing that bell ring from his grandmother's home on the lakeshore:

*It was a sad situation when somebody died. They always took the
coffin into the Chippewa City church and after the services they
carried the coffin in the back of a little pickup truck, or whatever
they had, and they'd just slowly go up to the Old Cemetery, with
the people following the truck. And the church bell would keep
ringing, and it would ring until after all the burial was done with;
when the people would leave it just kept ringing. I used to feel so
sad hearing that church bell ringing.*[8]

There are no stone angels or marble mausoleums in the Chippewa
City Cemetery. In fact, half the grounds are graced with only a few
markers, and most are unreadable or crumbling into the grass. I first
witnessed this graceful deterioration when I was a teenager, in the late
1980s. The road to the cemetery then was barely navigable. The grass
had grown up over the road and moose maple and dogwood tangles
crowded the edges, as if to say "keep out!" The cemetery had not
been mowed since the 1950s when the Boy Scouts had last served as a
cleanup crew. I felt a sense of both loss and belonging and a sense of
duty—in the old paper birch trees that marked the boundaries of the
field and in the crowds of wild daisies that seemed to take the serious
matter of grieving and honoring those buried there as their own sin-
gular responsibility.

Chippewa ceremonial spirit houses, date unknown. Courtesy of Cook County Historical Society.

According to Michael Morrison and others, the first burial plots in Chippewa City were located below the Old Road, very close to the lake. When people began building houses near the burial ground, the graves were moved to a new location above the road.[9] On Alta McQuatter's cemetery map, she confirms that twelve graves were moved from the lakeside to a new location up the hill and northeast of the churchyard.

In 1892, my great-great-grandparents Martell (Mathias) and Therese Anakwad procured a warranty deed for land on the hill, one-half mile northeast of the church. This half acre is known as the "Old Side" and served as the place of burial for the Chippewa City people until 1926. Some of the names Alta McQuatters has identified as buried there are Beargrease, LeSage, Wishkop, Massie, Anakwad, Newton, Conners, and Drouillard. There are only a few remaining grave markers on the "Old Side," but because we know they ran out of room on the eastern half, we can assume that many, many more family names prior to 1926 have been lost to history.

That year, the fisherman Claus C. Monker, and his wife, Christina Monker, one of a few non-Indian families to live in Chippewa City, donated a second plot of land west of the older plot. The deed drawn up between the Monkers and the Roman Catholic diocese of Duluth specifies:

> *The intention of this conveyance is that the premises herein described are to be used for no other purpose or purposes than a free burial ground principally, for the Chippawa [sic] Indians residing at and near said Chippawa [sic] Village in said Cook County.*[10]

This "new" section is still used today by Chippewa City families. Many people who have family members there remembered that the cemetery looked very different than it did when I first visited it in the 1980s. At one time, many of the graves were covered by wooden, ceremonial grave houses, which is a traditional Ojibwe way of marking a burial site. Also, because many people did not have the financial resources for a tombstone or more permanent type of marker, many graves were marked with stones or with wooden crosses, which are not equipped to withstand the elements over the course of time. Besides falling prey to natural causes, many grave markers were vandalized or stolen.

Gladys (Zimmerman) Beckwith described the graves as having "fancy fences around them" that were "always painted white and some of them stood quite high," or had "the house over them" and others still "just had tombstones."[11]

Gladys's sister Vivian recollected: "There used to be white, wooden crypts that were put over the grave. But they've all disappeared."[12]

The loss of the markers was part of a 1958 cleanup effort of the church and cemetery grounds, when many of the grave markers were inadvertently disposed of. Dorothy Johansen noted:

> *Somebody told me that the Boy Scouts went up there and cleaned it. Well, why did they haul everything away? So, you walk up there now, you don't know where anybody is unless they have a tombstone with a name on it, and some of them you can't even read.*[13]

Jim Wipson has relatives buried in both sections of the cemetery. He recounted a visit to the grounds:

> *I went to see that old cemetery. I was looking for my brother's grave, and I couldn't find it because they didn't have a marker on it. But some way or another, the Drouillards, they managed to put little signs on each one of them. And it's really sad looking at it, the whole family laid out there in that old cemetery . . . I wish they would do something about that old cemetery, but I guess they never will. You know, figure out who's who and where they are buried. You go in there now and you can't find nothing. It's really sad. I don't even know where my brother is buried.*[14]

Several of the people I interviewed about Chippewa City expressed their concerns about the condition of the cemetery. There have been a number of attempts over the years to clarify the boundaries of the cemetery grounds, as well as efforts to address drainage problems and encroachment. In a letter to the Cook County Board, dated May 15, 1967, Ignatius Candrian, vice president of St. John's Catholic Church in Grand Marais, asked for help in repairing the road to the cemetery, which suffered a washout that spring. At that time, the county took over care of the road and road maintenance, but the cemetery remained the responsibility of the Duluth diocese. In a letter to Will Raff, dated December 5, 1979, George Morrison wrote:

> *With the understanding that you are the best local historian, I want to ask you some questions in regard to a future plan I have in mind.*
>
> *In about two years I hope to retire from the U of M and move to the Grand Portage area. The plan I have is to have the old Chippewa Cemetery re-surveyed, possibly landscaped and to save any existing grave markings, and to erect a simple wood art monument with some kind of plaque with a listing of those buried there.*
>
> *My brother Mike has ideas with much of the physical part of this, but my part of it is with the monument itself.*[15]

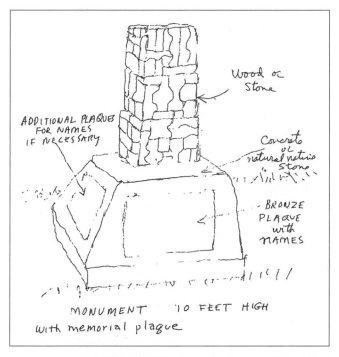

Cemetery monument sketch by George Morrison, 1981. Courtesy of Briand Morrison.

Raff responded on January 22, 1981; "We are in communications with State officials to have St. Francis Xavier Church and the Cemetery formally as State and National Historic Sites."[16] Raff also requested copies of the artist's preliminary plans for a monument.

George replied less than a month later with "the first rough sketch that I've had in my head for so long."[17]

The "Restore the Chippewa Indian Cemetery Committee" had its first meeting in September 1981. They made plans for a land survey and discussed the preservation of grave markers and possible landscaping. It is not clear what roadblocks the committee encountered, or who, specifically, was involved in the decision-making process at the time. However, a new land survey and report emerged six years later in 1987. Registered land surveyor Ken Hoffman recommended to the county attorney, Richard W. Johnson, that the church acquire an additional thirty-five feet on the east side of the grounds, because "The deed for the east parcel does not agree with the location of the graves."[18]

Neighbors Sally and David Eliasen agreed to have a quitclaim deed drawn up to correct the land title, deeding the thirty-five feet in question to St. John's Catholic Church. Since then, common complaints about the cemetery include ongoing drainage problems and damage to the oldest part of the cemetery during the spring, a lack of plot markers, and the slow encroachment of neighboring properties to the west, north, and east sides of the cemetery grounds. Possible encroachment was mentioned by Ken Hoffman, in his land survey letter: "The northerly fifty feet, more or less, of this west parcel is currently being used (innocently I am sure) by Ed Thoreson as a gravel storage area."[19]

There is a thin fringe of trees separating the piles of gravel on the west side of the cemetery from the graves of Louise, Peter, and George Beargrease, Jack Scott, Swamper Caribou, the mail carrier Louis Plante, and at least one hundred others. On a recent visit to the cemetery, the sight of an enormous mountain of gravel towering over the little cemetery seemed to symbolize the diminished place that Native American lives and history have in mainstream society. Concerns about the condition and care of the cemetery are long-standing with the families of the people who are buried there, especially Mike Morrison, who felt a responsibility to take care of the burial grounds. Taking matters into his own hands, he worked with St. John's Catholic Church in 2004 to construct fences along both sides of the road that divides the old side and the new. He had them painted white, and they now serve as representational guideposts. Like the painted-white spirit houses of the old days, they show where one world ends and another begins. I think of Mike every time I go back to visit the cemetery. He is there, close by, and because he shared his worry over the cemetery with me, it's now something that I, in turn, carry. His time and care fretting over the condition of the graves, and George's concern about having a place for the names that have been lost, should not be forgotten just because they are not here to remind us of it.

The cemetery is still owned by the Catholic diocese of Duluth and St. John's Catholic Church of Grand Marais, and though George's monument was never built, the church has now added the cemetery to its list of grounds that require regular mowing and upkeep throughout the summer. For now, the daisies have been given respite from their responsibility to grieve for all of the forgotten ones. The duty has been passed along and now belongs to all of us.

John Drouillard Dies at the Age of Eighty-Two

~&

Thursday, February 23, 1928

Last Friday morning at 8:30 John Drouillard passed away. He would have been eighty three on March 22. He was born March 22, 1845, at Monroe, Mich., near Detroit. Moved to Grand Portage with parents in 1852 and lived there until 1864 then moved to Bayfield. Fished along the North shore and at Isle Royale with father and brothers and has been a permanent resident of the county for the last fifty years or more. He was employed on various

*projects during his early years surveying, exploring, logging. He
was interpreter for the Grand Portage Indians for many years.
Deceased had been ailing for several years and died from heart
trouble and old age ailments . . . Funeral Monday, at 10am conducted by Father Thomas. Interment in the Catholic cemetery at
Chippewa City.*[20]

The obituary also includes a list of "survivors," including John's
brothers and sisters, nine of the twelve children who were born in
Chippewa City, as well as their mother, and John's "former wife, Mrs.
John Collins." History has not clarified when Great-grandmother
Elizabeth and Great-grandfather John split up, or whether, because
there is some question about their legal marriage, they ever actually
divorced.

In a telling omission from John's obituary, there is no mention of
his first wife Mary and the children he left behind in Bayfield. Searching for more information about Mary L. Bachand, the trail of evidence
about her fate ends with a very dark possibility. In 1883, three years
after their family is listed on the 1880 Bayfield census, a woman named
Mary Drouillard appears in the city directory for Detroit, Michigan.
It says, "Mary Drouillard, inmate, Little Sisters' Home for the Aged
Poor." A cursory search indicates that the "home" was a Catholic
charity home for "women, girls and the aged lonely." For anyone who
finds this troubling, understand that I do not know with certainty that
this is the Mary Drouillard who lived in Bayfield and was married to
John. But there are no further records for her in Bayfield, whether in
a census or on a death certificate. We are only left to wonder what
actually became of her and their children after John left permanently
for the North Shore in 1881. Mary and John do appear once more together on a document that surfaced much later. They are listed on the
1904 marriage license for Adele Drouillard, a young woman who was
born in Bayfield, Wisconsin, in 1881, who claimed them as her parents
on the day that she married a man named Howard Cross in Havre,
Montana.

If there is any insight to be
gathered about the undoubtedly complicated relationship
between my great-grandparents,
we'll most likely find it between
the years of 1884 and 1906, when
they brought twelve children
(Josephine, William, Charles,
James, Caroline, Alice, Mathilde,
John, Francis, George, Rose,
and Fred) into their family.
The Drouillards lived in two
worlds—that of John Drouillard,
a man who was more comfort-

John Drouillard and Elizabeth Anakwad,
early 1900s. Drouillard Family Collection.

able by himself in the woods than in a house raising children, and
Elizabeth Anakwad, a woman much younger than her common-law
husband, who taught her children to understand what it means to live
in two worlds at the same time.

We Are Buried Here

It's a natural thing to want to know where your ancestors are buried,
to have a place to bring flowers and tell the stories of the old ones to
the new ones of today. As many of the Chippewa City families know,
locating the place where your ancestor is buried has been difficult.
Alta McQuatters, a longtime Cook County Historical Society volunteer and archivist of the Shingibbiss family history, has been meticulously compiling the handwritten death records recorded by Father
Maurice and the roster of Catholic priests stretching back to Father
Simon. Using a map of both sides of the cemetery—the old and the
new—Alta has written in the names for a number of previously unidentified graves. On her map, you can locate where Lucy Caribou
and Philomene Evans are buried; the two sisters who lived apart in

life but are now next to each other on the "new" side of the cemetery. The Drouillards, Zimmermans, and Wishkops can be found on the map, and so can the Paros, Beckwiths, and some of the Anakwads. The pillars of St. Francis Xavier Church, Jim and Joe Morrison, are buried at Chippewa City, and so are their wives, Julia Morrison and Mary (Missabe) Morrison.

My great-great grandfather Marthias (Martell) Anakwad and my great-great grandmother Therese Anakwad are buried there, in the ground that they donated to the church so that there would be a place to bury the people who lived and died in Chippewa City. Great-great-grandfather died on March 1, 1910, when he was eighty-five. Great-great-grandmother Therese lived to be seventy-three years old. Her death date is recorded as November 8, 1915, at Grand Marais. They are both buried on the "old" side, but our family does not yet know exactly where to find them.

Antoinette (Tchingwe) Fillison lived to be seventy-five years old. She died on December 23, 1923, and is buried in the Chippewa City Cemetery, just up the hill from the church. Her grave is not far from

Congregation with Antoine Anakwad (left) and Father Simon in the back row. Courtesy of Michael Morrison.

the land that she and her husband, Antoine, deeded to the Catholic diocese so that St. Francis Xavier Catholic Church could be built. Antoine died three years after his wife, on June 5, 1926, at the age of ninety-two, and is buried in Chippewa City. They were Anishinaabe landowners, members of the Catholic church, and founding residents of Chippewa City. They lived through the time of the early treaties and through the reservation era. They resisted allotment and relocation. They persisted against forced acculturation, and through it all defined themselves by their actions and not their blood quantum. They generously gave up their ground so that their community would have a place to worship. They lived off of fish and wild game and drank from the pure and clean water of Lake Superior. Because of them, we still have a place to visit. This place doesn't promise to tell us everything that we would like to know, but it does give us a place to begin, as well as a place to end.

Patsy Drouillard Swanson with early modern transport, 1922. Courtesy of Patsy Drouillard Swanson Collection.

–➤ *Chapter 10* ←–

I GUESS SOMETIMES
I'M TORN

Life between Two Worlds

LIKE THE PIGEON RIVER, the waterway that straddles the border
between the United States and Canada, the North Shore Ojibwe also
straddled two worlds—that of the traditional Anishinaabe and that
of mainstream society. For many families, including the Drouillards,
two worlds collided through intermarriage with the French. For some
Anishinaabe families, living in two worlds was not the result of intermarriage but was instead brutally enforced by a string of treaty provisions and government assimilation programs specifically designed to
destroy everything it meant to be an "Indian."

Located on the Pigeon River, just upstream from the place where
our ancestors first arrived, the Pigeon River School, established in 1842,
was organized and operated by a Catholic missionary named Francis
Pierz. Pierz and his assistant served as teachers for twenty-eight boys
and twenty-seven girls. The curriculum was outlined as follows:

> *Children are not only taught religion but also such things as are
> conducive for the Indian lives . . . It is hoped this school will be
> kept up and promote the civilization of the Indians so that it will
> prove itself worthy of the kind of attention and posturing aid of the
> Government.*[1]

Since this first Catholic school was established on the banks of the
Pigeon River, Native people on the North Shore have been expected

to conform to a worldview that is different from the value system they were taught by their parents and grandparents before Europeans became the majority ethnicity in northern Minnesota. Most often, the European views on education, religion, land ownership, and family were forced on Native people against their will. Sometimes the people acquiesced voluntarily, as Espagnol did, when he converted to Catholicism in 1838 under the instruction of Father Pierz. But for other Anishinaabe people, such as Addikonse, who outright refused the ways of the Catholic church, there could be consequences. When Chief Addikonse would not convert, Father Pierz attempted to undermine his reputation as a leader of his people.[2]

In spite of the unrelenting pressure to take on the ways of the white man, Ojibwe people have successfully retained varying degrees of Ojibwe identity and the Ojibwe worldview. For most of the people I interviewed, this was a source of pride, just as their devotion to the Catholic religion was a source of pride. It's one of the commonalities that makes Chippewa City at the turn of the twentieth century a unique place in terms of cultural identity and the marriage of multiple worldviews.

Dorothy Johansen remembers having a strict upbringing in the Catholic church. She shared this story about her dad, Bill Drouillard, and a long-standing family tradition:

> My dad got a letter from his sister, Auntie Alice. My dad couldn't read, he never had any schooling, but he was a whiz at numbers. So, I read the letter to him, and she had wrote something in Indian. Well, of course, I couldn't begin to pronounce it, and he just grinned at me. He knew what it was. So afterward he went down and laid tobacco in the lake for Auntie Alice.[3]

When asked about her grandmother, Elizabeth (Anakwad) Drouillard, Dorothy speculated that "Grandma, being full-blooded Indian, she probably knew a lot of [traditional ways], but they went to the Catholic church so it isn't something they would have practiced."[4]

However, Dorothy later described one of her first memories of visiting her grandma's house in Chippewa City, where the family filled a spirit plate with food as a blessing to go along with their family meal:

> *They had a feast. And they had food on a plate and they set it over on the cupboard. I kept watching that plate because I wanted to see who was eating it! So, then, after they got done eating, Uncle Charlie [Drouillard] opened the wood stove and he pushed the ashes away, and let me scrape the food into the ashes.*[5]

Gladys Beckwith remembers visiting relatives' graves in the Chippewa City Cemetery and her mother's tradition of offering food: "a lot of times, we'd pack our lunch and we'd go to the cemetery and we'd have a dish for the person that was in the grave, and tobacco. So, I guess that's what you'd call combining."[6]

Jim Wipson discussed how his grandmother carried on this tradition in her everyday life:

> *My grandmother used to take a little tobacco and plant it certain places and give a little religious ceremony. They really strongly believed that it would bring good things. You know, even hunters did that before they'd go up in the woods.*[7]

Michael Morrison remembered that when he was a child there was a village of traditional people living within the larger village of Chippewa City. He recalled that at one time, traditional Midewiwin families lived along the lakeshore, across the bay from Thunder Hook Point. He would often sneak down to the shore and play with the children who lived there. He said that his mother would scold him for playing with "those Indians down there." Michael offered his wisdom regarding growing up somewhere between the two worlds:

> *I guess sometimes I'm torn between Indian religion and the Catholic religion. It doesn't bother me that I like to do things traditionally*

too. I think a lot of things that we did the white man inherited from us, and there's nothing wrong with going into the Indian religion too . . . Catholic church believed it was a sin to belong to other churches . . . other Indian beliefs, they believed they were pagans. The church is reformed now. Even some Catholic priests, Fr. Jim in Minneapolis, had a department of Indian work. He believes halfway between the Indian religion and the Catholic religion. He says the Mass, they have the same prayers in the Ojibwe language.[8]

Michael Morrison. Courtesy of Roberta Morrison.

Doctors and Early Health Care

Catherine Jones was married to Dr. Henry Jones, one of the first physicians to serve Grand Marais. In her diary, she recorded a number of her husband's house calls, which give a good indication of what local health care was like at the turn of the century. From Friday, December 2, 1898: "Dr. Jones went to Chippewa City to see a sick Indian, Leonce Caribou, and also some children at Frank LeSages."[9] Five days later she wrote:

> *Dixon came in for the last time and went out giving us a goodbye whistle as she passed out of the harbor. Leonce Caribou died this morning.*[10]

When Dr. Jones was the resident physician from 1898 until 1902, the Chippewa population was reliant on both Western medicine and traditional medicine practices. Throughout her diary, Mrs. Jones records specific times when Chippewa City residents called on Dr. Jones for medical assistance. On February 1, 1899:

*Shingibbiss called for some medicine for a woman with a sore
throat. She couldn't eat or drink.*[11]

In the next passage, Mrs. Jones explains the status of local health care:

*Mrs. Caribou fell on the ice and broke her wrist in the morning
and there was no one to come for her until evening. In the meantime, it had swollen so one of her neighbors clarified it, cutting
gashes from ½ to ¾ inch in length.*[12]

In the years after the Treaty of La Pointe and through the early
1900s, access to the local doctor in Grand Marais was described as
being sporadic at best. Michael Morrison, one of twelve children in
his family, was delivered at home in Chippewa City in 1921 by a midwife.[13] However, some of his sisters and brothers were born at the
Cloquet Indian Hospital, which was a government-run health facility
for members of the Lake Superior Chippewa bands. The hospital
served tribal members from Fond du Lac to Grand Portage. Dorothy
Johansen described what would happen in the case of serious injury
or illness:

*If I was ill, my sister Helen would take care of me. At that time,
they had an Indian hospital in Cloquet. So, if you had to be hospi-
talized, that's where you had to go. You'd have to hire someone to
take you or you'd go down in a government car. Maybe a brother
or some relative who had a car would take you down.*[14]

Despite the people's reliance on Western medical practices in the
early to middle twentieth century, the use of traditional medicine was
also recognized by the Chippewa City people. Jim Wipson described
his grandmother's knowledge of traditional medicines:

*She was a medicine woman and she could go in the woods and
you would be surprised the medicine she could find just by digging*

roots and certain trees, and she just knew what to get and how to
boil them, and how to process them.[15]

Grandpa Fred was born in Chippewa City and Grandma Lola
(Linnell) came to Mineral Center from Black River Falls, Wisconsin.
Although the family lived in Grand Marais, my grandfather kept
ties to Grand Portage, where a lot of relatives lived. My aunt Gloria
shared this story about her dad visiting one of the medicine men on
the reservation:

Daddy knew the medicine man up in Grand Portage. One time he
told me that he went up there to see him and he was out getting his
powers. He would go into the woods and climb a tree and stay up
there for seven days and seven nights. Daddy called him "Stump."[16]

Both Gladys Beckwith and Jim LaPlante remember visiting another Grand Portage medicine man, Alex Posey, while they were
living in Grand Marais and Chippewa City. In both cases, a family
member accompanied them from Chippewa City to Grand Portage,
where Mr. Posey performed traditional medicine ceremonies. Here
Gladys recounts her experience at a shaking wigwam ceremony at
Grand Portage when she was eleven years old:

If you had a sickness or something was wrong, they'd take you to
the medicine man. Well, I don't know what I had, but my Aunt
Alice [LaPlante] said we're going to take her to Grand Portage
to the medicine man. He had this tent out in the woods and my
mother kept saying, "Now you've got to believe!" There was a
fire in the tent. I didn't look and then something would shake the
tent! I don't think I was ever so scared in my life! But it must have
worked because I'm still here.[17]

Jim LaPlante remembers driving his mother (Alice LaPlante)
from Grand Marais to Grand Portage to visit Mr. Posey:

Alex Posey (*front right*) with drummers in Grand Marais. Courtesy of Cook County Historical Society.

He used to put that wigwam up in his kitchen. Then he'd turn around and back in there. Pretty soon everybody would be in there, some would be laughing, some would be talking, and some would be mad, and spirits would be coming in . . . He'd bring them in. They'd come in that hole in the top of the tent. And it's not just his voice you'd hear but you could hear the different sounds in the voices. There were a lot of spirits in there.[18]

As Milt Powell explains, the Native people living in town relied on each other for specific cultural things, especially in emergency situations, when only a certain kind of medicine would do, and the birth of a child and the life of a mother hangs in the balance:

Your grandma Lola [Drouillard] was hemorrhaging with Diane. She was in pretty bad shape . . . And your grandpa came up and he was pretty concerned. And my dad said, "OK. I know where some stuff is." It was in the middle of the night, and off they went. They got back three or four hours later and they cooked up this

brew . . . And I heard him tell your grandpa, "It tastes like hell,
but you have Lola drink a cup full of medicine every two to three
hours." And she cleared up. And your grandpa called my dad
after that "Doc."[19]

Ojibwe Language

In 1898, Catherine Jones recounted the use of translators for Chippewa patients during medical visits with her husband, Dr. Jones. And longtime Grand Marais resident Cac Hussey recalled that John Morrison Sr. "could talk Swede as good as he could Chippewa."[20]

In later generations, most of the people remember their grandparents and parents speaking their Native language, but in many cases, the language was not passed down to the younger people. The reasons for this are varied and are well documented throughout Native American history. In part, Native languages were systematically erased by government agents, schoolteachers, and non-Indian employers and neighbors. Jim Wipson spoke Ojibwe at home, but admitted that he did not speak the language elsewhere:

Everything my grandmother said to me was in Ojibwe and I had
to understand it . . . But the only thing is, I learned to talk English,
you know, going to school and everything. You had to talk English
when you'd go to school . . . We didn't dare speak Ojibwe around
Grand Marais because Grand Marais was terribly prejudiced
against Indians. If we'd start talking Ojibwe around them, well,
we'd've had black eyes.[21]

Dorothy Johansen fondly remembers hearing her older relatives speaking in Ojibwe:

Ojibwe was spoken in our house. My dad was very, very fluent at
it. A lot of people would say "Slow down, slow down" because he

would talk too fast . . . My sister Helen could speak real good. She could speak the hymns and I think she could write it.[22]

When asked why she did not speak the language, Dorothy Johansen admitted being afraid to speak Ojibwe when she was a child for fear of being scrutinized by others: "One of my relatives would always tell me, 'Shut up, you're murdering the language.' So, that's why every time I talked, I would think I was saying it wrong."[23]

Gladys Beckwith shared this story about how her mother, Josephine Zimmerman, and her aunts talked to each other when they got together for a visit:

My mother, my Aunt Tilly, and my Aunt Carrie Paro all go to Longview, Washington, to Auntie Alice's [LaPlante]. And when they talked it was part English or Indian. Well, Alice's daughter Virginia put a tape recorder under the table and she let them talk and carry on for quite a while.[24]

Gloria Martineau remembers her Drouillard relatives in Chippewa City and Grand Marais speaking to each other in Ojibwe, and although her father spoke fluently, the language was not passed on to his children:

My dad, he wouldn't teach us how to speak Indian. We really, really wanted to learn and he would say, "No, you don't need to know that." But whenever any Indians came, daddy talked Indian to them. And that's what we picked up, when we heard him say it.[25]

As children attended white schools and became more and more integrated into mainstream society, the Ojibwe language was spoken less and less. George Morrison recalled that, "Before I started school, Chippewa was spoken in the house, but after we went to school it got lost. Just a smattering of Chippewa was retained."[26]

If You're Part Indian, You're Indian, I Guess
~&

During the reservation period of American Indian history, when Indigenous people were being concentrated inside newly formed reservation communities, government agencies subjected tribes to a
system of determining tribal affiliation through blood quantum, or
degree of Indian blood. Today, each tribe has the ability to determine
the degree of blood quantum required for membership. Membership
in the Minnesota Chippewa Tribe dictates that an Ojibwe descendant
be one-quarter Ojibwe ancestry. This requires that at least one parent
has proven one-half Ojibwe heritage. This is complicated by the fact
that prior to 1961, the Minnesota Chippewa Tribe blood quantum for
membership was set at one-eighth degree of Indian blood. So, children of Ojibwe parents born prior to 1961 retain tribal membership.
However, children of the same parents born after 1961 do not have the
right to tribal membership. In many cases, this method of determining
Ojibwe ethnicity has split families of the same two parents into both
"Ojibwe" and "non-Native" based on their dates of birth. This is true
for many people in my family, where older cousins are enrolled at
Grand Portage, but younger cousins, who have the same parents, don't
qualify for tribal membership. Unlike other ethnicities, Native American people are constantly asked to prove who we are, and how much
we are. This way of defining identity was used as a tool to control the
way that Native people interacted with the various government agencies that could determine the rules about tribal enrollment, the rights
to own land or claim annuities, and create a way to structure the very
idea of "Indianness" by degree rather than by family descent. This
method of measuring our heritage would cause my family and many
other families what I like to call a crisis of continuation.

University of Minnesota professor Jill Doerfler has done extensive
writing and research on the quandary of Native American identity. In
her book *Those Who Belong,* she details how the Minnesota Ojibwe
historically based tribal identity on family lineage, treating all relatives
with one or more Ojibwe ancestors as tribal members. She quotes

White Earth Nation tribal elder William Anywaush, who, speaking at a membership hearing in 1941, testified in Ojibwemowin:

> *There was never in the past any mention of drawing any line; relationship was the only thing that was considered in the past. Even though the child had very little Indian blood, in considering relationship, he was still an Indian. One thing that these old folks over there urged me to do was to have mercy on my Indian people. Don't ever, as long as you live, discriminate against your fellow Indian.*[27]

Later in the meeting minutes, Mr. Anywaush reportedly "begged the delegates to be careful that they did not tie a knot which their children and grandchildren could not untie."[28] The one-quarter blood rule is closely aligned with the Indian Reorganization Act (IRA) of 1934, also known as the "Indian New Deal." It specified that "This federal legislation, initiated by Commissioner of Indian Affairs John Collier, was intended to recognize and strengthen tribal governments."[29]

In Minnesota, White Earth, Mille Lacs, Bois Forte, Fond du Lac, Leech Lake, and Grand Portage banded together to create a confederation called the Minnesota Chippewa Tribe (MCT). These bands, which share many familial and spatial ties, decided to work as a coalition government, as sanctioned by the Indian Reorganization Act, to create their own bylaws and charter, and ultimately create a constitution that would pertain to all of the people enrolled at these reservations.

At first, the MCT decided to follow traditional ways of determining identity, which based membership on lineage, family relationships, or residence on an Ojibwe reservation. The Bureau of Indian Affairs (BIA), a new government department housed in the Department of the Interior (formerly within the Department of War), was charged with overseeing tribal programs and relations. The BIA leadership urged the MCT to be more "exact" in the language used to define tribal enrollment. This would be the first of several attempts the BIA made to try to dictate the rules of tribal membership in spite of the tribe's right to self-determination. In 1942, after gaining the support of Francis J. Scott, the supervisor of the Consolidated Chippewa Agency, the MCT received a letter from Oscar Chapman, the assistant secretary of the Department of the Interior, stating:

> *If the Minnesota Chippewa Indians desire to share their property with a large number of persons who are Indians neither by name, residence or attachment but merely by the accident of a small portion of Indian blood . . . the Minnesota Chippewa Tribe must realize that every new name which they add to the membership roll will by that much decrease the share every member now has in the limited assets of the Minnesota Chippewa Tribe.*[30]

The MCT's fight to determine its own identity would continue for several years. Each time the Department of the Interior would add an increased threat to tribal funding or reservation programs in order to prevail. The Ojibwe people remained resolute and persevered in spite of the government's push toward termination, when a number of U.S. tribes ceased to be recognized by the federal government. Finally, in 1961, under continued pressure and threats from the BIA, the Tribal Executive Committee of the MCT passed a one-quarter blood quantum resolution. Even though the committee passed the law, one-third of the tribal delegates of the MCT who were present that day voted against it.

This regulation, which was strong-armed into existence by the U.S. government, divides Ojibwe people into ethnic compartments and plows through families using the arbitrary date of May 12, 1961, to determine who is, and who isn't, Ojibwe. In addition to this government rule, the sometimes murky record keeping of the time, or in some cases the degree of blood being determined by government agents who used unscrupulous methods to determine heritage, has contributed significantly to the problem of Ojibwe identity. Although many people are able to claim a "full-blood," or "four-fourths" grandmother or grandfather, a far fewer number of modern descendants are able to claim a four-fourths Ojibwe parent. And in some cases, blood quantum was unscientifically determined at birth, by a doctor or nurse who didn't know the family history and was unqualified to represent the heritage of a newly born baby.

The question of quantifying heritage affects many of the families with ties to Chippewa City or, like Irene Sullivan, the families that lived between Chippewa City and Grand Marais. She explained:

> *According to the records, my brothers and sisters, and there were six of us and we had the same mother and father, but [my sister's] records are listed as one-half Ojibwe. And with me, some papers I'm one-quarter and some papers I'm three-eighths. How is this possible?*[31]

George Morrison recalled his family's multicultural background and the effects that acculturation to mainstream society had on his grandparents and parents:

> *Both of my grandmothers were full-bloods, but by the time I grew up, a lot of their ways were gone. Even their religion was kind of gone. It was beginning to be influenced by the missionary ideas— the Catholic ideas. My grandfather was not totally Indian. He was Scottish and French. They lived in log cabins and they were eating white man's food and wearing white man's clothing.*[32]

For many people, Ojibwe heritage has little to do with blood quantum, but instead with the manner in which you grew up, who your family is, and the recognition of Ojibwe tradition within one's family. This belief is stated eloquently by Richard Anderson:

> *I'm not sure there are any full bloods left who lived in Grand Portage. I recognize the fact that it's not much great importance either. I think we say, if you're part Indian, you're Indian I guess. You never forget the old, so-called traditions, especially if you lived there.*[33]

Richard Anderson Sr. with clients at Grand Marais State Bank. Courtesy of Cook County Historical Society.

Most of My Friends Were Indians

Growing up Ojibwe in Grand Marais or Chippewa City required a certain degree of balance. For many people, growing up "part Indian" meant that they didn't fully fit into either world. It is this circumstance that makes Chippewa City unique in terms of Ojibwe identity and the connection to other people in the village and to relatives in Grand Marais. From the grandfathers and the grandmothers came the skills and knowledge needed to get by in both worlds. Gloria Martineau grew up in Grand Marais but had friends and relatives who lived in Chippewa City and Grand Portage. She shared how it felt to be caught between the two worlds:

> [Grandma Drouillard] looked really Indian. Somehow, I didn't feel really Indian when I was a kid. All of these people I'm talking about seemed more Indian than me. Even Uncle Willie, and he and Daddy were brothers. But Daddy was so different, you know? We lived in town and all that. But most of my friends were Indians.[34]

The question of Indian identity is difficult to define, and even more difficult to answer. It is most important to note that for the Grand Marais Chippewa people, mixed heritage was one of the commonalities that contributed to a unique identity among the people. Indianness as a *measurable* identifier became secondary to the shared experience of growing up part Indian in Chippewa City or Grand Marais, where being part Indian automatically made you an Indian.

Gloria Martineau. Photograph by the author.

Chippewa City is referred to as an "Indian settlement" in many of the historical texts, and there is much evidence showing that racial and cultural issues to varying degrees worked to keep the two communities separated from each other, both by geographic distance and socially. Although many "full-blood" and "mixed-blood" Native people lived within the city limits of Grand Marais, racial divisions developed between people with varying degrees of Indian blood and the white citizens of Grand Marais. Many of the people who were defined as "Indian" chose to attend the church in Chippewa City and participate in "Indian" events rather than those of their white neighbors. These divisions by blood and family relationship were heightened by divisions in geographic location. While the cultural and social divisions within the larger tribe are often invisible to the outside, the divisions are quite apparent to those who live with the paradox every day. Michael Morrison related his own experience with local prejudice based on where he lived:

> *Well, my mother and dad had a lot of friends, but as we were growing up as teenagers we didn't have very many friends from Grand Marais because we thought that we didn't want to associate because there was prejudice.*[35]

THE MISSION OF THE IMMACULATE CONCEPTION 1849

In 1849 two priests of the Society of Jesus, Father Jean-Pierre Choné and Father Nicholas Frémiot, established the Mission of the Immaculate Conception on the Kaministiquia River. From there the Jesuits travelled the north shore of Lake Superior on missionary journeys. They also supported Ojibwa demands for compensation for Indian lands acquired by the Crown in the region. Within five years the Mission, centred in an Indian village of about 30 dwellings, had a large church, a day school, and numerous outbuildings. Four Sisters of the Congregation of the Immaculate Heart of Mary arrived at the Mission in 1870 to teach and establish an orphanage. By 1908 the Mission had moved to sites located on this Reserve.

Erected by the Archaeological and Historic Sites Board,
Ministry of Colleges and Universities

Plaque at the site of the first Jesuit mission on the North Shore, at Fort William First Nations Reserve, Ontario. Photograph by Cathy Quinn.

→ *Chapter 11* ←

DIVIDE THE LAND,
DIVIDE THE PEOPLE

Land and Identity

THE SEPARATION OF PEOPLE into one category or another, based on the degree of ethnicity, either real or perceived, has been practiced throughout the ages on the North Shore. This ugly part of our history got its start well before the first Europeans were allowed to settle in Minnesota. Early on, dividing the people in order to gain control of land and resources was used as a tool to conquer not only the land, but also the spirit of the people living on the land.

Reverend Father Maurice dutifully and carefully kept the Catholic church records in good order, stretching back all the way to when the first church was built at Thunder Bay, Ontario, in the mid-nineteenth century. In sharing this history, he is also illuminating the role that Catholicism played in dividing the Anishinaabe into categories based on their real or perceived "Indian" identity. He said:

> *In 1849 or 1850 Father Shoney got all the Indians and the Métis and the non-Indians here at a general meeting. And that is when he said we will build a church at this spot and then the Indians can live on one side of the church and the Métis and non-Indians can live on the other side.*[1]

The church was placed, literally, at the center of the settlement, serving as the only "shared" space in the community. St. Francis Xavier in Chippewa City divided the people there into those who were Catholics and those who weren't. As the land becomes divided, so do the people on the land. George Morrison, who admitted experiencing prejudice as a young man in Chippewa City, reflected on how this changed after he moved to the city to study art:

> *Minorities—especially Indians or other groups of people—have become more or less integrated with the big society . . . When I went to New York and began to live with a lot of other people who did not grow up in my environment, I became a part of the big society. You always become one of them. Prejudice becomes less when you're in a big situation. Only when there is one group near another does friction exist. Prejudice comes into play when two groups meet more readily.[2]*

The existence of prejudice between Grand Marais and Chippewa City developed gradually. In the years of first contact, Europeans were the minority on the North Shore and were in many ways reliant on their Chippewa neighbors to get by. When the European population exploded in the late nineteenth century, the contact area between the Grand Marais Chippewa and the European settlers became much more defined. Along with the Europeans came the concept that land was something to be bought and sold, divided and redivided.

Beginning with the 1785 Treaty of Fort Mackintosh through the Indian Reorganization Act of 1934, the gradual loss of tribal land and the subsequent increase in contact between the Ojibwe and their European neighbors created a direct connection between land ownership and the ability of the people to survive in a sea of economic uncertainty and changing community relationships.

Community-Constructed Prejudice

So much of what has been written about Chippewa City and the Lake Superior Anishinaabe to date has come through the voices of non-Native people who see history from one side. It could be argued that it's actually good that these early written histories have been preserved as documents of the past because they can be used to explain why the words we use to frame the history of a place that we all share are so important.

Mrs. Edith (Mayhew) Strom shared this version of "Happy New Year," the same tradition described with a great fondness when I interviewed Mary Jane Hendrickson, Vivian Waltz, and Gladys Beckwith:

> *There were many things that the Indians did that have long passed away. There was Payment Day which always occurred on New Year's Day, and the government allotted a certain sum of money to every Indian family. They came into the village single file, everyone went to the bank and got their money and one time they were invited over to our house. Now an Indian woman was called a squaw and when she sat down, she always sat on the ground or on the floor. They always carried a white flour sack to put everything in. My mother passed cakes and cookies and she played piano and sang for them and the Indians called my mother's piano the noise-box. They didn't eat anything; pies, cookies, cakes, everything went in the flour sack. They stayed for quite a good while; the Indians were always very cordial, very friendly and very cheerful. The women, anyway, never forgot an event. They were very easily offended and it wasn't easy to overlook things.*[3]

Whereas Mary Jane, Gladys, and the others recount the tradition as though they have just lived it, Mrs. Strom takes the tone of a historian relating her colorful tales about a long-distant past. Words like "passed away," "was," and "they were" to describe the subjects of her story are used to put the tradition and the people into the ancient past. Her authoritative use of the racial and gender-based phrases—"an Indian woman was called a squaw" and "always sat on the ground or on the floor"; Indian women were "always very cordial, very friendly," yet were also "very easily offended"—paints a very one-sided view of history, and neatly, and without apology, places the women in her story so firmly outside of her history that they become almost inhuman. Attacking the Lake Superior Ojibwe people with words began with Alexander Henry on the Granite River and has continued on, one hundred years later, through the words of Edith (Mayhew) Strom and others. And words, like daggers, can become weapons if we're not careful.

In the interest of telling a more balanced local story, it is essential for a writer of history to differentiate between the words used by non-Native historians and figures from the past, and the words used by the people to describe themselves and their experiences. Because of Mrs. Strom's point of view as an esteemed resident of Grand Marais and as a second-generation Mayhew, it is assumed that she has given us a truthful assessment of history. However, given the historical reality of the time, her words are entrenched in the constructs that were firmly in place during her childhood in the early 1900s. These social constructions very much empowered her as a representative of the white community and gave validity to her highly subjective recollections of the past. By the early 1900s, the mainstream had successfully pushed the Ojibwe "other" into the historical background.

Because she saw Ojibwe people as figments of a distant past, or as characters in her fictional history, Mrs. Strom has no trouble seeing her Ojibwe neighbors as a source of entertainment and amusement. The following story illustrates this point and provides an interesting and sadly ironic view of how separate the citizens of Grand Marais and the people of Chippewa City had become in the eyes of a white-constructed history:

> And one Fourth of July (1898) there was an accident. All these fire-works were piled in one place and someone apparently dropped a match or something nearby to ignite all these fireworks. Well, all these Indian squaws were sitting around on the ground and all of a sudden, all these fireworks started to go off. There were pinwheels and the various kinds of fireworks and everything was shooting in different directions and these squaws never moved

so fast in all their lives. Well, fortunately, no one was hurt and nothing was burned but my father never ceased to laugh about that incident.[4]

This tale also appears in Will Raff's *Pioneers in the Wilderness*, the definitive history of Cook County. In Raff's version, he corroborates Mrs. Strom's statement that "no one had been seriously hurt, although a few people were slightly burned and several had their clothing more or less burned."[5]

Sadly, Raff, though a respected, prominent local historian, fails to recognize the dangerous stereotypes and cruel humor of this "colorful" local tale, which has been passed down through history within the Mayhew family to Edith, who was not yet born when this event took place—a perfect example of how words have extended lives, and how they can spread like a bad cough. You see, that dropped match that ignited the clothes of the women patiently waiting for the fireworks to start is just as incendiary as the words used by Edith Strom and Will Raff to tell the story. The kind of words that we use to build our collective American history are often made of cruel materials; ruthless and uncaring shards that are used to systematically discount and destroy Native people. As long as we continue to use words that separate us from each other to define who we are as a community and as a country, our paths will continue to diverge instead of intersect. And as we accumulate and embellish our own stories, we must take great care to acknowledge the voices of those who have become, in a sense, the unwilling victims of a specific time and place. George Morrison explained how the people of Chippewa City, his family and his people, were subjected to prejudice:

Because I think by and large there was some prejudice. I felt that, and I still feel it still exists. I think it's that same old prejudice of color. Because we were darker and poorer, we were apart from the white people in town. But there were of course so-called town Indians too. But even so, I know there was a distinction.[6]

George Morrison, *Rocks, Crags, Dark Water, and Sky*, 1982. Courtesy of Briand Morrison.

At the turn of the twentieth century, the families in Chippewa City were feeling the delayed effects of the Dawes and Nelson acts, which had gravely reduced the once-expansive land base of the Grand Portage band, while attempting to culturally assimilate (and by extension, annihilate) Native people. The methods they used to do this included forcing people off of their traditional homelands, creating laws that made traditional Indian religion and medicine illegal, and making Native children wards of the state by taking them away from their families and sending them to boarding schools. These places were, in many cases, far away from home. In some cases, children from all over Ojibwe country were sent to boarding schools in Canada and on the Red Lake Reservation. Dorothy Johansen and her brother George were sent to Catholic school at Red Lake at a time of family crisis:

> *My mother was sick, my dad he had a broken leg, and there was really nobody to take care of us. At that time, they were very, very strict and the state stepped in and they were going to take us, so the only way my mother could keep us was to let us go for a year to Red Lake. I think there were some [kids] from Red Lake and they probably come from other reservations too, I don't really know.*

Dorothy and her brother George (*front row*), her older sister Helen (*far right*), with their mother Margaret (Morrison) Drouillard and grandparents in Chippewa City. Courtesy of Dorothy Johansen.

While she was there, she received help and encouragement from a woman that she had never met:

> And at that time, well, they were called spiritual godmothers; somebody to write to you and stuff like that, and I remember at Christmas I got this great big package and I got a great big doll and candy. My spiritual godmother had sent me all this stuff. So, she was a really nice, nice lady. She was always writing to me, always sending me packages and my great-aunt, Mrs. Theresa Newton, made birch-bark baskets with all the quillwork and with the sweet grass and everything. And my mother bought one from her and I sent that to my spiritual godmother. I met her the day before we moved to Grand Portage. They came and they took pictures of her and I.[7]

The children who lived in Chippewa City attended school in Grand Marais. Jim Wipson described what it was like riding the school bus the mile from Chippewa City to the school building that was formerly located at Third Street and Broadway:

> I used to get on the bus at Chippewa City. They used to pick up all of these Croftville people. They were really unfriendly with us because we were Indians, you know? When we'd get on the bus they'd make smart remarks and some of them would dance up and down the aisle of the bus like Indians and make fun of us. It really tore our morale down. Of course, they're all grown up and got more sense now, I bet.[8]

Several people remembered feeling discriminated against at school, and Jim LaPlante found it hard to fit into both communities at times:

> When we would go to school it was "those dirty Indians . . ." That's the way it was, it was the shits. It wasn't like it is now. Everybody

wants to be Indian now. Before nobody wanted to be Indian; not even the Indian.[9]

When Dorothy Johansen attended high school in Grand Marais, she admitted that she felt more supported at school because of her connection to her Grand Marais relatives, who shared her Chippewa heritage, but did not live on the Grand Portage Reservation:

> *When I went to school I probably didn't feel as much as the other kids because I had so many relatives in Grand Marais. Doreen [Drouillard] was there and Fern [Boostrom] and all them. So, I felt better that way.*[10]

On his weekly walks into town with his grandmother, Jim Wipson described a warm, friendly place where they would share ice cream. But later in life it proved to be a place rife with discrimination, and where he no longer felt welcome:

> *There was a lot of discrimination in Grand Marais. In fact, the young ones used to make fun of Indians. They even made funny remarks against my grandma, which I didn't like. And I noticed it more when I was older, how the discrimination was there. But as a young boy, you don't pay attention much to it. You don't take it serious. But when I got older it really bothered me because I felt like an outcast in Grand Marais.*[11]

Jim was in the armed services during World War II. While on furlough, he went to a local establishment to enjoy a beer. He relates what it was like to be part Indian in Grand Marais in the 1940s:

> *Well, a lot of people couldn't tell I had Indian in me because you can see I don't show it that much. And I went into Jackson's and they were serving beer there and I was just enjoying myself. I was a young fellow, you know? And some Indians came by the front*

*and pounded on the window. And
Jackson yells, "What do you want?"
They said, "You're servin' that Indian
drinks in there. He's Indian." And so
Jackson came up and asked me, "Are
you part Indian?" I says, "Yeah." He
says, "Out! Get out! We don't serve
Indians in here!" So, he kicked me
out of the place.*[12]

Jim Wipson in military uniform.
Courtesy of Grand Portage
Museum.

Gloria Martineau described how
local prejudice created a double standard within her own family; a standard based on which family grew up in
Grand Marais and which family grew up in Chippewa City:

*Uncle Willie wanted my dad to buy liquor for him because they
wouldn't sell to him because he was an Indian. And the two of
them were brothers! That was the difference. I asked him why he
could go into the bar and drink and Uncle Willie couldn't and he
just said, "Never mind. I'll tell you someday."*[13]

While some Chippewa people lived with prejudice every day,
other Chippewa people don't recall feeling any discrimination to
speak of. When asked about experiencing prejudice in Grand Marais
while she was growing up, Gladys Beckwith replied, "No, I didn't. I
don't think there was anything like that that went on at that time."[14]

Her sister Vivian concurred: "I really don't think so."[15]

A possible explanation for this discrepancy may be found in this
admission by Richard Anderson, a tribal member who also grew up in
Grand Marais:

*I don't think any of that existed to any great extent between Grand
Marais and Grand Portage and yet some of the people in Grand*

*Portage feel that it went on . . . My friends there in Grand Marais
knew that I was Indian. They knew my family background. There's
always been a difference in the people who have lived on a reservation itself and others who are Indian and live off the reservation.*[16]

George Morrison offered this analysis, based on his own life
experience:

*Chippewa City was apart from the big town of Grand Marais in
terms of prejudice. That is one of the gripes I have against Grand
Marais or any small town. Prejudice against minorities without any basis. And I can still feel that same prejudice in Grand
Marais today. So, we were pretty much separate. We were scolded
to behave like white people in order to be proper. Dress clean. There
was an atmosphere of a lot of drinking, some violence and disease.
The Indians were poor and without education for the most part.
There was a lower standard of living. That may be why there was
prejudice.*[17]

Ojibwe Women and Land Acquisition
~&

The Cook County Recorder's office is an amazing place. Neatly filed
in the back room are carefully numbered volumes containing every
land transaction since the first homesteads were claimed in the mid-
nineteenth century. I was able to quickly find my great-grandmother's
land deed in Chippewa City. It's dated August 29, 1892, for a parcel
originally owned by her father Martell Anakwad. As was customary for Ojibwe people who did not speak or write English, both of
their "marks" are present and represented with an "X." Perhaps the
most interesting thing about the document is that she is listed by her
"married" name, "Elizabeth Drouillard," and Great-grandfather John
Drouillard is listed as a witness to the sale. The pair already had five
children by the time the land sale occurred, and they would eventually

have seven more. It's not clear why the land is in her name and not his, because he is known as having owned property all over Cook County during his lifetime. Perhaps because the parcel was located in Chippewa City the land was stigmatized as "Indian" land and considered a separate community. Or perhaps it was a simple land exchange between a father and daughter, which was the way a lot of land at Chippewa City changed hands prior to 1900.

The community divisions separating Native and non-Native were rooted in a number of factors including wealth inequality, cultural differences, and the physical segregation of people, based on the color of their skin and their degree of "Indian-ness," as was perceived at that time. At the very center of it all are the philosophical differences that exist about land as something to be owned, as well as the complicated history of how lands were acquired within ceded territory as part of the Treaty of 1854.

I discovered that it was not unusual for Ojibwe women to have title to lands newly ceded to them by the U.S. government. This trend goes all the way back to the 1854 Treaty of La Pointe and the issuing of "Half-Breed Scrip" patents to anyone who could claim a 50/50 blood quantum. Francis Roussain, the first "owner" of Artists' Point in Grand Marais, acquired the land through this treaty provision, as did a number of others who either claimed "half-breed" status or were married to Ojibwe women, thus allowing them to claim the land as the head of a mixed-blood family. The language of the treaty guarantees this and defined legal mixed-blood status as "both husband and wife of the same family."[18]

In 1855, the Indian agent Henry C. Gilbert was tasked with determining the number of people eligible to receive land under this provision of the treaty. It included all of the territory ceded by the Lake Superior Ojibwe bands, and specified that interested people receive a certificate prior to selecting their land, guaranteeing that the land would be secured to them by patent.

Gilbert initially identified 278 people who qualified for land selection under the treaty. They were all people who were able to provide "proof of residence among contiguous residences," as outlined by the treaty. This meant that only the people living in or contiguous to one of the eligible reservations would be given land.

Gilbert was relatively sympathetic to the plight of the Ojibwe people and believed in the autonomous ability of tribes to determine who qualified for membership. He wrote: "The Indians themselves, in council, by their own traditions and knowledge, will doubtless greatly aid in arriving at the facts regarding the ancestry of those who may claim under the provisions for mixed-bloods."[19]

The department also recognized that Gilbert acted in the best interest of the Ojibwe, in this telling account of how land patents were handled by the agent at the time of the claim:

Agent Gilbert himself did not put the claims of the white men upon the same level with those of the half-breeds, appearing from the fact that he collected, or allowed to be collected from them, a commission of $25.00 each, before deliver their scrip, those unable to pay such sum not receiving scrip, such not being the case with half-breeds, whose scrip was delivered without charges.[20]

In 1863, a new Indian Agent named Dole changed the scrip requirements, authorizing the selection of land by people living in the Twin Cities or other places outside of 1854 ceded territory. Between January 29, 1864, and June 9, 1865, 564 additional people were issued scrip under authority of the 1854 treaty. Then, on June 8, 1872, the U.S. Congress passed an act titled "An Act to Perfect Certain Land Titles Therein Described." This act stated that "innocent parties who had acquired locations made in good faith by claimants under 1854 Treaty might . . . perfect their titles . . . by paying not less than $1.25/acre."

After hearing testimony about the many fraudulent land claims made under the guise of being legitimate patents under the treaty of 1854, a department special commission delivered a report that "exposed a shockingly large number of fraudulent applications made by whites posing as Chippewa, by Indians applying more than once, by deceased half-breeds, and by husbands and wives each claiming head-ship for the same family."[21]

Of the group of white men posing as mixed-blood Chippewa, the commission stated bluntly: "It comes as no surprise that most of those innocent purchasers who were allowed to buy land under this act were lumbermen."[22] Not only were these fraudulent land claims made by falsifying information or claiming "half-breed" status that did not exist, but the actual construction of the treaty requirements had a built-in allowance that made it possible for white men to claim the blood of their Ojibwe wives to qualify for the accumulation of treaty lands.

When you dig a little deeper into the role that Indigenous women played in the success of westward expansion and land acquisition in Minnesota and the entire Great Lakes region, you'll uncover how Ojibwe women, through intermarriage with French or British fur trad-ers, permanently shaped the history of the fur trade and the success of early explorations. Both the Hudson's Bay Company and the North West Company followed the example of the voyageurs, knowing that intermarriage with the Indigenous daughters of tribal families would allow these "fur-trade husbands" to receive "reciprocal privileges such as free access to the posts and provisions" throughout the territory.[23] Intermarriage was sanctioned by many Indigenous societies, and in many cases, consent to marry was granted by the family and included the marriage of a daughter in exchange for an agreed-upon amount of trade goods. In the absence of white women at that time, marriage to an Indigenous woman was, for a trader, the only opportunity he would have to live a domestic life.[24]

Marriage to an Ojibwe woman was sometimes necessary for sur-vival itself, as was the case with George Nelson, who in 1815, while wintering over at his small outpost north of Lake Superior, was dan-gerously close to running out of provisions and would likely have starved to death if it weren't for his Ojibwe wife, who "during the month of February brought in fifty eight rabbits and thirty four par-tridges."[25]

Chippewa City Anishinaabe elder. Date unknown. Courtesy of Cook County Historical Society.

Ironically, in the early days of the fur trade, fully Indigenous women were considered the most desirable wives because of their knowledge and skills in the woods. Ojibwe women were often an essential part of moccasin making and preserving food that would last all winter. And because women were often responsible for collecting spruce gum and spruce roots for use in waterproofing birch-bark canoes, the traders employed their wife's skills to keep their boats seaworthy. By the early 1800s, marriage to a fully Indigenous woman became less desirable because fur traders and trappers were now more interested in the next generation of mixed-blood daughters—women who were seen as being acclimated to Western culture, while still being familiar with the ways of Indigenous culture. By 1806 the North West Company would formally prohibit its employees from marrying fully Indigenous women.[26] As more and more European traders and settlers moved westward, the role of Indigenous women in mainstream society became diminished. In 1830, Governor Simpson and another Hudson's Bay Company officer were wed to prominent British women, an ultimate show of status and wealth.[27] The tactic of marrying an Indigenous woman to gain status as a trader or businessman, or tailoring treaties to sanction the theft of an Ojibwe woman's cultural identity in order to gain access to land or timber, had proved to be fruitful, but was no longer necessary.

Kate Frost (*center*) and family, including Jim Wipson (with his hand in front of his face). Courtesy of Patsy Drouillard Swanson Collection.

This is how treaty lands were taken at the expense of Ojibwe women. They were taken by opportunists who were encouraged to falsify their own ethnicity and steal someone else's heritage, and by traders who were encouraged to marry Indigenous women in order to gain access to the land and resources. Certainly, although ill intent was not always the case with love and marriage, it did complicate the qualifications for land ownership at the time by clouding the definition of Ojibwe identity and who, historically, had the right to claim land as guaranteed by the Treaty of La Pointe. By purposefully co-opting the identities of Ojibwe women in order to gain a foothold on the landscape, these traders, prospectors, lumbermen, and land barons took what didn't belong to them. And by sanctioning the use of blood quantum as a tool to acquire, keep, and control Ojibwe homelands, the U.S. government has created a land and identity crisis that continues to divide us into little pieces, by exploiting the blood of our great-grandmothers, grandmothers, aunts, mothers, and sisters.

The view from Katie's Point in the early 1990s. Photograph by the author.

⟿ Chapter 12 ⟼

SIGNED WITH AN X

Katie's Point

THE FINAL LOSS OF LAND at Chippewa City happened in various ways. In some cases, the state took the land through eminent domain to build a highway. In other cases, the county asked citizens to pay property taxes that they could not pay. Further division of the land served to weaken an already dwindling community whose economic resource base was increasingly shrinking, as Jim Wipson observed:

> *It was just a little community, but it was pretty good sized. In fact, when you think about it, it was probably bigger than Portage in population. Now what has happened now, is that it has been taken over by the whites. Now there are hardly any Indians there at all.*[1]

Contributing to the decline was the departure of many men and women who left to serve in the armed forces during wartime, including Jim Wipson. Perhaps most significantly, in the years leading up to World War I, the people of Chippewa City were experiencing the gradual overtaking of the land base by white businesspeople and developers. As we will see, this last factor plays a very large part in the final decline of the community in the late 1930s.

The following is from an essay by Iva Claire Downey, a seasonal visitor to the North Shore:

> *Perhaps we had seen her many a time, sitting or almost squatting in front of the post office, while she waited for the mail to be distributed. Perhaps we had passed her again and again, limping her*

way to town on the road we frequented; the road between Grand
Marais and the Indian Village. The Indian Village lies a little over
a mile east of the town and consists of a weather-beaten church
and at least a dozen houses. Some of the houses are mere tar paper
shacks; some are white-washed log cabins and one or two others,
nicely painted clapboard dwellings. Only a few Indian families live
there, but each family has many children and big and little they
may be encountered daily on the old road, as they wend their way
to town for supplies.[2]

The woman in the story is Kate Frost, Jim Wipson's grandmother.
The story was written in 1931 during one of Downey's frequent visits
from Minneapolis. This was when Grand Marais was changing from a
logging and resource-based economy into a tourist economy, attracting people from all over the region who wished to enjoy the clean air,
water, and natural beauty of the area.

At the time, many people in Cook County were struggling to
make ends meet. Those most severely affected were people who made
up the lower class, who were, not surprisingly, mostly of Ojibwe descent. When this story was written, Kate Frost was one of the last
remaining residents of Chippewa City. Ms. Downey continued:

We never learned who she was until a certain Sunday afternoon
when we were out for a walk and happened to pass her lonely
cabin. Facing the Lake, it stood quite apart from the rest of the
village. It had a deserted, sealed-up appearance. Although this
was mid-summer, the storm windows had not been removed and
they were so covered with dirt and grime, one could scarcely see the
ragged curtains behind them.[3]

With her sad words Ms. Downey has effectively and sympathetically
conveyed the end of the narrative for Kate Frost and her home in
Chippewa City. But, just like Alexander Henry that day on the Granite
River, she is missing the most important part of the story.

Katie's Point

Kate's land on Thunder Hook Point was first homesteaded by Antoine Fillison in 1880 and registered on July 26, 1881. The land patent states:

> Homestead Certificate No. 950, Application 263: Whereas there has been deposited in the General Land Office of the United States a certificate of the Register of the Land Office at Duluth, Minnesota, whereby it appears that herewith to the Set of Congress approved May 20th, 1862, to secure homestead to actual settlers on the public domain and the acts supplemented thereto, the claim of Antoine Fillison has been established and duly consummated in conformity to law.[4]

This piece of land would encompass all of what was most commonly acknowledged to be Chippewa City. Although he was allotted land at Grand Portage as part of the Allotment Act of 1887, the land records show that Fillison never lived permanently at Grand Portage, choosing instead to homestead above the lake in Chippewa City. Listed as a "half-breed" on the 1930 Grand Marais census, Fillison should have been able to claim this land as part of the treaty of 1854 as "Half-Breed Scrip," just as Roussain had claimed Artists' Point. However, very few of the Ojibwe people who lost their traditional lands as part of treaty cession actually took advantage of this provision.

Martell and Therese Anakwad had acquired several lots from Mr. Fillison in 1884. The same plots were surrendered to the Grand Marais State Bank in 1904 and then bought back from the bank in 1910 by Kate's son Martin (also known as Martel) that same year. Martin transferred title of Lot 29 soon after. This land encompasses Thunder Hook, which was known by the people in Chippewa City as "Katie's Point." She lived at this location for many years, and it is where Jim Wipson was raised until he was ten. About his grandmother's land, Jim observed: "I think a lot of them didn't even understand that they were living on a reservation. See, the land was entrusted to them, wherever they lived, it was just like homesteading, I guess."[5]

There is also some indication that Kate and many of the people who lived at Chippewa City bought their plots of land from Fillison or others for a small sum of money, rather than seeking their own homestead. Richard Anderson explained: "Land was really cheap back in those days. You could buy an acre of land up here in Cook County for $3–4 an acre. So, I'm sure [Chippewa City] owned land there."[6]

There is also the possibility that some of the Ojibwe people on the North Shore received land through the Indian Homestead Act of 1884, but that was not the case with Antoine Fillison. The Indian Homestead Act was similar to the General Homestead Act of 1862 that allowed people to select their own parcels of land through the Duluth Land Office and settle within ceded territory in northern Minnesota for $1.25 per acre. That is how a number of early non-Native landowners acquired their acreage on the North Shore in the late 1800s. This

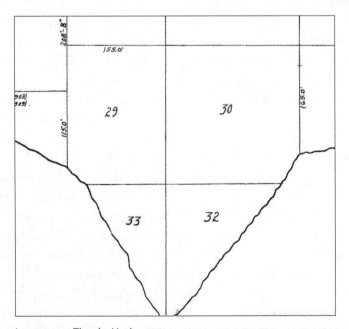

Lots 29–33 at Thunder Hook.

first wave of homesteaders includes Charles Johnson, who paid $1.25 per acre, for a total of 154 acres, on a land patent that was settled in the Duluth Land Office on November 15, 1891.[7] It is important to note that homesteaders were also able to acquire land through a provision of the 1889 Nelson Act, which released all unclaimed "agricultural" lands that remained after the government assigned allotments to tribal members.

City Taxes

Cook County had been charging residents property taxes since the 1890s, and by 1899 had already instituted a resolution for the Abatement of Delinquent Taxes in order to cover the growing cost of roads and public access to inland locations. In response, towns west of Hovland, eighteen miles east of Chippewa City, organized themselves into individual civic bodies in an effort to raise and manage their own revenue. Town halls sprang up all over the county, and the small municipalities were able to manage their own local affairs quite well until the population boom at the turn of the century, combined with the declining revenue from timber and mineral sales, resulted in the problem of delinquent taxes. In the economically depressed years of the 1930s the county proposed a new tax policy to be imposed on all property holders within the county limits. In support of this measure, the Cook County Board voted for the dissolution of any town that was "delinquent half of its taxes or has a valuation lower than $40,000.00, or if at least half of its area is owned by either federal or state government."[8] The towns affected by the law included Colvill, Hovland, Maple Hill, Lutsen, Tofte, Rosebush, Schroeder, and greater Grand Marais, an area that included Chippewa City and Croftville but did not include properties inside the city limits. Taxes were applied to both business properties and homes, and because of the designated treaty of 1854 reservation boundary, taxation did not apply to those tribal members who owned allotments at Grand Portage, but it did affect anyone who had acquired a land title outside of the reservation border. For the people of Chippewa City, the application of taxes would be the obstacle that would decide whether they would stay in their home at Chippewa City or be forced to move elsewhere. The increase of tax-delinquent land in Cook County was dramatic during that time period:

Year	Acres of tax-delinquent land in Cook County
1926	88,360
1927	18,160
1928	20,800
1929	15,840
1930	203,680

From Roy G. Blakey, *Taxation in Minnesota* (Minneapolis: University of Minnesota Press, 1932), 115.

Michael Morrison said this about his family's land at Chippewa City:

After our family moved to Duluth, that land was given to the state. Because my father didn't keep up on the taxes. If you didn't pay the taxes, it had to go back to the state. So, we don't own that land anymore. The State Highway Department has it now.[9]

It was at this time that much of the prime lakeshore along the Chippewa City bay was acquired by one of the prominent families in Cook County history, August Van Johnson and his sons, Charles (Charlie) J. Johnson and Van Johnson. Dora Kasames remembered that "all of the Indians knew [Van], they all trusted him."[10]

However, Charles and his brother, Van, were also responsible for taking advantage of their Chippewa City neighbors. Jim Wipson recounted how his grandmother lost her shoreline property in Chippewa City to Van Johnson:

I want to tell you about the man who confiscated our land and a lot of other people's land in Chippewa City. I bet he made a fortune. He talked real nice to my grandmother; he would say, "Hi, Katie. How are you?" My grandmother understood English, but she couldn't talk it very good, so she would say a couple of words in Indian and he would kind of know what she was talking about. And he would say, "Well, Katie, you need this and you need that," and my grandmother would say, "Yes, we need flour and we need pork." And he would say, "You just go up there to Tofte's, and I'll make out a slip for you and you can get all the food you want, whatever you want."

In the meantime, in the background, I guess, I started realizing that there was something behind it. And see, my grandmother couldn't pay taxes on the house. Why she had to pay taxes I don't even know, but for some reason they started taxing them from Grand Marais. Anyway, the man would go and pay my grandmother's taxes. And finally, he made her go and sign a paper, which she did with an "X" because she couldn't even write, and he told her that she could live in that log house until she died. So, my grandmother was agreeable, but when she died he took over all of that land there, all of that bay that belonged to my grandmother. Beautiful bay. And he didn't just do it with my grandmother, but with the other Indians too. So, after I came back here many years later, all of the Indian people had disappeared. Where they went, I don't know.[11]

August V. Johnson, father of Charles and Van Johnson, played a significant part in land and timber acquisition at Grand Portage and Grand Marais. Benefiting from the Allotment Act of 1887 and the Timber and Stone Act 1890, Johnson, who at the time was the Cook County Registrar of Deeds, wrote bids for, witnessed, and filed applications for land sales in his wife Stina L. Johnson's name. In the year 1919 alone, the U.S. government issued eighty-four patents for land sale. Twenty-nine of them were on the Grand Portage Reservation. August V. and Stina L. Johnson, along with their sons, were the buyers for many of these sales. By 1936, as a shareholder in the Lake Superior Realty Company, Charles Johnson's son, Lloyd K. Johnson, owned eight thousand acres of land at Grand Portage.[12] In an interview with Pat Zankman, former museum director of the Cook County Historical Society, Lloyd K. Johnson was asked about how he and his family acquired land on the reservation. He gave this explanation:

> We were interested in having the highway go down through Grand Portage and across the Pigeon River where we had our little gift shop and then continue on ... But you want to remember this was during the depression and nobody had money enough to pay taxes on their land so you could buy it for a period of time at unbelievable prices. And of course, neither Van nor I had any money at all but we would buy and sell timber and be able to get enough money, usually, to be able to turn the corner and to have another piece. So, anyway, we bought the [six thousand acres] of the Grand Portage Company.[13]

Zankman asked how his family came to own land at Chippewa City. He replied: "I don't know how it was acquired, but it was Chippewa City. The Chippewa were moving into town." Zankman asked for clarification: "So, the land became available and [Van] purchased it when they moved into town. Is that what you are saying?"

Mr. Johnson replied, "I think so."[14]

During the late nineteenth century, most of the Ojibwe people could not yet read or write English proficiently. In order for any Ojibwe person to sell his or her allotted lands, a fee patent had to be requested by the potential seller. An interested buyer could also instigate a sale by asking that a fee patent be issued. Once a patent was issued by either party, the land was taxed for sale and sold. The land abstract for Government Lot 3(W), unofficial Plat Lots 3–33, Section 22, Township 61 North, Range 1E, has 184 entries, beginning with the original homestead patent from the United States of America to Fillison in 1880 and through later transactions in the 1970s. According to the abstract, in 1925 a quitclaim deed for Katie's Point was drawn up between Kate Frost and S. L. Johnson—Stina L. Johnson. August V. Johnson is listed as registrar and witness to the deed, along with his youngest son, Victor Johnson. Curiously, the original land sale occurred on December 31, 1925, but was never officially recorded until October 16, 1963, thirty-seven years later. There is no clear explanation for this long delay in registering the paperwork. However, in the upper-left corner of the document a typed note by County Treasurer Ethel Jacobson clarifies that the transaction was "Exempt from State Deed Tax."[15] A clerk at the treasurer's office helped me to clarify the note. She explained that land sales not subject to a deed tax indicated that no money changed hands at the time of the sale. In other words, Stina Johnson, the proxy buyer of the land, never actually paid Kate Frost any money for the sale.

In early 1933, a company called "Ogema" replaces individual names on land transactions involving the Johnson family. Ogema Realty, co-opting the Ojibwe word for "chief," is the corporate land-development company owned by the heirs of August V. Johnson and his two sons. Ogema used to have a nondescript office downtown on Wisconsin Street, just across from the harbor. The building's quiet exterior gave no indication of the sheer amount of acreage acquired by the family over the years. Yet somewhere behind the shuttered facade was the truth about how August Van Johnson and his family came to own nearly all of the lakeshore at Chippewa City. For many years, it was hidden in plain sight, inside dusty boxes containing a mountain of land abstracts and quitclaim deeds. The former Ogema office was razed in 2018, and, like other old remnants that once provided clues about the story of Chippewa City land, has been dismantled and buried beneath the beach gravel of history. But the past, like a bit of beach glass, has a way of resurfacing. You'll find it encapsulated in the worn letters on an old realty sign emblazoned with the face of an Indian chief in full headdress—alone, his people nowhere in sight. He has his eyes fixed on the horizon, and the nameless Ogema puffs on his pipe, an offering of perpetual peace and friendship.

Chippewa City real estate sign. Author's collection.

Kate Frost was allowed to stay in her house on Katie's Point until she died three years after signing the land over to Johnson. Her grandson Jim speculated about how she died:

> *My grandmother, they didn't know what was wrong with her . . . She couldn't eat . . . when I think about it, she might have had cancer and didn't know it. But they took her to St. Mary's Hospital in Duluth and they just treated her with pain killers until she died . . . they buried her in Duluth in a Catholic cemetery.*[16]

By the time of Kate Frost's death in 1928, many of her Chippewa City neighbors had already left the area. When the U.S. government adopted the Indian Reorganization Act in 1934, Native American people were encouraged to return to their home reservations and take shelter in this new policy that encouraged tribal sovereignty and self-government. In 1941, the population at Grand Portage numbered 199, plus one hundred other band members who lived at Grand Marais. It is reported that between 75 and 90 percent of these Ojibwe people were practicing Catholics who also used traditional medicines.[17] When the last Mass was held at the Chippewa City church on Christmas 1936, the community had dwindled into only one or two families.

Years later, I asked Jim Wipson what he remembered about the waterfront where he used to live with his grandma, out on Katie's Point. This is what he said:

> There's trees all over the place. Now, how these trees came about to grow I don't know. I heard an old saying that even birds can plant trees. [smiling] But the point almost looks the same yet. I didn't walk down there. Of course, the beach along the bay there, from Chippewa City going out to the point, it used to be a little wider. It was so much bigger than it is now . . . And you used to stand on Highway 61 and you could look right down and see the whole lake, real clear. You can't do that now, there's so many trees.[18]

Forest fire above Grand Marais, 1907. Courtesy of Cook County Historical Society.

→ Chapter 13 ←

JIIGEWAYAAZHAGAMAY

She Walks along the Water's Edge

THE LOSS OF KATIE'S POINT is just one example of how land, and the people on the land, eroded away at Chippewa City. Some of the other factors contributing to the decline of the community include the expansion of Highway 61 north to Canada in the late 1920s, which physically cut through the community, and the devastating forest fire in 1907, which forced people to abandon their homes.

Carol Hackett is Gladys Beckwith's daughter. She experienced the decline of Chippewa City firsthand, during her childhood in Grand Marais:

> *When I was growing up, during the late 1940s and 1950s, there were not very many Indian people living in Chippewa City. I know my mom said that there were several families that lived down by the Lake, but I couldn't tell you what their names were. There had been a big fire sometime before I was born, and I think many of the people moved into town and to other places. All that remains of Chippewa City is the house we lived in, a couple of other houses, the church, and the two cemeteries.*[1]

Edith (Mayhew) Strom provided an outsider's glimpse into an increasingly dark time in the history of Chippewa City and the Grand Marais Chippewa, when many people suffered from health problems and disease:

*I don't think of anything else particular that the Indians did that was unusual. Of course, they're mostly gone now and that custom will never come back. When the Indians passed away, they usually had one of two diseases. They either had tuberculosis, we used to call it consumption, or they had what was called dropsy. I never remember seeing an Indian wear a pair of glasses. They must have had wonderful eyesight. They did all this fine beadwork and needlework and embroidered moccasins and they must have done it in the daylight. Some of them . . . they not only had wigwams but they had a house. The wigwams were dark.*²

Tuberculosis moved through the northern villages, infecting high numbers of Ojibwe people, including Shingibbiss's grandson White Sky, who fell ill in 1913 and did not recover from the disease. George Morrison famously lived with tuberculosis of the hip, and his brother Michael Morrison contracted the disease when he was eighteen years old and was also fortunate enough to survive the experience:

*At an early age, eighteen years old, I developed tuberculosis. So, I was sent off to a sanitarium in Walker. I used to visit some family down by the point in Grand Marais. There on the shore. And I'd play cards with him, almost every day. And he'd cough. And then after that I developed tuberculosis. That was when I started to learn how germs were carried from one person to another. I never really was bitter about it because during the time after I went to the sanitarium was when he passed away.*³

An influenza outbreak in 1918 affected many Chippewa City families, including the family of legendary John Beargrease, who had died from complications of tuberculosis in his home town of Beaver Bay. Shortly after his death in 1910, his wife Louise and several members of the Beargrease family moved back to Chippewa City, her home village. She died there on December 11 of influenza, eight years after her husband's death. She and John's seventeen-year-old son George and her brother-in-law Peter died the following day. As the historian Will Raff wrote:

When the influenza epidemic of December 1918 swept through the area, Louise Wishkop Beargrease died, along with two other members of the Beargrease family. The local newspaper reported their deaths and the sad fact that all three were buried together, "laid in the same grave" in the Chippewa Cemetery.[4]

For many years, there was an old wooden signpost leaning up against a birch tree on the grounds of the Chippewa City Cemetery. Carved in neat letters, it said: "Indian Grave—Joe Beaver. Carried mail with dog team for N. W. Company," with an arrow pointing into the trees, close to where his fellow musher John Beargrease's family is buried. It's sad to think of them so far away from John's grave in Beaver Bay. But every year with the running of the John Beargrease Sled Dog Marathon, racers from all over the country pass along the same trail that John and his dogs knew so well. A musher friend who has done the trek many times confided that each time they pass by John's grave, they put down some tobacco on the trail, just a small gift, to thank him for his years of bravery and hard work—a way to honor him and his team of dogs, who helped to deliver the mail to the far reaches of Chippewa City and beyond.

Between 1920 and 1930, the trail once used by Beargrease had become an expansive, scenic highway connecting Duluth to the Canadian border. What began as a narrow path through the woods then became a trail for dogsleds and horses. For years after that, the thoroughfare was only able to accommodate horse-driven coaches. By the 1920s, Model Ts were able to make the trip, and soon after that, what was then a craggy, gravel road became a two-lane paved artery suitable for all manner of cars, trucks, and buses. The construction of this road, Highway 61, effectively cut Chippewa City and east Grand Marais in two, separating the church from the cemetery and forcing the destruction of many of the community's homes and community gathering places. Irene Sullivan observed:

> We hated it when the highway went through because it went right through the middle of our little community. I think it happened when I was about ten years old. They had to tear down some of the homes and many people moved away. Eventually all the houses except one disappeared, and they built the Aspen Lodge there and several big buildings, including that nursing home.[5]

Irene also recalled that before the highway was constructed, the houses were positioned in a circle: "my Aunt Josephine, they were neighbors with the Zimmermans. It was a wonderful area there, it was sort of rounded and it reminded me of the movies and the stagecoach days."[6]

Aerial view of Chippewa City with arrows marking the Old Road, 1934. Government Land Office.

Irene's cousin, Vivian Waltz, described how the State Highway Department got her mother Josephine Zimmerman's land in east Grand Marais: "They took part of mother's land to build that highway. They said that they would either buy it from her or they would just use it. I know she was so mad."[7]

For some people, the building of a brand-new highway on top of what was once a dirt pathway to and from Chippewa City became more of a hazard than a boon. Jim Wipson shared this story about Antoine Anakwad, who lived with his mother, Marie Anne Wabibinens (Weetch):

> *One night I think he had too much to drink and he was trying to come home. He had to walk home from Grand Marais to Chippewa City. I guess he was wobbling along the road and he just got hit by a car. They said it was a local person from Grand Marais that hit him and killed him. So, after that Weetch lived all by herself.*[8]

By the late 1930s, nearly all of the families who had lived in Chippewa City had moved elsewhere. Many of them moved to Grand Portage and worked on infrastructure and tribal building projects funded by the Indian Reorganization Act. Some people moved to Duluth to find work or join family there, and some people relocated to other Ojibwe reservations where they had family members or other social ties. Much of this upheaval was part of the government effort to relocate people off of tribal lands and send them to urban areas with the promise of jobs.

Six Petticoats

Great-grandmother Anakwad's home is listed on the 1930 Grand Marais census. Her name is recorded as "Elizabeth Drouillard—Head of Household. Sixty-eight years old. Widowed." It indicated that she never attended school and could not read or write English, nor could she speak English. According to the census taker, she was born in Minnesota to a "Mixed-blood" father and "Chippewa" mother. It also states that the value of her house was one thousand dollars and that her occupation at the time was "basket weaver." Two people were living with her, both listed as grandsons; Adam Roach, eighteen years old, and Irwin Wiggins, eight years old.[9]

Great-grandmother Anakwad was followed from house to house by fire. It may have been a result of having a lot of birch bark and other highly flammable materials in her house, the materials she used to make baskets and makuks to make a living. George Morrison suggested a more macabre explanation:

> She actually had another house that burned down and there were rumors that someone had put a curse on her. It may have been part of the old Indian magic that they used against each other. My grandmother practiced that kind of magic, but in a harmful way. Once her face became twisted and distorted; like you see in the Iroquois twisted face society—the masks and such. The Chippewa were originally from that part of the country and the magic came with them. When my grandmother's face became grotesque, she suspected it was another old lady who had put a spell on her. She had her own antidote and she must have applied it in the right way because her face went back to normal.

George smiled at me and then said: "I wouldn't tell many people that because that kind of thinking is all behind the new generation. If you had grown up in Chippewa City with that thinking, then you would have been a part of it."[10]

Irene Sullivan described the day her grandmother died:

> She lived in Chippewa City. And they say she had two houses that burned down. It was a two-story frame house in Chippewa City. After that burned she lived near us in Grand Marais in a small

house. That's where she lived and that's where the house burned down. Then my mother Carrie and my sister Violet went there, but it was already too late, the door had jammed and her clothing was all a fire. You know in those days those old ladies wore about six petticoats. You know we used to call them old ladies but they were only about forty-five years old.[11]

Irene's cousin Vivian Waltz was also there and witnessed a terrible sight.

I was over to my mother's house and we were cleaning out the attic . . . I had lived next door and I had left my little girl sleeping, so I was going to go over and check on her. And I opened my mother's back door and there was my grandma standing on her porch, just screaming, and her clothes were on fire. So, we all went over and got her off the porch and rolled her on the ground. But she died. She must have been smoking in bed and then her curtains caught on fire.

I asked Vivian, "Is that what they think happened?"

She nodded and said, "Um-hmm."

I stated, "She had more than one house fire."

"I know." She said.

"So, she smoked cigarettes?" I asked with a degree of surprise.

And Vivian replied, "I think she rolled her own."[12]

She died in 1940 when my dad, Francis, was five years old. He remembers someone yelling about a fire, and watching his dad run out of the house and down the path to where his grandmother lived. In a tragic twist of fate, the fire started on a holiday, when the construction crew that was putting in sewer lines along the newly built highway was not there. Had they been there working that day, Irene Sullivan theorized, they might have been able to help put the fire out.

Great-grandmother is buried in Chippewa City. I have searched for her grave and was not able to find a stone or a marker with her name on it. Rereading Dorothy Johansen's interview provided me with a clue.

She recalled: "I don't think there's a stone . . . it's a great big square, cement thing, and it's all caved in . . . But that's where Grandma is, and then right next to her is [grandson] Adam Roach."[13]

Thanks to the work of Alta McQuatters, we can now find their two graves, side by side, on the cemetery map. Grandmother and grandson are located just above our Drouillard and Dahl relatives on the "New" side. Adam's life, like Great-grandmother's, was ended by a tragic accident. Adam Roach was a brother to Jim, Elizabeth, and Virginia LaPlante, all children of her daughter Alice (Drouillard)

Great-grandmother Elizabeth Anakwad, 1930s. Courtesy of Vivian Waltz.

LaPlante. Just twenty years old, Adam had spent three years at Isle Royale, where he was employed by Helger Johnson as a fisherman. According to the newspaper report:

> *The unfortunate young man, who drowned while engaged in his work, had not been home for a year and a half. He was making arrangements at the time of his death, to come to Grand Marais for a visit with his many relatives here. He had made his home since a young boy with his grandmother, Mrs. John Collins.*[14]

Widowed by John Drouillard in 1928, Great-grandmother Elizabeth is known to have married a man named John Collins sometime after 1930. In later documents, she is identified as Mrs. Elizabeth Collins, but little is known about him, if they were officially married, or if they lived under common law. It's yet another missing piece of the family puzzle. These portions of her life, like some of the people she loved, have been lost to the elements—taken by fire and the forces of wind and water that eventually break everything down in the end. I find it appropriate that her last name, "Cloud," is not of this earth—at least not in same way that fire and rocks and trees are. To me, Great-grandmother Cloud is somewhere between us, here on earth and up there in the sky—ishpiming (above). You can find her inside the rolling banks of precipitation that create storms out over Lake Superior. You can see her gathering in wisps at the top of the tallest mountain. Sometimes she is adrift across a bright blue sky, like puffs of smoke from a hand-rolled cigarette. And often, you can feel her covering the land with heavy layers of white, like the ruffled and lace petticoats hidden underneath the wool of an old woman's skirt.

Jiigewayaazhagamay—She Walks along the Water's Edge
~&

In some ways, you could say that Great-grandmother died from lack of water. When she needed it desperately to put the fire out, it wasn't there to save her. When the first Ojibwe people arrived on the North Shore, they had already been on the water for thousands of years. As modern people, we are conditioned to believe that land ownership and the quest for land acquisition and *property* are what define us as successful in this world. In reality, the nature of human relationships to the earth are more closely related to water then they are to land. When Great-grandmother and her family were forced to move their homes to make way for a new highway, the people became uprooted. Throughout history, our sense of belonging to our homelands is made insecure by the whims of those who are more powerful than we are. The history of Minnesota land acquisition is driven by the displacement and relocation of Anishinaabe people. In every government action beginning with Jay's Treaty all the way through the modern fight to uphold tribal sovereignty and treaty rights, Ojibwe people have been cut off from our traditional homelands. And when we no longer know the land, we risk no longer knowing who we are. In some ways, the modern approach to property ownership has created the propensity to *defend* what we own, and not truly understand the inherent value of the places that we call home. When we cut territories into pieces, we create the problem of having turf rather than community. When we define people by degrees of blood, we are, in effect, dividing ourselves into pieces, just as the treaties carved up the land.

Since I started down the Old Road back to Chippewa City, I've been searching for answers to a number of questions. With the help of my elders, I've been able to explore the places of the past and see what their lives were like so many years ago. They told me what they felt was important to remember, and helped me to understand what things are OK to let go. I've discovered some uncharted territory and uncovered some hard truths about family history. Together, they've added their knowledge and experience to the historical record and added their voices to the cacophony of local history. But after we've solved the mysteries and wandered down spurs that led us to unexpected discoveries, at what point do we know when it is time to turn around and come home?

The answer, I believe, is at the water. All along the Old Road we hear the sounds of the lake. It comes at us from one side, ever present, and always changing. From every vantage point and from every angle, the lake defines where the land stops and where the water begins . . . jiigewayaazhagamay . . . "she walks along the water's edge." When you come from a place where it's possible to walk west and walk north and walk east, but not ever south, you learn to understand that everything we do becomes a part of the lake.

We live in a place where osmosis in unavoidable. The lakes and rivers here in northern Minnesota raised us. The fish and water beings raised us. The *manoomin* and maple sap, they raised us, too, and we, in turn, become them. As Professor Collins pointed out in Ojibwe class, foods are living things, unless they aren't. Rocks are living things with a spirit, because they are always in a state of change. The jagged rocks

THE BEACH, GRAND MARAIS, MINN.

Vintage postcard, Grand Marais beach. Courtesy of Cook County Historical Society.

on Artists' Point are always in a state of flux. The beach gravel gently working its way into smaller and smaller pebbles is undergoing the inevitable and dynamic process of metamorphosis. Because everything changes, and because everything *is changing,* we can no longer count on the land to show us who we are. Because for many of us, the processes of history have complicated what it means to have a homeland. Inside the context of Native American history, land has become an intangible part of our Native heritage. With each treaty and government act, the grasp on our homelands has become shiftless and untrustworthy. But when you are raised by water, it has a forceful way of showing you what your limitations are—which rocks are slippery and how far you can safely go without getting lost. If you grow up walking along the water's edge, you can always find your way back home. You just find the direction of the lake and walk south until you can't walk anymore. And when you eat and drink and breathe it, you learn to respect its mood swings, and marvel at its colors. And when you know this, you begin to understand what it means to be from somewhere. I think Great-grandmother would understand this because her life was of the water and died in spite of it. I know that my grandfather Fred would agree, because he spent his life on the water and fed his family because of it. And I feel with certainty that my sister and I were taught by our parents to trust that the way of the water is the truth. Water, like love, and like family, can never be ignored and must always be protected. This is what I want my nephew to understand. Then he, too, will always know how to find his way back home.

My dad Francis Drouillard and my nephew Francis Endrizzi: Francis x 2, Grand Portage. Courtesy of Dawn Drouillard.

Betsy Bowen, painting of St. Francis Xavier Sacristy. Courtesy of Betsy Bowen.

→ *Epilogue* ←
A RETURN HOME

THERE IS A STORY that my dad tells with great relish about my great-uncle, Charlie Drouillard, the same man who knew how to fry up donuts in bear grease. One day Uncle Charlie was walking home to Chippewa City from Grand Marais, where he had been undoubtedly enjoying the social hour at one of the local taverns. He walked the path that he had walked for years, the Old Road that connected Grand Marais and Chippewa City and all points east or west. Uncle Charlie walked on, seemingly oblivious to the fast-moving cars and errant honking that followed him along his trail. He was soon stopped by the local authorities who asked him why, in heaven's name, was he was walking down the middle of the highway.

"I am *Charlie Drouillard,*" he replied, "and you built the road on my trail!"

Charlie Drouillard (*in white gloves*) with horse carriages in front of Babb home in downtown Grand Marais. Courtesy of Cook County Historical Society.

Although the village of Chippewa City is no longer visible and the original houses have all been replaced by new buildings, those who once lived there still consider it to be their home. Vivian Waltz, the daughter of Mrs. Josephine Zimmerman, the first person to be confirmed at St. Francis Xavier Church, was asked if she still considers that area to be Chippewa City. Without hesitation she responded, "Yes."[1]

Jim Wipson told the story of visiting Katie's Point on the bay at Chippewa City:

> *I went there to show my wife where my grandmother and I lived when I was a boy and a big sign there says, "Private Property." And my wife said, "We better not go in there, or they'll arrest you!" I said, "Hell, I lived here even before this house was even here." So, I walked in and the gentleman that owns the house is a scientist and he's a real nice guy. And I started telling him how my grandmother had a log cabin just over from his house and he was pretty amazed when I told him about it. There's a big point that goes way out. Anyway, this white guy that I talked to said they want to build condominiums on that point. There's a lot of wildlife and it would be a dirty shame if they tore down all that stuff and built condominiums there.*[2]

Many others have wanted to visit the site of their former home. Jim LaPlante said, "I haven't walked through there lately, I don't know, one of these days I'll try."[3]

Dorothy Johansen once tried to find the location of her father's fish house on the shore at Chippewa City:

> *The kids and I went in [the church] and I said that what I would just love to do is walk all over down there, where the homes were, where our house was, where my dad's fish house was, but I'd be trespassing all over the place. Irene and I tried to drive down the Old Road and just before you could get to my dad's house, there was a great big chain across the road.*[4]

Blocked trail. Photograph by the author.

Evidence of when the Old Road became impassable is found in this local news report from 1904:

> The road crew finished grading the shore road east to the township line and broke camp the first of the week. The boarding camp has been closed. A reduced force is now engaged on St. Paul avenue, which is to be opened up and extended eastward to connect with the shore road. On account of the closing of the old Chippewa City road, which passed over private property, this latter improvement became an absolute necessity. Upon the completion of this extension road work will be suspended for the season.[5]

An old city plat map outlines how the early planners intended to develop the streets of downtown Grand Marais. The location of the cranberry bog, remembered by Irene Sullivan, is colored in with blue pencil and marked in red. A point on the map concurrent with the location of the East Bay Hotel is labeled "C. J. Johnson's Barn & Stables, Shop, etc."

Old city plat map, marked with C. J. Johnson's stable. Government Land Office.

Based on the memories of Jim Wipson and others, we know that the Old Road from Chippewa City came out in town, close to the water:

> It's still there but it's not usable hardly. I don't think anybody uses it. I think you can still walk it. And the upper road is the modern highway and this lower road follows the bay for a while and then it comes out in Grand Marais. Now, if that road still comes out in Grand Marais, I don't know. One of these days I'm gonna go down there and trace it out. If you can't drive it I'm gonna walk it. I'm going to go down to Chippewa City and start on that road just to bring back memories, if nothing else.[6]

It is this strong connection to our homelands that lies at the center of who we are, and it explains why the people who were born and raised in Chippewa City have maintained such a strong bond with both the physical place and each other. George Morrison described why he eventually came back to Cook County:

Even after my father died in 1949 and my family was gone, I would come back. One thing that made me come back is the land. I feel a reverence for the land and the lake. You come back to your own environment and how you grew up. Maybe you are drawn to the people too—those you grew up with. A certain relationship to those people and a relationship to the land, rocks and trees. This may have influenced my art to a certain degree. The way driftwood is indirectly related to nature.[7]

St. Francis Xavier and the Chippewa City Cemetery serve as physical testaments to these Chippewa City traditions. As monuments to the Grand Marais Chippewa, they are still used and honored by those who remember what life was like at that time and place.

In 1916, a new Catholic church was built in Grand Marais. Masses alternated between the two churches for a time, but gradually attendance at St. Francis Xavier dwindled down, as people left Chippewa City. The church stood vacant for thirty-four years. The foundation began to buckle and the roof began to sag. In 1970, the Cook County Historical Society, under the direction of Olga Soderberg and St. John's Catholic Church of Grand Marais, planned together for the restoration and repair of the building in the hope of rededicating the church in time for its seventy-fifth anniversary. In the years following, a new foundation was laid, extensive restoration was done on the interior, and a new roof was added. On July 4, 1975, Rt. Rev. Msgr. Stephen Anderl, M. Div., spoke at the rededication ceremony for "the first religious edifice" in the area.[8]

With the help of the Cook County Historical Society, the church was listed on the National Register of Historic Places in 1985. In 1995, a jointly sponsored hundred-year anniversary event took place at St. Francis Xavier. George Morrison was the guest speaker at the event. A eucharistic liturgy was also held in the morning before Mr. Morrison's presentation. In 1995, the church was still owned and maintained by the Diocese of Duluth and St. John's Catholic Church in Grand Marais, one hundred years after the first services were held there.

On March 17, 1998, the church was given to the Cook County Historical Society by the Diocese of Duluth and St. John's Catholic Church, to ensure that the historic church would "continue and not deteriorate."[9] Soon after, the Historical Society received a matching grant from the state to make repairs on the roof, in addition to a five thousand-dollar donation from the Grand Portage Band of Chippewa. Through other donations, a new organ was purchased to temporarily replace the original, which was in the possession of a private owner until 2015. Bob Swanson and museum director Carrie Johnson, along with some strong helpers, brought the original instrument back from the Twin Cities in what Bob likes to call "The Story of the Organ Transplant."

Regarding the legacy of the church, Pat Zankman of the Cook County Historical Society explained: "It is intended that the church will serve as a focal point for those who wish to research and document their family histories as related to the church and its community."[10]

The years between 1936 and 1998 were difficult for many people with roots in Chippewa City. Michael Morrison, in particular, described his concerns about the church over the years:

> I guess I inherited my feelings from my father because since that church was built in 1895 my grandfather took care of a lot of things that needed to be done around the church and also the cemetery. So then after my grandfather died in 1936, my father inherited his job, and I guess after my father died I took it upon myself to take care of it. Being away from Chippewa City, living in Duluth and Minneapolis, occasionally I would come up and take over the summer care [of the church]. I feel more comfortable now since I know that it's all in the hands of the Historical Society.[11]

There was just one more road left for me to explore. But this time I had a map. It's a hand-drawn, geographically accurate depiction of the old road to the Drouillard/Anakwad sugar bush just above Croftville.

Created by R. Emerson Morris, whose family lives close by, it indicates the precise location of where Kate Frost, the Wishkops, Antoine Anakwad, and some of their Drouillard relations would set up their maple harvest in the spring, with their birch-bark teepees, boiling kettles, and homemade wine.

Chippewa City church, 1895. Courtesy of Cook County Historical Society.

With the help of my friend J.D., who interpreted the map, and Robin and Mark Johnson (of the Matt Johnson family), who let me park my car at their garage, I set out from where the old road used to head uphill to the maple woods. It was a beautiful spring day and the walking was easy—at least at first it was. I followed the path uphill where it crosses a glacial esker that runs along the ridge. Just past that there was a dip where the trail disappeared into deep mud and the road ahead was obscured by a thick tangle of windfalls, completely blocking my way forward. Sizing up the depth of the mud with the height of my rubber boots I decided that I must try to forge ahead. Nearly losing one of my boots in the quagmire, I started to laugh about my predicament. Here I was nearly finished with the story, and once again faced another impasse—this one looked to be wicked. But then I thought about how Great-grandmother Anakwad had taken off in a spring storm for the sugar bush, her children in tow, bound and determined to get to work. I thought about Shingibbiss and how, at eighty years old, he walked the steep incline into the trees to do what he had been taught to do every spring. And I thought about Kate Frost and Jim Wipson, who had taken this very road up to their spring camp, where there was a stream of fresh water, a crust of snow underfoot, and the promise of maple sugar candy from the kettle waiting for them. Holding on to a sturdy tree, I pulled my boot out of the mud, wound my way through the tangle of trees, and steered myself back on the road.

MIIGWECH

MIIGWECH TO MY ELDERS, who generously shared their life stories with me: Gladys Beckwith, Barney Drouillard, Robert Drouillard, Mary Jane Hendrickson, Dorothy Johansen, my aunt Gloria Martineau, George Morrison, Michael Morrison, Alice and Milton Powell, Vivian Waltz, and Jim and Lorraine Wipson. I can still hear your voices as clearly today as I did more than thirty years ago when I recorded my first interview. I am thankful for the shared history of Bill Amyotte, Richard Anderson, Dora Kasames, Jim LaPlante, Irene Sullivan, and Father Maurice, whose audiotaped interviews and stories housed at the Grand Portage National Monument greatly enrich this book.

To the Chippewa City family members—Michelle Hoy, Rick Anderson, Lani Blackdeer, Carol Hackett, Briand Morrison, Roberta Morrison, Chris Powell, Claudette Puccia, Patty Pilon Rogers, Mary Stack, and Sue Zimmerman: thank you for sharing your family stories and photographs as part of the Chippewa City collective history. I am so happy and thankful for your confidence and support.

To Dave Cooper, Tim Cochrane, and Steve Viet of the Grand Portage National Monument; Mary Ann Gagne at the Grand Portage Museum; and Carrie Johnson, Pat Zankman, Martha Marnocha, and Alta McQuatters from the Cook County Historical Society: miigwech for doing the good work of tracking and cataloging history and for supporting this project for so many years. Many of the beautiful and telling photographs included in *Walking the Old Road* come from these three amazing collections and provide breathtaking documentation of life on the North Shore at the turn of the twentieth century.

To my teachers and teacherfriends—Collins Oakgrove, Judith Daniels, Ruth Voights, Jean O'Brien, Carol Miller, Ron Libertus, JoAnn Krause, Judith Trollander, Sharon Smith, Percilla Garrigan, Keith Secola, Linda LeGarde Grover, Stephan Hoglund, Julie King, Merrie Brantseg, Debbie Benedict, Chel Anderson, Shoshanna

Matney, Julie Louise Koski, Betsy Bowen, Cheryl Conklin, Joan Farnam, Carol Thomas, Claire Carrier, and Clea Korf: you have inspired me to be a better reader, storyteller, listener, and writer, and I am forever thankful.

Extra special thanks to Bob Swanson, who has contributed so much to Grand Portage and Bois Forte Anishinaabe history and has worked very hard to keep the Chippewa City story alive. Many of the images from Chippewa City are part of the Patsy Drouillard Swanson Collection, generously shared by Bob, Patsy's son. Bob, it is an honor to be your friend and your Drouillard/Anakwad cousin. Miigwech for your good words, for the tears and for the laughs.

Walking the Old Road as a book with pages, pictures, and maps would not exist without the help of Phil Anderson, Ken and Molly Hoffman, J. D. Lehr, Tom McCann, and Jim Raml. Thank you, friends, for patiently reading through early incarnations of the manuscript; for plotting points on a map; and for helping me to connect the physical place of Chippewa City with the written history of the people. You all made the story better.

With much gratitude to the Arrowhead Regional Arts Council, which provided me with writing and editing support during the winter of 2017. This help and encouragement allowed me to stretch my writing muscles and dig into the process of transforming an (at times) clinical academic thesis into something else entirely.

If our communities are to heal from the wounds of the past, historical truths, like sunken barrels of wartime munitions, must be brought to the surface, carefully uncapped, and responsibly disposed of so no further harm can be done. For this reason, I am thankful for the good work of Joan Gardner-Goodno at the Lloyd K. Johnson Foundation, for her wisdom and clarity regarding the delicate process of acknowledging the painful truths of history while striving to make our community the best that it can be.

To Erik Anderson, Kristian Tvedten, David Thorstad, Rachel Moeller, and everyone at the University of Minnesota Press: thank you for your kind and thoughtful care of the Chippewa City story and for your guidance and gentle trust at each and every mile marker. Miigwech.

To my family—Cathy Quinn, Joyce and Francis (Poot) Drouillard, Dawn Drouillard, Mike and Francis Trout Endrizzi, Grandma Lola and Grandpa Fred, Grandma Freda and Grandpa William, and all of my aunts, uncles, cousins, and dearly supportive friends: gizagi'in. I am stingy with you.

NOTES

Prologue
1. James Wipson, interview with the author, Grand Portage, Minnesota, March 11, 2001.
2. Robert Swanson, "Bimaadizi Aadizookaan," unpublished, 2016.

1. We Used to Sneak in There and Play
1. Dorothy Johansen, interview with the author, Duluth, Minnesota, January 25, 2001.
2. Margot Fortunato Galt, *Turning the Feather Around* (St. Paul: Minnesota Historical Society Press, 1998), 21.
3. Michael Morrison, "19th Century Town," Cook County Historical Society, June 1975, unpublished.
4. Land Warranty Deed, 1887, U.S. Government Document, Cook County Registrar of Deeds, Grand Marais, Minnesota.
5. Dorothy Johansen, interview with the author, Duluth, Minnesota, January 25, 2001.
6. James Wipson, interview with the author, Grand Portage, Minnesota, March 11, 2001.
7. Letter from Josephine Zimmerman to Olga Soderberg, *Cook County News Herald*, 1971.
8. Olga Soderberg, "History of St. Francis Xavier," Cook County Historical Society, 1975, unpublished.
9. Ibid.
10. Vivian Waltz, interview with the author, Duluth, Minnesota, March 31, 2001.

2. A Gateway for the Ages
1. George Morrison, interview with the author, Grand Portage, Minnesota, October 1987.
2. Ibid.
3. Timothy Cochrane, "L'Espagnol: Grand Portage Band Chief," May 2000, unpublished, 15.
4. William W. Warren, *History of the Ojibway People* (St. Paul: Minnesota Historical Society Press, 1994), chapter 4.
5. Author's note.
6. Warren, *History of the Ojibway People*, 79. The migration of the Anishinaabe from the east is supported by Warren and others but is not

necessarily believed by all Anishinaabe people. Some Ojibwe people in Grand Portage and elsewhere believe that the people have always lived in Ojibwe country and did not, in fact, migrate from another place.

7. Warren, *History of the Ojibway People*, 96.
8. Ibid., 83–84.
9. Ron Morton and Carl Gawboy, *Talking Rocks* (Duluth: Pfeifer-Hamilton, 2000), 73.
10. Carolyn Gilman, *The Grand Portage Story* (St. Paul: Minnesota Historical Society Press, 1992), 32.
11. Minnesota Chippewa Tribe, *Kitchi-Onigaming—Grand Portage and Its People* (Cass Lake, Minn., 1983), 7.
12. Warren, *History of the Ojibway People*, 56.
13. Ibid., 82.
14. Louise Erdrich, *Books and Islands in Ojibwe Country* (New York: Harper Perennial, 2003), 7.
15. Warren, *History of the Ojibway People*, 36.
16. Anton Treuer, *Ojibwe in Minnesota* (St. Paul: Minnesota Historical Society Press, 2010), 6.
17. Gilman, *The Grand Portage Story*, 33.
18. Melissa L. Meyer, *The White Earth Tragedy: Ethnicity and Dispossession at a Minnesota Anishinaabe Reservation, 1889–1920* (Lincoln: University of Nebraska Press, 1994), 13.
19. Ibid., 15.
20. Ibid.
21. Minnesota Chippewa Tribe, *Kitchi-Onigaming*, 7.
22. Gilman, *The Grand Portage Story*, 35.
23. J. Arnold Bolz, *Portage into the Past: By Canoe along the Minnesota–Ontario Boundary Waters* (Minneapolis: University of Minnesota Press, 1960, 1988), 45.
24. Ibid.
25. William H. Raff, *Pioneers in the Wilderness* (Grand Marais, Minn.: Cook County Historical Society, 1981), 124.
26. Jack Blackwell, *Boundary Waters Boy* (Grand Marais, Minn.: Northern Wilds Media, 2018), 71.

3. At the Pleasure of the United States

1. Timothy Cochrane, *Gichi Bitobig–Grand Marais* (Minneapolis: University of Minnesota Press, 2018), 100.
2. From author's conversation with Timothy Cochrane, author of *Minong—The Good Place Ojibwe and Isle Royale* (East Lansing: Michigan State University Press, 2009).

3. Dorothy Dora Whipple, *Chi-mewinzha: Ojibwe Stories from Leech Lake* (Minneapolis: University of Minnesota Press, 2015), 11.
4. John B. Arnold, *A Story of Grand Portage and Vicinity* (Minneapolis: Harrison and Smith Co., 1923), 28.
5. Minnesota Chippewa Tribe, *Kitchi-Onigaming*, 45.
6. Cochrane, "L'Espagnol," 19.
7. Gilman, *The Grand Portage Story*, 110.
8. Minnesota Chippewa Tribe, *Kitchi-Onigaming*, 8.
9. Cochrane, "L'Espagnol," 122.
10. Meyer, *The White Earth Tragedy*, 37.
11. Treaty with the Chippewa, Article 6, October 4, 1842.
12. Treaty with the Chippewa of the Mississippi and Lake Superior, Article 1, August 2, 1847.
13. Timothy Hegney, *Schools Annual Report, Grand Portage, 1856,* Commissioner of Indian Affairs, 1857.
14. Minnesota Chippewa Tribe, *Kitchi-Onigaming*, 50.
15. Commissioner of Indian Affairs, "Annual Report of Grand Portage Indian School, Minnesota Territory, from October 1, 1856, to September 17, 1857." U.S. Government Publication, 1857.
16. Ibid.
17. Unknown author, "The Drouillard Family of Grand Marais, Minnesota," Early Cook County History, *Cook County News Herald,* December 10, 1925.
18. Ibid.
19. Cochrane, "L'Espagnol," 40.
20. Edmund J. Danziger Jr., "They Would Not Be Moved: The Chippewa Treaty of 1854," *Minnesota History* (spring 1973): 178.
21. Gilman, *The Grand Portage Story,* 110.
22. Ibid., 109–10. With Ojibwe translations from the unpublished notes of Alta McQuatters, Lutsen, Minnesota, 2017.
23. Gilman, *The Grand Portage Story,* 109.
24. Ibid.
25. *Annuities List of the 1854 Treaty,* United States Department of the Interior, 1854.
26. Raff, *Pioneers in the Wilderness,* 5.
27. Minnesota Chippewa Tribe, *Kitchi-Onigaming*, 15–17.
28. Bill Amyotte, interview with Donald Auger and Paul Driben, Grand Portage National Monument, Grand Portage, Minnesota, 2000.
29. Raff, *Pioneers in the Wilderness,* 16.
30. Ibid., 4.

4. Here Were Many Wigwams

1. Joseph Alexander Gilfillan papers, Minnesota Historical Society Collection, St. Paul, Minnesota, v. 17.

2. Dr. F. B. Hicks, "Historian Tells of Early Beginnings of Grand Marais as an Indian Trading Post," *Duluth Tribune,* October 6, 1929, 1.

3. Ibid.

4. United States Engineers Office, "History of Grand Marais Harbor," unpublished report, Duluth, Minnesota, 1939, 2.

5. Hicks, "Historian Tells of Early Beginnings of Grand Marais as an Indian Trading Post," 1.

6. Grand Marais Map, 1900–1910, as reported by M. J. Humphrey, April 1979, and revised by John Blackwell Jr., May 3, 1979. From the Cook County Historical Society collection, Grand Marais, Minnesota.

7. Raff, *Pioneers in the Wilderness,* 16.

8. Lloyd K. Johnson, interview with Pat Zankman, Cook County Historical Society, Duluth, Minnesota, 2003.

9. Catherine Jones, unpublished journal, Cook County Historical Society, Grand Marais, Minnesota, November 2, 1898—November 14, 1900.

10. Raff, *Pioneers in the Wilderness,* 350.

11. Catherine Jones, unpublished journal, April 1899.

12. Irene Sullivan, interview with Donald J. Auger and Paul Driben, eds., *Grand Portage Chippewa: Stories and Experiences of Grand Portage Band Members,* Grand Portage Tribal Council, Sugarloaf Interpretive Center Association (Grand Portage, Minn., December 2000), 33.

13. Ross R. Cotroneo and Jack Dozier, "A Time of Disintegration: The Coeur d'Alene and the Dawes Act," *Western Historical Quarterly* (October 1974): 405.

14. Ibid.

15. Meyer, *The White Earth Tragedy,* 38.

16. *Treaty with the Chippewa, September 30, 1854,* United States government document, article 2, section 7, 3.

17. Auger and Driben, *Grand Portage Chippewa,* 112.

18. Raff, *Pioneers in the Wilderness,* 16.

19. Cac Hussey, interview transcript, Cook County Historical Society, 2003.

20. Certificate of the Register of the Land Office at Duluth, No. 41, Chippewa Certificate No. 107, Department of the Interior, General Land Office, Washington, D.C., November 20, 1866.

21. Raff, *Pioneers in the Wilderness,* 16.

22. Marian Boyd Winter, "Sketch—Roussain Eustache and Francis," unpublished, Fond du Lac, Minnesota, 1931, 6. Minnesota Historical Society Collections, Minnesota History Center, St. Paul, Minnesota.

23. *Treaty with the Chippewa, October 4, 1842,* United States government document, article 4.
24. *Treaty with the Chippewa, August 2, 1847,* United States government document, article 4.
25. *"Half-Breed Chippewa Scrip Locations,"* Certificate No. 107, Department of the Interior, General Land Office. Washington, D.C., November 20, 1866.
26. Meyer, *The White Earth Tragedy,* 40.
27. Ibid.
28. U.S. Federal Census, Fond du Lac, Minnesota, 1860.
29. Raff, *Pioneers in the Wilderness,* 353.
30. Ibid. It should be noted that one of the early Grand Marais grocery businesses is still operated by the Matt Johnson family, whose patriarch, Mathias Johanasen, emigrated from Norway. The Johanasen family is not related to Charles Johnson, whose ancestors originally came from Sweden.
31. United States Engineers Office, "History of Grand Marais Harbor, Minnesota," 4.
32. U.S. Census, Grand Marais, Minnesota, 1880.
33. *Schedule of Land Allotments,* United States Government document, 1889.
34. Meyer, *The White Earth Tragedy,* 52.
35. Arnold, *A Story of Grand Portage and Vicinity,* 45.
36. Gilman, *The Grand Portage Story,* 118.
37. Meyer, *The White Earth Tragedy,* 52.
38. Ibid.
39. Danziger, "They Would Not Be Moved," 181.
40. Minnesota Chippewa Tribe, *Kitchi-Onigaming,* 53.
41. Ibid.
42. Fortunato Galt, *Turning the Feather Around,* 26.
43. Raff, *Pioneers in the Wilderness,* 15.
44. Ibid., 18.
45. Ibid., 41.
46. Minnesota Chippewa Tribe, *Kitchi-Onigaming,* 54.
47. Ibid.

5. Nishkwakwansing

1. James Wipson, interview with the author, Grand Portage, Minnesota, March 11, 2001.
2. U.S. Census, Bayfield, Wisconsin, 1870.
3. Dora Kasames, interview with Donald Auger and Paul Driben, Grand Portage National Monument, Grand Portage, Minnesota, 2000.

4. Raff, *Pioneers in the Wilderness,* 292.
5. Auger and Pal Driben, *Grand Portage Chippewa,* 33.
6. Raff, *Pioneers in the Wilderness,* 269.
7. Author unknown, "Pigeon River Road to Open Soon," *Duluth Tribune,* October 6, 1929.
8. Author unknown, "A Cold Bath," *Duluth Herald,* August 5, 1899.
9. Raff, *Pioneers in the Wilderness,* 298.
10. Ibid., 309.
11. Baptism Record, Anna Louise Scott, March 2, 1885, unpublished.

6. Nokomisag miinawaa Mishoomisag
1. James Wipson, interview with the author, Grand Portage, Minnesota, May, 27, 2001.
2. Gilman, *The Grand Portage Story,* 119.
3. Auger and Driben, *Grand Portage Chippewa,* 83.
4. Cochrane, *Gichi Bitobig–Grand Marais,* 133.
5. Betty Powell Skoog, *A Life in Two Worlds* (Lake Nebagamon, Wis.: Paper Moon Publishing, 1996), foreword by Justine Kerfoot, xii.
6. Blackwell, *Boundary Waters Boy,* 72–74.
7. Lloyd K. Johnson, interview with Pat Zankman, Cook County Historical Society, Duluth, Minnesota, 2003.
8. Raff, *Pioneers in the Wilderness,* 235.
9. Gloria Martineau, interview with the author, Grand Marais, Minnesota, April 2001.
10. Ibid.
11. Ibid.
12. Francis Drouillard, interview with the author, Grand Portage, Minnesota, May 2010.
13. Ibid.
14. Raff, *Pioneers in the Wilderness,* 56.
15. Shingibbiss obituary, *Cook County News Herald,* Grand Marais, Minnesota, April 25, 1907
16. Ibid.
17. Author conversation with Alta McQuatters, 2017.
18. Catherine Jones, unpublished journal, Cook County Historical Society, Grand Marais, Minnesota, November 2, 1898—November 14, 1900, 5.
19. Gilman, *The Grand Portage Story,* 119.
20. Dora Kasames, interview with Donald Auger and Paul Driben, Grand Portage National Monument, Grand Portage, Minnesota, 2000.
21. Gloria Martineau, interview with the author, Grand Marais, Minnesota, April 2001.

22. James Wipson, interview with the author, Grand Portage, Minnesota, May 27, 2001.
23. Dragos D. Kostich, *George Morrison: The Story of an American Indian* (Minneapolis: Dillon Press, 1976), 16.
24. Auger and Driben, *Grand Portage Chippewa*, 110.
25. Michael Morrison, interview with the author, Grand Portage, Minnesota, October 27, 2001,
26. George Morrison, interview with the author, Grand Portage, Minnesota, October 1987.
27. Dorothy Johansen, interview with the author, Duluth, Minnesota, January 25, 2001.
28. James Wipson, interview with the author, Grand Portage, Minnesota, May 27, 2001.
29. Ibid.
30. Ibid.
31. Irene Sullivan, interview with Donald Auger and Paul Driben, Grand Portage National Monument, Grand Portage, Minnesota, 2000.
32. Compendium, Office of Light House Inspector, Eleventh District, Detroit, Mich. April 17, 1875, Letter Book 366, dated March 15, 1875, page 158 enclosure, unpublished.
33. Baptism record, Josephine Drouillard, July 2, 1884, unpublished.
34. Baptism record, Charles Drouillard, May 7, 1887, unpublished.
35. Baptism record, Rose Drouillard (Anakwad), July 18, 1903, unpublished.
36. "Long and Arduous Trip," Bayfield County Press, reprinted from the *Duluth News Tribune,* May 23, 1891.
37. "Early Cook County History," *Cook County News Herald,* December 10, 1925.
38. James Wipson, interview with the author, Grand Portage, Minnesota, May 27, 2001.
39. George Morrison, interview with the author, Grand Portage, Minnesota, October 1987.
40. Vivian Waltz, interview with the author, Duluth, Minnesota, March 31, 2001.
41. Dorothy Johansen, interview with the author, Duluth, Minnesota, January 25, 2001.
42. Sue Zimmerman, interview with Donald Auger and Paul Driben, transcript located at Grand Portage National Monument, Grand Portage, Minnesota, 2000.
43. Gladys Beckwith, interview with the author, Grand Marais, Minnesota, March 10, 2001.

7. *Indian Maidens and Plastic Tomahawks*

1. Jim Anderson, "Trestle Pine Days," *Cook County News Herald,* January 10, 1994.
2. Kenneth MacKenzie, Grand Portage census, August 1885.
3. James LaPlante, interview with Donald Auger and Paul Driben, Grand Portage National Monument, Grand Portage, Minnesota, 2000.
4. James Wipson, interview with the author, Grand Portage, Minnesota, May 11, 2001.
5. Gilman, *The Grand Portage Story,* 115.
6. Milt Powell, interview with the author, Grand Marais, Minnesota, December 13, 2011.
7. Catherine Jones, unpublished journal, Cook County Historical Society, Grand Marais, Minnesota, November 2, 1898—November 14, 1900, 6.
8. Auger and Driben, *Grand Portage Chippewa,* 9.
9. George Morrison, interview with Donald Auger and Paul Driben, Grand Portage National Monument, Grand Portage, Minnesota, 1999.
10. Raff, *Pioneers in the Wilderness,* 355.
11. Michael Morrison, interview with Donald Auger and Paul Driben, Grand Portage National Monument, Grand Portage, Minnesota, 2000.
12. Milt Powell, interview with the author, Grand Marais, Minnesota, December 13, 2011.
13. Gladys Beckwith, interview with the author, Grand Marais, Minnesota, March 10, 2001.
14. Auger and Driben, *Grand Portage Chippewa,* 107.
15. Michael Morrison, interview with the author, Grand Portage, Minnesota, October 27, 2001.
16. Raff, *Pioneers in the Wilderness,* 69.
17. Memory shared with the author by Mark Johnson, unrecorded, 2016.
18. James LaPlante, interview with Donald Auger and Paul Driben, Grand Portage National Monument, Grand Portage, Minnesota, 2000.
19. Auger and Driben, *Grand Portage Chippewa,* 47.
20. Cochrane, *Gichi-bitobig—Grand Marais,* 113.
21. Bill Amyotte, interview with Donald Auger and Paul Driben, Grand Portage National Monument, Grand Portage, Minnesota, 2000.
22. Cac Hussey, interview transcript, Cook County Historical Society, 2003.
23. James Wipson, interview with the author, Grand Portage, Minnesota, May 27, 2001.
24. Ibid.
25. James LaPlante, interview with Donald Auger and Paul Driben, Grand Portage National Monument, Grand Portage, Minnesota, 2000.

26. Ibid.
27. *Cook County News Herald,* December 13, 1923.
28. Gloria Martineau, interview with the author, Grand Marais, Minnesota, April 2001.
29. James Wipson, interview with the author, Grand Portage, Minnesota, March 11, 2001.
30. Michael Morrison, interview with the author, Grand Portage, Minnesota, October 27, 2001.
31. Dorothy Johansen, interview with the author, Duluth, Minnesota, January 25, 2001.
32. Dora Kasames, interview with Donald Auger and Paul Driben, Grand Portage National Monument, Grand Portage, Minnesota, 2000.
33. Robert Drouillard, Cook County Historical Society videotaped interview, Grand Portage, Minnesota, August 2000, videotape located at Cook County Historical Society, Grand Marais, Minnesota.
34. James Wipson, interview with Donald Auger and Paul Driben, Grand Portage National Monument, Grand Portage, Minnesota, 2000.
35. Ibid.
36. Catherine Jones, unpublished journal, Cook County Historical Society, Grand Marais, Minnesota, November 2, 1898—November 14, 1900, 8.
37. Raff, *Pioneers in the Wilderness,* 60.
38. Ibid., 66.
39. Ad clipping, on file at University of Minnesota Library, Duluth, Minnesota.
40. Carl Gawboy and Ron Morton, *Talking Rocks: Geology and 10,000 Years of Native American Tradition in the Lake Superior Region* (Duluth: Pfeifer-Hamilton, 2000), 44.
41. James Wipson, interview with the author, Grand Portage, Minnesota, March 11, 2001.
42. Gloria Martineau, interview with the author, Grand Marais, Minnesota, April 2001.
43. Ibid.
44. Michael Morrison, interview with Donald Auger and Paul Driben, Grand Portage National Monument, Grand Portage, Minnesota, 2000.
45. Edith (Mayhew) Strom, interview with Cook County Historical Society, Grand Marais, Minnesota, 1982, transcript located at Cook County Historical Society, Grand Marais, Minnesota, 3.
46. Vivian Waltz, interview with the author, Duluth, Minnesota, March 31, 2001.

8. A Call from Longbody

1. Raff, *Pioneers in the Wilderness*, 55.
2. Ibid., 52.
3. Ibid., 51.
4. Catherine Jones, unpublished journal, Cook County Historical Society, Grand Marais, Minnesota, November 2, 1898—November 14, 1900, 12.
5. Ibid.
6. Edith (Mayhew) Strom, interview with Cook County Historical Society, Grand Marais, Minnesota, 1982, transcript located at Cook County Historical Society, Grand Marais, Minnesota, 2.
7. James Wipson, interview with the author, Grand Portage, Minnesota, March 11, 2001.
8. Catherine Jones, unpublished journal, Cook County Historical Society, Grand Marais, Minnesota, November 2, 1898—November 14, 1900, 12.
9. Ibid.
10. Lloyd K. Johnson, interview with Pat Zankman, Cook County Historical Society, Duluth, Minnesota, 2003.
11. Catherine Jones, unpublished journal, Cook County Historical Society, Grand Marais, Minnesota, November 2, 1898—November 14, 1900, 18.
12. "History of the Grand Marais Harbor," United States Engineers Office, unpublished report, 1939, 4.
13. James Wipson, interview with the author, Grand Portage, Minnesota, May 27, 2001.
14. Dora Kasames, interview with Donald Auger and Paul Driben, Grand Portage National Monument, Grand Portage, Minnesota, 2000.
15. Gloria Martineau, interview with the author Grand Marais, Minnesota, April 2001.
16. Dorothy Johansen, interview with the author, Duluth, Minnesota, January 25, 2001.
17. Dora Kasames, interview with Donald Auger and Paul Driben, Grand Portage National Monument, Grand Portage, Minnesota.
18. Richard Anderson, interview with Donald Auger and Paul Driben, Grand Portage National Monument, Grand Portage, Minnesota, 2000.
19. Barb Dahman, "From the Editor," *Moccasin Telegraph*, Grand Portage Tribal Council, October 1996.
20. Catherine Jones, unpublished journal, Cook County Historical Society, Grand Marais, Minnesota, November 2, 1898—November 14, 1900, 19.
21. Frances Densmore, *Chippewa Customs* (St. Paul: Minnesota Historical Society Press, 1979), 114, 116.
22. "Local Football," *Cook County News Herald*, Grand Marais, Minnesota, September 28, 1901.

23. Author unknown, *Cook County News Herald*, Grand Marais, Minnesota, January 6, 1900.

24. Mary Jane Hendrickson, interview with the author, Grand Portage, Minnesota, 2001.

25. Catherine Jones, unpublished journal, Cook County Historical Society, Grand Marais, Minnesota, November 2, 1898—November 14, 1900, 5.

26. James Wipson, interview with the author, Grand Portage, Minnesota, May 27, 2001.

27. Vivian Waltz, interview with the author, Duluth, Minnesota, March 31, 2001.

28. Gladys Beckwith, interview with the author, March 10, 2001,

29. James Wipson, interview with the author, Grand Portage, Minnesota, May 27, 2001.

30. Gloria Martineau, interview with the author Grand Marais, Minnesota, April 2001.

9. We Are Buried Here

1. Shingibbiss obituary, *Cook County News Herald,* Grand Marais, Minnesota, April 25, 1907.

2. Catherine Jones, diary manuscript, 1889–99, unpublished, courtesy of the Cook County Historical Society, Grand Marais, Minnesota.

3. Dora Kasames, interview with Donald Auger and Paul Driben, Grand Portage National Monument, Grand Portage, Minnesota, 2000.

4. Mary Jane Hendrickson, interview with the author Grand Portage, Minnesota, 2001.

5. Michael Morrison, interview with the author, Grand Portage, Minnesota, October 27, 2001.

6. James Wipson, interview with the author, Grand Portage, Minnesota, May 27, 2001.

7. Dorothy Johansen, interview with the author, Duluth, Minnesota, January 25, 2001.

8. James Wipson, interview with the author, Grand Portage, Minnesota, May 27, 2001.

9. Michael Morrison, interview with the author, Grand Portage, Minnesota, October 27, 2001.

10. Cook County Warranty Land Deed, 8-Deeds 248, September 1, 1926, recorded June 10, 1930, unpublished.

11. Gladys Beckwith, interview with the author, Grand Marais Minnesota, March 10, 2001.

12. Vivian Waltz, interview with the author, Duluth, Minnesota, March 31, 2001.

13. Dorothy Johansen, interview with the author, Duluth, Minnesota, January 25, 2001.
14. James Wipson, interview with the author, Grand Portage, Minnesota, May 27, 2001.
15. Letter to Will Raff from George Morrison, December 5, 1979, unpublished, courtesy of the Cook County Historical Society.
16. Letter to George Morrison from Will Raff, January 22, 1981, unpublished, courtesy of the Cook County Historical Society.
17. Letter to Will Raff from George Morrison, with original sketch, February 4, 1981, unpublished, courtesy of the Cook County Historical Society.
18. Letter to Richard W. Johnson from Ken Hoffman, April 16, 1987, unpublished, courtesy of the Cook County Historical Society.
19. Ibid.
20. John Drouillard obituary, *Cook County News Herald,* February 23, 1928.

10. I Guess Sometimes I'm Torn

1. "History of Cook County Schools," author unknown, Minnesota History Center, St. Paul, Minnesota, 2.
2. Cochrane, "L'Espagnol," 23.
3. Dorothy Johansen, interview with the author, Duluth, Minnesota, January 25, 2001.
4. Ibid.
5. Ibid.
6. Gladys Beckwith, interview with the author, Grand Marais Minnesota, March 10, 2001.
7. James Wipson, interview with the author, Grand Portage, Minnesota, May 27, 2001.
8. Michael Morrison, interview with Donald Auger and Paul Driben, Grand Portage National Monument, Grand Portage, Minnesota, 2000.
9. Catherine Jones, unpublished journal, Cook County Historical Society, Grand Marais, Minnesota, November 2, 1898—November 14, 1900, 3.
10. Ibid.
11. Ibid., 7.
12. Ibid., 24.
13. Michael Morrison, interview with Donald Auger and Paul Driben, Grand Portage National Monument, Grand Portage, Minnesota, 2000.
14. Dorothy Johansen, interview with the author, Duluth, Minnesota, January 25, 2001.
15. James Wipson, interview with Donald Auger and Paul Driben, Grand Portage National Monument, Grand Portage, Minnesota, 2000.

16. Gloria Martineau, interview with the author, Grand Marais, Minnesota, April 2001.

17. Gladys Beckwith, interview with the author, March 10, 2001.

18. James LaPlante, interview with Donald Auger and Paul Driben, Grand Portage National Monument, Grand Portage, Minnesota, 2000.

19. Milt Powell, interview with the author, December 13, 2011, Grand Marais, Minnesota.

20. Cac Hussey, interview transcript, Cook County Historical Society, 2003, 33.

21. James Wipson, interview with the author, Grand Portage, Minnesota, March 11, 2001.

22. Dorothy Johansen, interview with the author, Duluth, Minnesota, January 25, 2001.

23. Ibid.

24. Gladys Beckwith, interview with the author, Grand Marais, Minnesota, March 10, 2001.

25. Gloria Martineau, interview with the author, Grand Marais, Minnesota, April 2001.

26. George Morrison, interview with the author, Grand Portage, Minnesota, October 1987.

27. Jill Doerfler, *Those Who Belong: Identity, Family, Blood, and Citizenship among the White Earth Anishinaabeg* (East Lansing: Michigan State University Press, 2015), 40.

28. Ibid., 41.

29. Ibid., 32.

30. Ibid., 43.

31. Auger and Driben, *Grand Portage Chippewa*, 18.

32. George Morrison, interview with the author, Grand Portage, Minnesota, October 1987.

33. Auger and Driben, *Grand Portage Chippewa*, 2.

34. Gloria Martineau, interview with the author, Grand Marais, Minnesota, April 2001.

35. Michael Morrison, interview with the author, Grand Portage, Minnesota, October 27, 2001.

11. *Divide the Land, Divide the People*

1. Reverend Father Maurice, interview with Donald Auger and Paul Driben, Grand Portage National Monument, Grand Portage, Minnesota, exact date unknown.

2. George Morrison, interview with the author, Grand Portage, Minnesota, October 1987.

3. Edith (Mayhew) Strom, interview with Cook County Historical Society, Grand Marais, Minnesota, 1982, transcript located at Cook County Historical Society, Grand Marais, Minnesota.

4. Ibid.

5. Raff, *Pioneers in the Wilderness*, 332.

6. George Morrison, interview with the author, Grand Portage, Minnesota, October 1987.

7. Dorothy Johansen, interview with the author, Duluth, Minnesota, January 25, 2001.

8. James Wipson, interview with the author, Grand Portage, Minnesota, March 11, 2001.

9. James LaPlante, interview with Donald Auger and Paul Driben, Grand Portage National Monument, Grand Portage, Minnesota, 2000.

10. Dorothy Johansen, interview with the author, Duluth, Minnesota, January 25, 2001.

11. James Wipson, interview with the author, Grand Portage, Minnesota, March 11, 2001.

12. Ibid.

13. Gloria Martineau, interview with the author, Grand Marais, Minnesota, April 2001.

14. Gladys Beckwith, interview with the author, Grand Marais, Minnesota, March 10, 2001.

15. Vivian Waltz, interview with the author, Duluth, Minnesota, March 31, 2001.

16. Auger and Driben, *Grand Portage Chippewa*, 14.

17. George Morrison, interview with the author, Grand Portage, Minnesota, October 1987.

18. Department of the Interior Report, "Half-Breed Scrip: Chippewas of Lake Superior, the Correspondence and Action" (Washington, D.C.: U.S. Government Printing Office, 1874), 14.

19. Ibid.

20. Ibid.

21. Danziger, "They Would Not Be Moved," 185.

22. Letter to Mr. Edwin Demery, area director, Minneapolis Area Office, Bureau of Indian Affairs, from the U.S. Department of the Interior, Office of the Solicitor, Fort Snelling, Twin Cities, Minnesota, July 3, 1980.

23. Sylvia Van Kirk, "The Role of Native Women in the Fur Trade Society of Western Canada, 1670–1830," *Frontiers* 7, no. 3 (1984): 10.

24. Ibid.

25. Ibid.

26. Ibid., 11.
27. Ibid., 12.

12. Signed with an X
   1. James Wipson, interview with Donald Auger and Paul Driben, Grand Portage National Monument, Grand Portage, Minnesota, 2000.
   2. Iva Claire Downey, "Kate Frost," unpublished essay, 1931, located at the Cook County Historical Society, Grand Marais, Minnesota.
   3. Ibid.
   4. Land Warranty Deed, 1887, United States Government Document, located at Cook County Registrar of Deeds, Grand Marais, Minnesota.
   5. James Wipson, interview with the author, Grand Portage, Minnesota, March 11, 2001.
   6. Richard Anderson, interview with Donald Auger and Paul Driben, Grand Portage National Monument, Grand Portage, Minnesota, 2000.
   7. Record of Patents Delivered, 1884–1903, Duluth Land Office Register, Minnesota History Center, St. Paul, Minnesota.
   8. "Tax Delinquent Towns to Be Dissolved," *Duluth Herald*, December 12, 1935.
   9. Michael Morrison, interview with the author, Grand Portage, Minnesota, October 27, 2001.
   10. Dora Kasames, interview with Donald Auger and Paul Driben, Grand Portage National Monument, Grand Portage, Minnesota, 2000.
   11. James Wipson, interview with Donald Auger and Paul Driben, Grand Portage National Monument, Grand Portage, Minnesota, 2000.
   12. Auger and Driben, *Grand Portage Chippewa,* 54.
   13. Lloyd K. Johnson, interview with Pat Zankman, Cook County Historical Society, Duluth, Minnesota, 2003.
   14. Ibid.
   15. *Land Deed Record Number 36,* October 16, 1963, Cook County Recorder's Office, Grand Marais, Minnesota.
   16. James Wipson, interview with the author, Grand Portage, Minnesota, May 27, 2001.
   17. Gilman, *The Grand Portage Story,* 12.
   18. James Wipson, interview with the author, Grand Portage, Minnesota, May 27, 2001

13. Jiigewayaazhagamay
   1. Auger and Driben, *Grand Portage Chippewa,* 73.
   2. Edith (Mayhew) Strom, interview with Cook County Historical Society,

Grand Marais, Minnesota, 1982, transcript located at Cook County Historical Society, Grand Marais, Minnesota.

3. Michael Morrison, interview with the author, Grand Portage, Minnesota, October 27, 2001.

4. Raff, *Pioneers in the Wilderness*, 311.

5. Auger and Driben, *Grand Portage Chippewa*, 32.

6. Ibid., 1.

7. Vivian Waltz, interview with the author, Duluth, Minnesota, March 31, 2001.

8. James Wipson, interview with the author, Grand Portage, Minnesota, May 27, 2001.

9. Fifteenth Census of the United States: 1930, Department of Commerce—Bureau of the Census, Grand Marais Village, Cook County, Minnesota.

10. George Morrison, interview with the author, Grand Portage, Minnesota, October 1987.

11. Irene Sullivan, interview with Auger and Driben, Grand Portage National Monument, Grand Portage, Minnesota, 2000.

12. Vivian Waltz, interview with the author, Duluth, Minnesota, March 31, 2001.

13. Dorothy Johansen, interview with the author, Duluth, Minnesota, January 25, 2001.

14. Adam Roach, obituary, *Cook County News Herald,* May 3, 1933.

Epilogue

1. Vivian Waltz, interview with the author, Duluth, Minnesota, March 31, 2001.

2. James Wipson, interview with Donald Auger and Paul Driben, Grand Portage National Monument, Grand Portage, Minnesota, 2000.

3. James LaPlante, interview with Donald Auger and Paul Driben, Grand Portage National Monument, Grand Portage, Minnesota, 2000.

4. Dorothy Johansen, interview with the author, Duluth, Minnesota, January 25, 2001.

5. "Road to Chippewa City Closed," author unknown, *Cook County Herald,* Grand Marais, Minnesota 1893–1909, October 1, 1904, Minnesota History Center, St. Paul, Minnesota.

6. James Wipson, interview with the author, Grand Portage, Minnesota, March 11, 2001.

7. George Morrison, interview with the author, Grand Portage, Minnesota, October 1987.

8. St. Francis Xavier dedication, text, Cook County Historical Society collection, Grand Marais, Minnesota, 1975.

9. "Church Celebrates 100th," author unknown, *Cook County News Herald*, June 26, 1995, Grand Marais, Minnesota.

10. Ibid.

11. Michael Morrison, interview with Donald Auger and Paul Driben, Grand Portage National Monument, Grand Portage, Minnesota, 2000.

INDEX

"Act to Perfect Certain Land Titles, An," 237
Addikonse (Little Caribou), 18, 65–67, 86, 91, 93, 102, 110, 115, 117–18, 210
American Fur Company, 57–58, 62, 87, 102
Amyotte, Bill, 68, 154, 277
Anakwad, Antoine, 127, 129, 160, 206, 259, 275
Anakwad, Elizabeth, 4, 15, 28, 91, 104, 133, 137–38, 146, 153, 167, 205, 262
Anakwad, Martell, 15, 199, 206, 235, 245
Anakwad, Mathias, 102
Anakwad, Therese, 15, 199, 206, 245
Anderson, Richard, Sr., 222
Artists' Point, 77–79, 82, 236, 245, 265
assimilation, 84, 92, 97, 109, 158, 180, 209

baptisms, 18, 20, 110–12, 127, 134, 137
Beargrease, John, 3, 108–9, 135, 256–57
Beargrease, Louise, 4
Beckwith, Gladys, 11–12, 20, 117, 127, 139, 151, 189, 199, 206, 211, 214, 217, 227, 234, 255, 277
Bineshiikwe, 34–35
Binesiwabe, 102
Birch Terrace Supper Club, 70–71
Blackstone II (Chief), 118–19, 123
blood quantum, 50, 83, 207, 218, 220–21, 236, 241

Blue Sky, 52, 123, 263
boarding schools, 180, 231
burials, 126

Caribou, Dave, 119
Caribou, Joe (I-ah-be-dway-waish-kung), 66, 93, 104, 114, 117–18, 125
Caribou, Louise Anna, 117
Caribou, Lucy, 120–21, 126, 165, 205
Caribou, Swamper, 119–20, 142, 202
Chippewa City Cemetery, 197, 206, 211, 257, 273

Dahmen, Mary (Morrison), 184
Dawes Act (Allotment Act), 77–78, 84, 91–92
Deschampe, Theodore, 182
Downey, Iva Claire, 243–44
Drouillard, Archange Chauvin, 62
Drouillard, Bill (William), 11, 145, 146, 182, 197, 210
Drouillard, Charlie, 142–44, 269
Drouillard, Francis (Poot), 2, 117, 266
Drouillard, Fred, 135, 137, 147, 157
Drouillard, John, 4, 62, 88, 102–4, 107, 132–33, 135–37, 153, 203, 205, 235, 262
Drouillard, Nelson (Narcisse), 59, 61, 103, 111

Espagnol, 55, 115, 154, 210
Evans, Philomene (Caribou), 121–23, 205

Father LaMarche, 16, 128
Father Maurice, 110, 112, 134, 205, 225, 277
Father Simon (Lampe), 16–17, 21, 22, 205
Father Specht (Joseph), 14, 16, 18, 111
Fillison, Antoine, 13–14, 245–46
Fillison, Antoinette, 14
fishing, 30–33, 53, 55, 57–58, 60, 72–73, 80–81, 86, 88, 102, 145–47, 182
forest fires, 22, 96, 254–55
Fort Misery, 57–58
Frontierism, 172
Frost, Kate (Catherine Anakwad), 1, 91, 98, 100, 111, 131, 135–36, 145, 155, 188, 190, 240, 244, 245–47, 251–52, 275–76

Gagnon, Pete, 146
Gilbert, Henry C., 62–63, 65, 118, 236–37
Godfrey, Josephine, 62–63
Good Harbor Hill, 152, 193–94
Grand Marais harbor, 68, 72–73, 82, 87–90, 96–97, 104, 123, 133, 166
Granite River, 41–42, 162, 228, 244
Greysolon, Daniel (Sieur du Lhut), 39
Groseilliers, Chonart des, 38

Hackett, Carol, 255, 277
Half Breed Scrip, 82, 84
Hedlund, Albertina, 20–21
Hegney, Timothy, 60–62
Hendrickson, Mary Jane, 117, 187, 195, 227, 277
Henry, Alexander, 41–44, 162, 228, 244

Hicks, F. B., 72–73, 284
Homestead Act, 14–15, 92, 246
Howenstine, Samuel, 62, 82, 86, 88, 94, 118, 124, 145, 185–86
hunting, 45, 54–55, 67, 72, 86, 119, 125, 144–45, 147, 164
Hussey, Cac, 82, 154, 216

Indian Reorganization Act, 2, 115, 219, 226, 252, 259

Jackson's Café, 182–83, 233
Jay's Treaty, 56, 263
Johanasen, Mathias, 152
Johansen, Dorothy, 11–12, 17, 117, 128, 131, 139, 146, 159, 182, 197, 200, 210, 213, 216–17, 231, 233, 261, 270, 277
Johnson, August J., 20
Johnson, August Van, 96, 248, 251
Johnson, Charles (Charlie, Chas), 74–76, 86, 96, 119, 136, 145, 189, 247, 250
Johnson, Lloyd K., 74, 178, 250, 278
Johnson, Matt (Johanasen), 152, 276
Johnson, Stina, L., 96, 249, 251
Johnson, Van, 96, 248–49, 251
Jones, Catherine, 74–75, 125, 148, 161, 173, 175–80, 184, 187, 195, 212–13, 216

Kanipi Lake, 118
Kasames, Dora, 104–5, 117, 126, 148, 159–60, 181–82, 195, 248, 277
Kitchi Onigaming (Grand Portage), 35, 47

Lac La Croix, 34, 44, 118–19, 123
LaPlante, Jim, 19, 22, 91, 110, 127,

145, 152–53, 157, 186, 190, 214, 217, 232, 262, 270, 277
logging, 88, 92, 136, 145, 171, 204, 244
Longbody (Cognoshowa), 73, 171–91
Mabel's Café, 168, 182
Martineau, Gloria, 117, 120, 126, 147, 158, 165, 181, 190, 217, 222–23, 234, 277
Mayhew, Henry (Hazeal), 85, 86, 89–90, 94, 104, 124, 133, 145, 171, 176
Maymashkawaush, 55, 88, 110, 115
migration (Anishinaabe), 33–35, 44, 47, 50
Monker, Claus, 153, 199
Morrison, George, 3, 10–12, 26, 28, 53, 84–85, 93, 111, 117, 128, 130, 148, 190, 201, 217, 221, 226, 229–30, 235, 260, 272–73, 277
Morrison, James (Jim), Jr., 13, 17, 111, 128, 129, 142, 175
Morrison, James, Sr., 13
Morrison, John, 14, 20, 152, 216
Morrison, Michael, 13–14, 142, 148, 159, 166, 196, 198, 206, 211–13, 223, 248, 256, 274, 277
Mount Josephine, 63–65, 100, 104

Naniboujou, 34, 162–64
Nelson Act, 92–93, 97, 180, 230, 247
North West Company, 57, 238, 240

Oakgrove, Collins, 5, 35–36, 38, 277
Ojibwe language, 5, 15, 17, 36–38, 59, 81, 101–2, 128, 133, 212, 216–17, 219, 236
Old Road, the, 13, 28, 100–101, 104,

117, 198, 244, 264, 269–72, 274, 276

Pierz, Francis, 209–10
Pigeon River, 25, 30, 31–34, 38–41, 44–47, 56–57, 62, 67–68, 89, 107, 110, 209, 250
Pioneers in the Wilderness (Raff), 80, 106, 119, 229
Plante, Louis, 107–9, 202
Pond, Peter, 42
population (Cook County), 22, 45, 60–61, 88–89, 95, 97, 162, 173, 180, 212, 226, 243, 247, 253
Posey, Alex, 214–15
poverty, 23, 91
Powell, Milton, 117–18, 150, 215
prejudice, 23, 223, 226, 229, 234–35

Radisson, Pierre-Esprit, 38, 73
Raff, Will (Bill), 68, 74, 80, 82, 86, 93, 106, 119, 137, 148, 171–72, 201–2, 229, 257
religion, 33, 124, 180, 209–12, 221, 231
Roach, Adam, 260–62
Roussain, Francis, 77–78, 82–85, 236, 245
Roussain, Zoe, 82–86

Saganaga Lake, 41–42, 54, 57, 146–48, 150
Saganagons Lake, 118
schools, 25, 28, 59–62, 80, 103, 130, 153, 159, 171, 180–81, 190, 194, 209, 216–17, 231–33, 260
Scott, Katherine Boyer (Maggie), 68, 80–81, 111
Shingibbiss, 15, 52, 91, 118, 123–25, 193–94, 205, 213, 256, 276
Shingibbiss, Margaret, 123, 125

Soderberg, Olga, 19–20, 273

St. Francis Xavier Catholic Church, 10–11, 13–15, 17–23, 25, 102, 104–5, 111–12, 126, 127, 134, 137, 195, 202, 206–7, 225, 268, 270, 273

Strom, Edith (Mayhew), 166, 174–75, 227–29, 255

sugar bush, 119, 127, 153–55, 194, 274, 276

Sullivan, Irene, 76, 106, 132, 221, 258, 260–61, 271, 277

Swanson, Bob, 4, 274, 278

taxation, 247–48

Thomas, Joe, 126, 148

Thunder Hook Point (Katie's Point), 1, 158, 190, 211, 245–46

Timber and Stone Act, 93–95, 97, 249

totems (*doo-daims*), 33–34, 39, 57

tourism, 104, 140, 162, 164–66, 168, 244

trapping, 60, 74, 128, 145, 148–50, 164

Treaty of Greenville, 56

Treaty of La Pointe, 1842 and 1854, 34–35, 58, 65–68, 77–78, 80, 103, 213, 236, 241

Treaty of 1783, 56

Wakelin, Ed, 82, 86, 94, 145

Waltz, Vivian, 12–13, 20, 23, 117, 139, 168, 187, 189, 227, 259, 261–62, 270, 277

Warren, William, 33–34, 36, 39, 43

Waywaygewam, 65

Weetch (Marie Ann Wabibinens), 126–27, 161, 259

Wipson, James (Jim), 1, 11, 18, 98–99, 116–17, 126–27, 131–32, 136, 138, 154–56, 158, 161, 164, 175, 181, 188–90, 194, 196–97, 200, 211, 213, 216, 232–34, 240, 243–45, 248, 253, 259, 270, 272, 276, 277

Wishkop family, 4, 13, 16, 108, 112, 199, 206, 257, 275

Zankman, Pat, 74, 250, 274, 277

Zhaganasheence, 65, 67, 102, 115

Zimmerman, Josephine, 19, 217, 259, 270

Zimmerman, Susan, 167

STACI LOLA DROUILLARD lives and works in her hometown of Grand Marais, Minnesota, on the North Shore of Lake Superior. A Grand Portage tribal descendant, she began interviewing Chippewa City elders in 1987. She has degrees from the University of Minnesota and the University of Minnesota Duluth.